FIRE IN THE WATER, EARTH IN THE AIR

Fire in the Water

CHRISTOPHER J. OGLESBY

Christopher Oglesby

2015

For Ashley Monical
You can relate, I'm sure,
Loads of best wishes
for your recording, etc.!
CO

Earth in the Air

LEGENDS OF WEST TEXAS MUSIC

UNIVERSITY OF TEXAS PRESS AUSTIN

Requests for permission to reproduce material from this work should be sent to:
   Permissions, University of Texas Press, P.O. Box 7819, Austin, TX 78713-7819
   www.utexas.edu/utpress/about/bpermission.html

∞ The paper used in this book meets the minimum requirements of ANSI/NISO Z39.48-1992
(R1997) (Permanence of Paper).

LIBRARY OF CONGRESS CATALOGING-IN-PUBLICATION DATA
Oglesby, Christopher J. (Christopher Joseph), 1965–
   Fire in the water, earth in the air : legends of West Texas music /
Christopher J. Oglesby.— 1st ed.
      p.   cm.
   Includes bibliographical references (p. 281), discography (p. 241), and index.
   ISBN-13: 978-0-292-71419-9 (cloth : alk. paper)
   ISBN-10: 0-292-71419-x (cloth : alk. paper)
   ISBN-13: 978-0-292-71434-2 (pbk. : alk. paper)
   ISBN-10: 0-292-71434-3 (pbk. : alk. paper)
      1. Musicians—Texas, West—Interviews. 2. Artists—Texas, West—Interviews. 3. Texas,
West—Social life and customs—Anecdotes. I. Title.
   ML394.O32 2006
   781.64092'2764847—dc22   2006003690

This book is dedicated to
the memory of my mother,
who loved language, art, and religion

CONTENTS

An intriguing but significant dilemma in writing a book about the talented musicians, writers, and artists from Lubbock, Texas, and the surrounding area is the sheer volume of material. There is no way I could mention them all, let alone interview even a majority of the fascinating artists with Lubbock connections. I do not intend that this chronicle be taken as an all-inclusive slate of important artists from the South Plains. The interviewees in this book were simply the ones whose paths crossed mine and who were gracious enough to share time discussing their lives in West Texas. Many talented folks have gone unnamed and that is regrettable. However, time and space do limit us all. I would like to express my highest regards for anyone who considers him- or herself an artist and has survived on the High Plains.

ACKNOWLEDGMENTS

The author thanks all the artists who shared their stories for this book, as well as their respective spouses who facilitated in many different ways. I thank my own wife for her patience and support. Shannon Halley's influence has been incalculable, but most of all she connected me with my publisher, the University of Texas Press. Luke Torn was my developmental editor and helped me organize the original manuscript. Allison Faust and all the editorial staff at UT Press have been encouraging and helpful. Thank you to my copyeditor, Paul Spragens. Also, the following people provided assistance or support that is much appreciated: my parents, my sister Elizabeth, Paul Bullock, Mike Burk, Jack Burk, Alan Crossland, John Scott, Scott Jensen, Eddy Patterson, Robert Patterson, John X Reed, Bené Bertrand, Conni Hancock, Traci Hancock, Charlene Hancock, Craig Barker, Miz Ayn, Steve Long, Johnny Hughes, Rob Weiner, Angela Paschal, Kent Mings, John Nelson, David Teneyuque, Dee Purkeypile, Tanya So, David Keller, Trent and Diane Hunt, Deanna Shoemaker, Steve and Jennifer Graves, Tracee Hoffman Brown, Trey McClendon, Gina Space, Hal Nelson, John Fillipone, Jay Hataway, Rose Rosenblatt and Marion Lipschutz of InCite Pictures, Jordan Weeks, Cari Collins, John and Maureen Chambers, Leslie Hodge, Chris Barnes, Kelly and Shanna Weiss, Nicole Taylor, Dr. James Harper, Dr. Bruce Clarke, and John T. Davis.

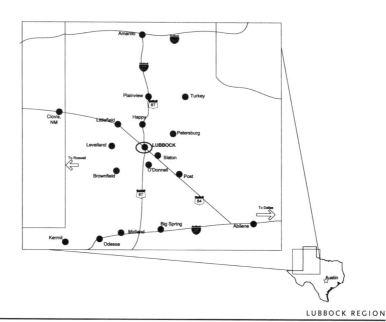

LUBBOCK REGION

Texas Tech University
Lubbock Christian University
Hospital
DOWNTOWN
Buddy Holly Park
Mackenzie Park
Lubbock International
South Plains Mall
The Strip
(Package Liquor Stores)

Ursuline Street
Erskine Street
4th Street
19th Street
34th Street
50th Street
Brownfield Highway
82nd Street
114th Street

Frankford Ave.
Slide Road
Quaker Ave.
Indiana Ave.
University Ave.
Milwaukee Ave.
Avenue Q
Avenue A
Martin Luther King Jr. Ave.

Clovis Highway
Loop 289
Main St.
Broadway
East 19th Street
East Loop 289
Spur 331
Slaton Highway US 84
Idalou Highway

Lubbock
"The Hub of the Plains"

CITY OF LUBBOCK

xii

FIRE IN THE WATER, EARTH IN THE AIR

Fire in the Water, Earth in the Air

CHRISTOPHER J. OGLESBY

Since Lubbock is the place where the earth is in the air and the fire is in the water, it's naturally got to be the place where the music gets tied up in knots and comes out unraveled.

—JIMMIE DALE GILMORE

I grew up like most other folks in Lubbock. I went to church, where my mom taught Sunday school, every Sunday until I moved out of my parents' house to attend Texas Tech University. Like many other Tech students in the 1980s, I found my weekend rituals at Fat Dawg's, the Main Street Saloon, the Texas Spoon Café, and P. J. Belly's. I discovered, as everyone who has lived there knows, that all the social and cultural action in Lubbock happens either in churches or bars. After eighteen years of going to church every Sunday morning with my mother, Saturday night at Fat Dawg's saloon became both school and church to me. The sober Presbyterians on 33rd Street did not offer the spiritual revival of a Joe Ely show, with Jesse Taylor on electric guitar, Lloyd Maines on pedal steel, and often Rolling Stones saxophone player Bobby Keys blowing the crowd to high heaven with exultant solos.

When I learned as a teenager that Buddy Holly had attended Roscoe Wilson Elementary, Hutchinson Junior High, and Lubbock High, the same public schools I attended, I became enchanted knowing an artist of worldwide importance could come from my seemingly normal neighborhood. After receiving two degrees from Texas

Tech University, I moved to Austin, where I became more aware that Lubbock's fame for producing songwriters, musicians, and artists is equal to its renown for cotton, conservatives, and windstorms. I have interviewed many of these artists over the years, searching for an answer to that oft-asked question: "Why Lubbock?" This book is the product of that exploration.

FIRE IN THE WATER

In 1989 the first President George Bush responded to accusations that the U.S. economy was adrift in malaise, "All the people in Lubbock think things are going great."[1] Since then, Lubbock has been considered a leading standard-bearer for American conservatism. Much of the Lubbock community is proud of that fact. Nowhere does the GOP enjoy such universal popularity as it does in Lubbock. In the 2004 election, 75 percent of those voting a straight ticket in Lubbock County voted Republican. Among the seven largest metropolitan areas in Texas, Lubbock County had the highest percentage voting for George W. Bush in 2004, also 75 percent. Ranked in 2005 as the second-most-conservative U.S. city, Lubbock proudly occupies the vanguard of the Republican Revolution of the early twenty-first century.[2] This is despite the irony that would-be assassin John Hinckley was living in Lubbock in 1981 when he bought the gun he later used to shoot President Reagan.

Perhaps equally as ironic, on March 10, 2003, Lubbock native Natalie Maines was one of the first to publicly question the war agenda of fellow West Texan President George W. Bush. Natalie made her now famous statement, "Just so you know, we're ashamed the president of the United States is from Texas," between songs in Shepherd's Bush Empire, an intimate London concert hall that seats fewer than 1,500 people. She did not intend to issue a formal statement to the press or anticipate the reaction. In case you missed it, she caught a lot of flak for it back in the USA, and not the least of the criticism came from Lubbock. A sample of the hundreds of open letters addressed to Natalie Maines and posted to the Web site of the leading country music station in Lubbock said: "For you to travel to a foreign land and publicly criticize our Commander in Chief is cowardice behavior. Would you have so willingly made those comments while performing for a patriotic, flag-waving crowd of Texans in Lubbock? I would imagine not. I am returning to you each and every Dixie Chicks

CD and cassette that I have ever purchased."[3] Furthering the irony, Natalie's uncle Kenny Maines happened to be a popular Republican Lubbock County commissioner at the time.

It is not an overgeneralization to say that, to many in Lubbock, the terms liberal and progressive are insults often spoken with disdain equal to that associated with such loaded words as faggot or nigger. In a 2005 PBS documentary film about the effects of Lubbock's "abstinence only" sex education policy, the Lubbock pastor who directs the city's True Love Waits sex education program expresses a prevalent local attitude when he states, "The terms Christian and liberal are like oil and water. It is true that Christianity is the most intolerant of religions, and I'm proud of that."[4]

It is frequently said that Lubbock has a church on every street corner. Of course, that is exaggeration. However, Lubbock does have many more than its share of churches. There are almost eight times as many churches per capita in Lubbock than in the United States as a whole.[5] Broadway Street in downtown Lubbock is dominated by six major churches on a one-mile strip, each church an entire block long. The three largest churches on this devout avenue, Broadway Church of Christ, First United Methodist, and First Baptist, are among the largest congregations in the world of their respective denominations. Of the other churches in Lubbock, forty-eight are Baptist, thirty are Church of Christ, and twenty-six are Methodist.[6]

West Texas is a land of paradoxes. Despite such avid church attendance, Lubbock has double the national average of sexually transmitted diseases in teenagers and has among the highest teenage pregnancy rates in the country.[7] These facts support the theory: Tell a kid enough times not to do something and the kid will figure out that it must be fun for some reason. That alone may be enough to explain the wealth of rock 'n' roll, country, blues, and jazz artists who come from Lubbock.

Many people from West Texas believe its most valuable natural resource to be the character of the people who reside there. Even the most rebellious rock 'n' roll prodigals from Lubbock concede that West Texas people are exceptional in their commitment to values such as hard work, honesty, charity, and friendliness. Mac Davis, who coined the phrase "Happiness is Lubbock, Texas, in my rearview mirror," when asked about his hometown, replies, "Let me put it this way: If I was going to have a flat tire without a spare, Lubbock is where I'd like to be."

However, in conservative Lubbock, one frequently is deemed to fall into one of two groups; one is either a "partier" or a "churchgoer." The churchgoers govern the town, while the partiers serve as the vocal counterculture. This duality is frequently the cause of much friction for the Lubbock music community. Musicians who must ply their trade in nightclubs and bars are almost always considered partiers and therefore on the underside of the community. But such subterranean friction creates powerful, potentially earthshaking energy. Place into this environment an artistic individual who sees reality a little differently than the rest, someone with creative genius, and we have an awesome potential for a new synthesis, and we're all a little bit closer to the truth for it.

When I began my quest to chronicle the legends of Lubbock music, I spoke with guitar player Jesse Taylor, the first white man to ever play at the original Stubb's Barbecue in East Lubbock. I told Jesse about being young and going with my dad to the now legendary Stubb's. My dad was the basketball recruiter at Texas Tech during the late 1960s and '70s, and he brought the first black collegiate basketball players to Lubbock in 1969, not without controversy. Also, books on the subject of barbecue have cited my dad as one of the foremost authorities on Texas barbecue joints. Although he is not much of a loud music fan, my dad had no qualms about taking me over to Lubbock's east side (which means the black side of town) in search of the best barbecue in West Texas. However, very few other white people ever made the journey to the east side to visit Stubb's, at least not until Jesse Taylor and Stevie Ray Vaughan started rocking the joint at Stubb's Sunday Night Jams. Being over there in the dark side of one of the most white-bread towns in America, I remember thinking, even as a youth, "There is something cool here. Why doesn't anyone in Lubbock know about it or acknowledge it?" C. B. Stubblefield ("Stubb") closed the small barbecue restaurant in 1984 due to poor finances, and moved to Austin, where several of his friends such as Joe Ely were living. Shortly before he died in 1997, Stubb reopened Stubb's Barbecue in downtown Austin, where it is now one of the premier live music venues in the Live Music Capital of the World.

I told all this to Jesse Taylor during our first phone conversation and he agreed. "Sometimes I think that Lubbock will never change," Jesse responded. "They don't know what genius they have from right there in Lubbock. They could have built recording studios and turned Lubbock into the Nashville of Texas music but they just turn their backs." He added: "But Austin is almost the same. It's not at all like Lubbock in that Austin is very open-minded and liberal, but even in Austin, the people here don't have any idea how much all us guys from Lubbock have done. I'll go on tour with Bob Dylan or Bruce Springsteen and when I get back to Austin people come up to me and say, 'Hey, Jesse, why haven't you been playing down at the Saxon Pub lately?' People just don't know what they have here."

A verse from the Bible has resounded in my mind as I have studied the paradox that is West Texas music and art. "No prophet goes without honor, except in his own country and among his own kin, and in his own home" (Mark 6:4). Perhaps any examination of conservative West Texas must begin by considering the Bible.

The King James Version of the Bible is the seminal text of the English language. Until the late nineteenth century, the KJV was commonly the only book most English speakers owned or read. It has been said that every metaphor, symbol, and story theme in the English language is based on the sacred stories in the King James Bible, and with good reason: These are very good stories. Virtually all truths are contained in this contradictory, poetic, magical epic of humanity's violent struggle to enter the Kingdom of God.

The fact that the Lubbock community remains deeply immersed in the language and themes of the Bible in a way that may have become unpopular as America has entered the twenty-first century may be one explanation why Lubbock is noted for producing such exceptionally talented storytellers, poets, and lyricists.

EARTH IN THE AIR

Moreover, we must consider the uniqueness of the land of West Texas. People in Lubbock thrive in a territory of boundless horizons. In the vast emptiness of the South Plains, there is limitless room for the dreams of creative spirits.

However, to most folks, the land around Lubbock appears to be a broad, flat expanse of nothingness. There are no natural trees, no hills, no streams. For the predominantly Anglo-Saxon Protestant farmers who chose to settle in this unlikely semiarid landscape at the end of the nineteenth century, all Lubbock had to offer was the soil, and plenty of it. As historian Richard Mason explains, the cotton industry has been predominant on the High Plains of West Texas since emigrants, mostly from the Deep South states, fled the ravages of the boll weevil and sought inexpensive lands and a chance for a future out West.[8]

The land was inexpensive because no white man had figured out how anyone could live out there on the vacant plains. However, these thick-skinned, no-nonsense immigrants settled on this inhospitable prairie to work the land for all the wealth to be reaped from it, not to enjoy the scenery. No one in his or her right mind settled in West Texas without being focused on the soil alone. Most westward-moving, prosperity-seeking Americans were bypassing the empty outback and forging on to the lush West Coast, to California, Oregon, and Washington. Only the truly imaginative saw prosperity on the empty, arid central grasslands.

Naturalist and Texas Tech professor Dan Flores has noted Americans' historical attitudes toward the Plains:

> For a species whose evolution was shaped so much by a plains setting, we humans—especially we Americans—have never found much to admire in plains country other than skies. This is another aspect of our cultural preparation; since the time of Thomas Jefferson, scenery for Americans has meant mountains. . . . This discourages plains people. They look around them at the smooth line of the horizon, see no mountains in any direction, and accept the widespread consensus that the region is unlovely and, perhaps, not much worthy of love.[9]

Many of the people who settled in West Texas brought with them the true American spirit of rugged individualism. Being isolated from the rest of the nation by endless miles of empty prairie, many West Texans discovered that if any joy was to be found in life it was to come from deep inside the heart, mind, and soul. When exposed on the West Texas plains, you are the tallest vertical object around, all that is between the land below and the sky above. It's easy, standing there in that vast sea of prairie, to see the face of God staring back.

"Nothing else to do" is the frequent answer to the question "Why do so many innovative musicians come from Lubbock?" This void, the absence of external natural stimulation, as for the biblical holy men in the Sinai desert, can cause an individual to journey into the hidden spaces inside the human heart and mind, perhaps to discover marvelous mysteries deep within the spirit of mankind. With no surrounding external beauty, a sensitive individual tends to search for beauty and truth deep inside the heart and mind. Stimulation must come from within because there damn sure is nothing outside there on the plains to stimulate the mind, nothing other than the drive for survival in that vast island of prairie.

Necessity is the mother of creation. Lubbock needed beauty, poetry, humor, and it needed to get up and shake its communal ass a bit, or go mad from loneliness and boredom; so Lubbock created the amazing likes of Jimmie Dale Gilmore, Butch Hancock, Terry Allen, and Joe Ely.

But first there was Buddy Holly. Buddy, the putative father of American rock 'n' roll, was certainly a prophet of his age, an age awash in broadcasted recorded music. All our twenty-first-century minds, regardless of geography and language, are filled with the sounds of the Beatles, the Rolling Stones, Bob Dylan, Elton John, the Clash, the Ramones, etc., and all of these influential artists were directly and indelibly inspired by Buddy Holly.

If one takes the time to go to Lubbock, Texas, and speak with people who lived there at the time Buddy Holly was growing up, one will discover that many of Buddy Holly's former peers and neighbors think very little of the man who became a worldwide icon of the rock 'n' roll era. They do not think poorly of him; most everyone who knew Buddy agrees that he was a good-hearted boy. Rather, most people who grew up in Lubbock with Buddy Holly think very little about him at all. It doesn't take long in Lubbock to realize that most really did consider Buddy Holly an oddball. Of course, prodigies often do seem odd and out of place in mundane surroundings.

According to his contemporary Lubbockites, Buddy always had that strange misfit demeanor that seems so poignantly illustrated by those startling horn-rimmed glasses that were his trademark. Most people in Lubbock, other than a few teenagers like Sonny Curtis, Bobby Keys, and Waylon Jennings, paid little attention to young Buddy Holly. After all, he was just a boy the entire time he lived there. He had been out of Lubbock High School for only three years before his fateful death in the winter of 1959. Buddy was already recording by the age of fourteen. People in Lubbock simply remember him, if at all, as "that crazy boy who always carried around a guitar," a miscreant kid piddling away his time with electronic noise.

In the religious, agricultural town of Lubbock, one is respected if he works hard and has something to show for it. Music is appreciated, but only as something you do in your free time, not as an occupation. For many years after Buddy's death, the Lubbock community paid little regard to the earthshaking influence their most famous child had on the world.

Buddy went directly from local teenage misfit to international rock 'n' roll messiah in four short years. Buddy's creative vision would change the world for us all.

While Elvis will always be the King of Rock 'n' Roll, Buddy Holly is most certainly its George Washington. Buddy Holly gave hope to all the outcasts, misfits, artists, dreamers, shakers, wailers, and moaners of the world that if goofy old Buddy Holly could make it, they could, too. As Paul McCartney of middle-class Liverpool observed, "Buddy Holly gave you confidence. He was like the boy next door."[10] Buddy Holly and the Crickets were literally the first garage band, a self-contained four-piece ensemble: two guitars, bass, and drums, and a charismatic singer out front, writing and recording their own songs. This would prove to be the standard for all rock 'n' roll bands to come.

However, it is easy to make heroes out of the dead, because the dead can be whatever we want them to be. One aim of this book is to honor Lubbock's living artists, to recognize their various contributions to art, music, and culture in Texas and the world.

Several generations of artists and writers have emerged somehow from Lubbock to influence popular music and art in significant and subtle ways. So the question is posed: Why does an isolated, conservative agricultural town like Lubbock, Texas, generate such innovative artists in numbers that seem so disproportionate to its population?

Is it the UFOs, the famed "Lubbock Lights" that hovered over West Texas in the 1950s? Is it the call of the crazy Comanche wind? Could it be the 360° vista of flat horizon that makes you feel smack dab in the center of the universe? Or is it just so damn boring out in the literal middle of nowhere that even the most mundane moments seem miraculous? Some say the lack of stimulation in the environment creates the perfect zendo.[11] Some say there is nothing else to do but make music and dance. The answer may be an unspoken magic in the soil, water, or the incessant wind. Perhaps it is the eccentric and innovative culture of the people who have settled and thrived in Lubbock. A place of howling dust storms and magic rainbows, paradox and prairie dogs, the religious right and Zen mystics, flying saucers and shooting stars, supernatural outlaws and perfect masters of self, Lubbock, Texas, is certainly a place that engenders strong emotions, as evidenced by the interviews in this book.

AUSTIN, TEXAS, 2005

1. "President Defends Pace of Administration," *Washington Post,* March 8, 1989.

2. Bay Area Center for Voting Research study ranking political leanings of cities with populations greater than 100,000. Provo, Utah, was number one; Abilene, Texas, was number three.

3. Radio station KLLL-FM Web site (http://www.klll.com).

4. Ed Ainsworth, as quoted from the film *The Education of Shelby Knox,* InCite Pictures, New York, 2004; original PBS television air date June 21, 2005.

5. In 2001, there were 574 churches in Lubbock for a population of 199,564 (source: 2001 SBC Lubbock Yellow Pages), compared to 102,775 churches nationwide for the total U.S. population of 281,421,906 (source: National Council of Churches membership statistics).

6. It is interesting to note that fourth and fifth on the list are Assembly of God, thirteen, and Mormons, eleven (source: 2001 SBC Lubbock Yellow Pages).

7. Ceci Connolly, "Sex Education, Texas-style," *Washington Post,* February 16, 2003.

8. Richard Mason, "The Cotton Kingdom and the City of Lubbock: South Plains Agriculture in the Postwar Era," in *Lubbock from Town to City,* ed. Lawrence Graves (Lubbock: West Texas Museum Association, 1986), pp. 1–2.

9. Dan Flores, introduction to *Canyon Visions,* by Dan Flores and Amy Cromley Winton (Lubbock: Texas Tech University Press, 1989), p. 2.

10. http://www.dallasobserver.com/issues/2001-02-01/music.html.

11. A "zendo" is a space in which one practices Zen meditation.

THE LEGENDS

TERRY ALLEN is an accomplished sculptor, painter, playwright, filmmaker, songwriter, composer, and musical performer. Terry graduated from high school at the age of seventeen and promptly left Lubbock to attend the Chouinard Art Institute in Los Angeles. He received his Bachelor of Fine Arts degree in 1966, and by 1970 had earned his first of four grants from the National Endowment for the Arts. He was awarded a Guggenheim Fellowship in 1986. His visual art can be found in major public collections such as the Metropolitan Museum of Art and the Museum of Modern Art in New York, and the Los Angeles County Museum. Terry Allen has recorded eleven albums of original music. *Rolling Stone* magazine granted a coveted five-star ranking to his album with the Panhandle Mystery Band, *Lubbock: on everything,* and four stars to his *Silent Majority: Greatest Missed Hits.* Terry Allen's songs have been performed by such diverse and innovative artists as Lowell George, David Byrne, Bobby Bare, Ricky Nelson, Lucinda Williams, and Robert Earl Keen. Terry now lives and works in Santa Fe with his wife, actress and writer Jo Harvey Allen.

Terry Allen

TERRY: I think it's funny that all of that stuff happened in Lubbock, thinking back on it now, because there wasn't any evidence to me that there was anything going on in Lubbock when I was there. All I basically wanted to do was get out. I desperately needed to get out of Lubbock, for a whole combination of reasons.

CHRIS: You moved away from Lubbock at the age of seventeen. As a teenager in Lubbock, what was on your mind?

TERRY: In my own particular case, I didn't really want to be anything, and that scared me because everybody I knew wanted to be something when they got out of high school. They knew what they were going to study. They had a plan. I had no plan. I couldn't relate to anything that these people wanted to be. I was kicked out of high school twice: once for doing porno drawings on people's notebooks, for a quarter; and then I got kicked out for playing a song I wrote which was called "The Roman Orgy." I had tried out for this assembly at Monterey High with a Bo Diddley song, and then for the assembly I sang my own song. My peers liked it but it got me in big trouble with the powers-that-be and they kicked me out.

It's interesting that the two things I got in trouble for constantly were the two things that I ended up doing. I don't do porno drawings on notebooks anymore, but I'm not above it.

So there was rock 'n' roll. It's very hard to explain all that to people who didn't live through it, what an incredible impact and how dangerous it was when it first hit. It was like the Atomic Bomb. Rock 'n' roll was a huge influence on me. That, and the Beats, which Lubbock got a weird little dose of toward the end of the '50s. We had a couple of coffeehouses, with people hanging out in berets and sunglasses and leotards, reading poetry and playing bongos, kind of Lubbock's twisted idea of what it would be like to be in New York or San Francisco. I can remember my wife Jo Harvey and I, when we were dating, would go stand under the Great Plains Life Building, the tallest building downtown, and put our chins right on the bricks and look straight up at the sky and imagine that we were in New York or some big city, far away. All of our longings were about somewhere else.

I've discussed this with Jimmie Gilmore, Joe Ely and Butch Hancock, Jesse Taylor

VERTICAL VIEW OF METRO TOWER

and all those people who are now known as the Flatlanders. See, I knew everybody but Joe back in high school, because Joe was like four years younger than me. Jimmie and Butch, I knew in high school but not from any music point of view. And I knew Jo Carol Pierce and Jesse Taylor, because they went together some back then. But I never knew them in a musical context. I didn't even know about the Flatlanders until I went back to Lubbock later, because I had gone to California right after high school and they didn't form the Flatlanders until much later. Talking about it now, I always tell them: "You stayed in Lubbock to become Flatlanders, and I was just flat out of there." That's the truth. But all of that longing was shared. There was something going on there, and I think rock 'n' roll had a lot to do with the heart of it.

Also, there is the desolate landscape and horizon, all of the mythic things you hear about Lubbock; I think they're real, because you do see things different when you live on flat land.

I can remember little spot images which are wonderful to me; maybe twenty or thirty carloads of people going out to those cotton patches and forming a circle with the cars and everybody tuning into the same radio station and turning the headlights on and having a big dance in the middle of this ring of lights. And I always imagined what it would be like to go over in an airplane or flying saucer and see what was going on down there.

They did the same things with fistfights. Fistfights were very formal affairs in those days. If it was night, you'd call somebody out or they'd call you out and you'd pick a place. And it was nearly all the ways out to the south side of 82nd Street, which everybody used as a drag strip back then. There were no houses out there then; 50th Street was the last line of where the tract homes stopped and you hit the cotton patches. You'd drive out there and two guys would face off in the middle of these headlights and go at it.

But I think, always, it went back to that dirt somehow. When there was some drama going on, it ended up out there in the damn cotton patch with the radio playing.

You think about all the memorable first things that happened to you; what were the common denominators? It was always a car. It was always a radio. It was always whiskey or beer or bootleg liquor, because Lubbock was dry in those days.

That was the big enterprise: "How do you get liquor?" Mexico is where everybody went, to Juárez and Acuña, and brought back carloads full of whiskey and beer and raffled them off. I remember being in the Triple S Drug Store parking lot across from the old Hi-D-Ho on 34th and Flint, and standing out on Friday or Saturday night on the hood of your car and auctioning off what you brought back from Mexico. And that's how people made their money.

CHRIS: Just right out in public?

TERRY: Yeah. I mean, you'd see the cops coming and instantly hide it, you know. But they knew it was going on. Cops were kind of a different breed then, too, you know. But I'm certainly not one that's ever been very endeared by cops.

I know that when Joe got inducted into that Buddy Holly Walk of Fame, he told me he almost laughed when he was on the podium because they were handing him this award and saying all this great stuff about him and he was looking at these "dignitaries," people who were the upper crust of Lubbock who were doing this presentation, and Joe looking over at the jail and remembering being in there for some standard delinquent misdemeanor, and just trying to make the leap in his head from the Lubbock County jail to that goofy ceremonial stage.

That's a classic paradox, honoring the prodigal son. I don't think that's particularly unique to Lubbock but it is overt there because it is such a conservative place. I know that there was big-time living hell in Lubbock over the statue of Buddy Holly being put up in the first place. I guess they'd much rather have a statue of some Christian general armed to the teeth. But the irony of it is that Buddy Holly was armed to the teeth because he's got that big Stratocaster, you know, and that was a vicious weapon when he was living there in Lubbock. Now he's this huge export of the city; Buddy Holly is the dream child for the Chamber of Commerce. There's a saying in Lubbock: You do not want to die in the summer because you cannot get into the cemetery for all the tourists from England crammed in looking at Buddy Holly's grave.

But back to the religion thing; in Lubbock, any kind of erratic behavior is considered not moral, and the list of what is considered deviant behavior is incredibly long in that part of the country. I can remember huge record burnings at the fairgrounds in the '50s. The preachers from all of the churches would band together and make these pleas to the youth of the city to come and get rid of this devil music. Anything that enticed you in any way, whether it was sexual or not, any sensual kind of pleasure was a threat. And I mean a major threat in those days, and it still is, it seems.

There was a definite phenomenon that happened there, I think, for anybody that had a curious urge. Making music, or any kind of art, I think for people that do it and continue to do it, making anything is a personal necessity. It doesn't mean their life is going to be any better because they do it; in lots of cases their life is worse, actually.

But it is a need that you can't teach. You can't make another person have that creative need. It's like this book you're writing: Writing is that same need, the something you need to do, even though you may not understand why you need to do it.

There was a group of people in Lubbock for whom that's how the dice rolled. It happened to a certain generation there. That need became apparent. And I think it was music that got it going for a lot of us. When ol' Presley, or Perkins, or whichever one you heard first, said, "Don't step on my blue suede shoes," that was an anthem. It was a total anthem, and you didn't even know it was an anthem at the time. It just hammered a bell. It didn't have anything to do with all the shit they were laying on you, whether it was the churches or the schools. It was something about *you*. And I think it isolated you. It isolated me. It made me totally unsure of myself as a person, made me want to leave Lubbock, go look for something that was mine.

It's a funny thing, though, because there's something about Lubbock that is not neurotic. There's not a lot of self-pity floating around in that town, which you find in a lot of other places. It's like people in Lubbock decide who they are and what they are and "Fuck you, if you don't like it."

When I was a little kid, my dad ran Fair Park Coliseum and that's where they had the wrestling matches every week. My mother used to sell tickets to the wrestling matches at Wiley's Drug, and I would go across the street to the courthouse and sit and listen to old men sitting out in front of the courthouse whittling or playing checkers and forty-two. To this day, I remember a hard bitterness there toward changing times, but also a deep pride. It was like: You do what you say you're gonna do. You dance with the one you brung; that system of values, which I think is also very ingrained there in Lubbock.

So it's that spooky double edge of deeply believing those values you grew up with, but at the same time wanting desperately to do something of your own and all of a sudden that desire slams you head-on with all these people and values you were raised to respect. It is mind boggling, you know, especially when you're a kid.

CHRIS: I'd like you to talk about *Chippy*, the musical play you and Jo Harvey did, with a Lubbock all-star cast including Joe Ely, Butch Hancock, and Jo Carol Pierce.

TERRY: *Chippy* originated when we got these old diaries from Joe Sears and Jaston Williams, who have an act called *Greater Tuna*. They had come across these great old diaries of this woman who had made her living as an oil field prostitute in West Texas during the Depression. They were amazing to read, but Joe and Jaston didn't know what to do with them. They knew Jo Harvey was out performing her one-woman shows, so they thought she might be interested and sent them to her. She loved them, but didn't know what to do with them either.

It was a fluke they were ever made into a play like it was. The way that happened was, one night Jo Harvey and I were having supper with a guy from Charlotte, who we knew from having done a play at the Spoletto Festival. He had been the director of the festival but he had left and ended up as the director of the Santa Fe Opera. We were having supper with him, and we started talking about how this group of people, all from Lubbock, had always wanted to do something together but it just never worked out. And we also said how it would take a lot of money to get everybody to stop what they were doing and get under one roof to work on something together.

The next day, this guy calls us and says he'd pitched the idea to the American Musical Theatre Festival in Philly, and they thought it would make a really neat musical play. So we were in this dilemma: What do we do now? We called everybody up, and they were all excited, but we had no clue where to start. We got together in Austin and talked about all kinds of ideas; how the whole thing takes place in a honky-tonk or the honky-tonk parking lot. Then Jo Harvey remembered the diaries. So we later faxed the diaries to everybody. Everybody read them and said, "It's great because, for one thing, it's like all of our relatives were her johns." Once we got into reading the diaries and finding out about her, we began to build an idea of how it might work, making up about as much as we found out, but trying to make her real. She actually called herself Chippy, which is West Texas slang for an easy pickup. We tried to make her into a human person of that era instead of some kind of dramatic cartoon. It was very fertile ground for all of us to work in because it was what we knew.

She had roamed all over West Texas. She was a generation removed from us; it was the fucking Depression, but everybody our age in West Texas had it nailed into us how rough the Dust Bowl was, how hard those times were. The diaries were a dense, true history. She documented every song on the jukebox, every movie that played, every band in every juke joint, a total descriptive history. It was the time of Bob Wills and all those touring bands, which are an indelible influence on anybody who likes music and grew up in that part of the country. It was our musical inspiration for the play. Chippy and her times ran through all of our bloodlines.

So that's how *Chippy* came about: This bunch of Philly Yankees financed the whole thing. We did a workshop for two weeks in front of audiences in Philly, and then the following year did a full run in Philly, and then took it to the Serious Fun Festival at the Lincoln Center in New York.

We put out a record of the songs on Hollywood Records. We wrote all the songs in the play individually and together, most specifically for the play but some were songs we had written earlier but worked with the play.

CHRIS: I know that you are friends with David Byrne of the band Talking Heads. And Jo Harvey is great in his 1986 film *True Stories*. That is such an astonishing movie for me to watch, being from Lubbock, because that "fictional" West Texas town is so much like the Lubbock that I know. For David Byrne to come from Rhode Island or New York City or wherever and make a film that so captures the weirdness of life in West Texas in such an observant way, that's pretty amazing to me. I know that some of the music in the movie is performed by you and the Panhandle Mystery Band. And Jo Harvey almost steals the show as "The Lying Woman." How did y'all meet David Byrne and get involved in that classic film?

TERRY: Actually, I met David when he was making *True Stories*. David was listening to my album *Lubbock: on everything* a lot because he was shooting that movie about Texas. He was listening to a lot of Texas and Tejano music to get the feel. He asked me to write a song for the film with him and that's how we became friends. We continue to do stuff off and on. David and I are real opposite in lots of ways. We write music very different. We have different avenues of how we get information. But our common ground is curiosity. He is one of the most remarkably curious people on all levels of anyone I have ever met. He's incredibly visual, which I think, actually everybody from Lubbock is really visual (although David isn't from Lubbock, of course; he's from Baltimore).

It's storytelling. When there's really nothing visual there, you become very imaginative and inventive in making what is there into "another there." I have great respect for people who do that. It's how you survive.

In a lot of ways, David Byrne reminds me of Joe Ely. There is an intensity about Joe and David that is very similar. They are both probably the most uninhibited and intense stage performers of anybody I know. They're my two favorite people to watch play in your living room or on a stage or wherever because it's never dicking around. If they are singing you a song, they're singing it full-tilt boogie. I like that a lot. I like that passion. It's complete respect for what you're doing, and that always comes out. It's true with Joe. It's true with David. I think that is what music and life has to be about.

CHRIS: Everything is so well defined in Lubbock, so curiosity is an important factor in this equation; curiosity and the drive to explore. One begins to ask, "Surely everything can't be so plain and simple as it is in Lubbock?"

TERRY: There is a community expectation in Lubbock. It's another irony because you also have there the Grand Pioneer Spirit, the individual who stands alone. Man, those people had some hard bark on them, the people that settled that murderous place. It's not a pleasant place to live.

Lubbock is a most mysterious place, to be so normal at the same time. Well, I don't know if "normal" is ever the word I would use for Lubbock. I made that perfect circle of really hating it, and then coming back when I did *Lubbock: on everything*, it was like coming to terms with a whole lot of things between myself and that town. It was like the first time I really saw Lubbock.

It was strange because I had written all of these songs and expressed this total hostility about the place, and it literally wasn't until we were listening to the mixes that it dawned on me: Not one of those songs were really hostile about that place. I realized then that I felt something completely opposite inside myself. That took me back because, here I am thinking, "Goddamn, I never want to go back there again." Every time before when I'd go back, I would get on that Loop 289 that circles the city and drive around it, over and over. I would think, "I better get off here," and then, "Nah, I ain't getting off here. I'll get off the next place." I would make these circles for hours driving

TERRY ALLEN AND STUBB IN FRONT OF STUBB'S, 1980.

around that stupid Loop in Lubbock. Because there was no reason to get off of it, you know? It was like I was going to turn to butter, going 'round and 'round like that.

But when I went back and made that record, everything changed, my attitude and all of it; well, nearly all. I really liked Lubbock, really liked its goofiness. I couldn't help myself. I really like its Nazi core. And yeah, on another level I still despised part of it, too.

CHRIS: I know one of your favorite spots in Lubbock was Stubb's Barbecue on East Broadway. Tell me about your friendship with Stubb and your involvement in the Stubb's Memorial in Lubbock.

TERRY: I met Stubb in 1977 when I came back to Lubbock to record *Lubbock: on everything*. My old friend and fellow artist Paul Milosevich told me I needed to meet Stubb so he took me out to his barbecue place. Stubb was in there by himself, listening to that great jukebox of his. We spent the next four hours talking, and I loved him right off because there wasn't a word that came out of his mouth that wasn't like a poem. Stubb's use of the English language was about as unique as anyone I've ever known.

I had told Stubb I was recording the album, and the next night we started at about two in the morning. About that time, Stubb showed up at the studio with piles of free barbecue for us all. Richard Bowden had hitchhiked in from Austin for the gig and was starving; he was a vegetarian and he even ate some ribs! Since that time, Stubb's Barbecue became my focal point in Lubbock. It got to where as soon as I got to town, I would drop Jo Harvey off at her folks' and go immediately to Stubb's to hang out with him.

The first time I played with the Panhandle Mystery Band in public was at Stubb's after the release party for the *Lubbock: on everything* album. I went back as much as I could for a series of shows we did at Stubb's. The late '70s and early '80s was such a fertile time for music in Lubbock, and Stubb was an integral part in all the musicians' lives then. He'd show up at just the right time with food and was our best friend, and that carried over when he moved to Austin until the time he died.

Stubb's funeral was in Lubbock and it was a typical Stubb's gathering; half the audience was white and the other half was black, with Stubb in the middle wearing that goofy denim cowboy hat he always wore. Joe Ely, Jesse Taylor, and I sang at the funeral.

For several years afterwards, Paul Milosevich and I were talking about how we should do some sort of memorial for Stubb, something right where all of that great music happened. By this time, the old property had been torn down and there was nothing left but the concrete slab and the linoleum floor. There were a bunch of telephone poles and junk piled up on the lot. The city government was initially very resistant to contributing to build anything on East Broadway, because of the part of town. The guy who owned the land said he would donate the property if the city would maintain it. Since the city initially wouldn't give us any money for the memorial, we raised the money ourselves. Ely and I did a benefit concert at Fair Park Coliseum and had big buckets where people could throw money into. We also did benefit shows in Austin and Dallas. Paul's ex-wife Debbie Milosevich was on Lubbock's Art Commission and came up with the idea to sell bricks for $150 each, with donors' names engraved on them, to frame the property with a brick walkway. We raised about two hundred thousand dollars. The city felt left behind, I think, and eventually gave us another twenty-five grand.

I did the bronze sculpture of Stubb. People donated time and money to build a brick wall for the memorial plaque. And we put plaques on the linoleum floor where things were, like the jukebox, the pit, the pool table, the booth where his pals Little Pete and Cuz frequently sat, et cetera. It was very much a communal effort by the musicians and other people who loved Stubb. It took about five years to come to fruition. The memorial is officially called *Barbecue Beyond the Grave*.

The sculpture of Stubb was one of the most emotionally and physically difficult pieces I ever made, but I am perhaps as proud of that sculpture of Stubb on East Broadway in Lubbock as I am of any piece of work I've ever done. It is a tribute to what Stubb did in Lubbock, what nobody else really did, which is wiping out the color lines, the racial divide. I hope that the people of Lubbock can recognize what a valuable contribution he made.

Amarillo Highway (for Dave Hickey)

from the album Lubbock: on everything

I'm a high straight in Plainview
Side bet in Idalou
an' a fresh deck in New Deal
Some call me high hand,
an' some call me low hand,
but I'm holding what I am . . .
The Wheel

'Cause I'm a panhandlin'
Man handlin'
Post holin'
High rollin'
Dust Bowlin' Daddy
I ain't got no blood veins
I just got them four lanes
Of hard . . . Amarillo Highway

I don't wear no Stetson
But I'm willin' to bet son
That I'm a big a Texan as you are
'Cause there's a girl in her bare feet
Asleep on the back seat
An that trunk is full of Pearl and Lone
     Star

Gonna hop outta bed
Pop a pill in my head
Bust the Hub for the Golden Spread
Under blue skies
Gonna stuff my hide
Behind some power glide
An get some southern fried . . . back
     in my eyes

As close as I'll ever get to heaven
Is makin' speed up ol' 87
That hard-ass Amarillo Highway

Flatland Farmer
from the album Lubbock: on everything

He's a flatland farmer
Who flatpicks an old guitar
Yeah he's a flatland farmer
He flatpicks an old guitar
He don't make no money
But he can out-pick them Nashville stars
The people come in pick-ups
They travel in from miles around
Ahhh the people come in pick-ups
They travel in from miles around
Yeah they park in his front yard . . .
    sit on his ground
An they eat fried chicken to that flatland
    sound
Eat a little . . .
Well they call mighty Nashville
Music City USA
Yeah they call that god-all-mighty
    Nashville
Music City USA
But get out of the city to where the
    farmer plays
An you're into real music country with-
    out them city ways
Get with the flatland farmer
Who flatpicks an old guitar
Get with the flatland farmer
Who flatpicks an old guitar
An closest you'll want to any Music Row
Is a long dirt furrow where cotton grows
Grow . . .
Get with the flatland farmer
Who flatpicks an old guitar
Yeah, get with the flatland farmer
Who flatpicks an old guitar

He don't make no money
But I'll tell you, that boy can
Out sing
Out pick
Out play
Out drink
Out pray . . . and out lay
Any of them Nashville stars

The Wolfman of Del Rio

from the album Lubbock: on everything

He took his first release on a highway
In a 1953 green Chevrolet
And he was carryin' an awful load
For just a 15-year-old
'Til he laid his mind
On the center line
An turned up the radio
Goin' a hundred miles an hour
Down the blue asphaltum line
Listening to the Wolfman of Del Rio
An he didn't give a damn
About the trouble he was in
Yeah deep down in his soul
He just wanted . . . to go
An you can tell by the look on his face
He's all caught up with the need
To trade in some emptied out spaces
For some speeeeeeed
An that good ol' American Dream

She took her first release on the back seat
Of a 1961 black V-8 Ford
An she just give up all control
On that vinyl tuck-and-roll
Breathin' hard
With a dark-eyed boy
That she barely even knowed
Goin' a hundred miles an hour
Down the blue asphaltum line
Listenin' to the Wolfman of Del Rio
An she didn't give a damn
About the trouble she'd get in
Deep down in her soul
She just wanted . . . to flow
An you can tell by the paint on her face

She's all made-up for the need
To trade in some emptied out places
For some speeeeeeed
An that good ol' American Dream

An now they circle one another
Armed with the lives from their past
An they fight to the death for their lies
'Til the bad feelings pass
Then they sit
An they smoke
An they drink
An they talk and talk and talk and talk
An then they stalk around
Like they're lookin' for something
    they've lost
But can never again be found
An it's crazy
Yeah, crazy in the backyards, the
    bedrooms, the kitchens
Crazy out in the streets

Through all their cities
An even smaller towns
It most certainly seems
Some disease of the dreams
Has been goin' 'round
Yes, it most certainly seems
Some disease of the dreams
Has been goin' 'round
Goin' a hundred miles an hour
Down the blue asphaltum line
Listenin' to the Wolfman of Del Rio

Gimme a Ride to Heaven Boy
from the album Bloodlines

I was caught up with myself
On the highway at night
Drivin' like a bat outta hell
When I beheld an amazing sight
It was a lonely apparition
By the roadside standing there
With his thumb out in the wilderness
And a halo in his hair

Chorus:
He said, "Gimme a ride to heaven boy
I'll show you paradise
Yeah gimme a ride to heaven boy
My name is Jesus Christ"

So I come screeching to a halt
I said, "Hop on in"
He said, "Thanks a lot for the lift
I forgive you of your sins
Yeah I just come from Jerusalem
Where things are going bad
Ahhh gimme a ride to heaven boy
I need to talk to my dad"

Well I didn't know what to do
So I jammed her down in gear
Kind a kicked my feet beneath the seat
I was trying to hide the beer
but he just grinned and said, "My
    friend,
I know you must think it's odd
But you got nothin' to fear about
    drinkin' a beer
If you share it with the son of God"

Chorus repeats

Well I saw good news in his baby blues
So I stomped it on the floor
I said you have to show me how to get
    there
I ain't been before
"Well it's a hard place to find," he said
"But I'll give you a little clue
It ain't somewhere up in the air
It's sittin' right here inside with you"
Then right in the middle of that perfect
    smile
From his robes he pulled a gun
And stuck it up beside my head and
    said,
"How's this for Kingdom Come?"
Well I pulled off scared but I heard him
    say
As he left me beneath the stars
"The Lord moves in mysterious ways
and tonight, my son . . . He's gonna use
    your car"

Chorus repeats

Flatland Boogie

from the album Human Remains

Up on the Caprock
Me and my baby ride
Goin' a hundred miles an hour
Cause this old Ford can still fly
Got Four Roses in a sack
An we ain't lookin' back tonight

Some top 40 Shorty's
Singin' on the radio
And there's cotton fields forever
On both sides of the road
It's still the Flatland Boogie
But where did the Wolfman go?

Chorus:
Old photographs turn yellow
Times they come and go
But we can still do the boogie
From the High Plains to Mexico
Some old Angel from Amarillo
Must be helpin' us to hold it on the road

Moonlight's a fallin'
Look at that caliche glow
An old coyote's a howlin'
Doesn't know he's too old
Headlights a shinin'
On all we ever need to know

Cross the Llano Estacado
Baby's still by my side
Ain't no reason to stop
And there ain't no place to hide
You want to Flatland Boogie
Better flat out come and ride

Chorus repeats

RICHARD BOWDEN is one of the original members of Terry Allen's Panhandle Mystery Band. He spent over ten years in Lubbock playing fiddle with the Maines Brothers Band. Richard now lives in Austin, where for several years he was a member of the sardonic Austin Lounge Lizards. Retired from group life, Richard still performs regularly with Lubbock artists Cary Swinney, Terry Allen, and others.

Bowden

RICHARD: My dad had a record deal when I was a kid. He eventually gave up on professional music and became an economics professor, but he never stopped playing and singing, with Mom and us kids harmonizing. My folks got me piano lessons and made me play trumpet in school band. I hated both. When I was sixteen years old my dad was teaching at Texas A & M. Living in College Station, I was lucky to meet a great Texas bluesman, Mance Lipscomb, who would come up from Navasota to play at a coffeehouse there He allowed me to visit his home, showed me pictures of him with Bob Dylan, and showed me how he used a pocketknife to play slide guitar. He was so generous. I tried to do what he showed me on my guitar, but never could get it.

In the summer of 1969 I hitchhiked to the Woodstock Music Festival. Woodstock was a life-changing experience for me. When I came back to Texas for my last year of high school, I was determined to get into music somehow. My mom had her old violin in a closet and let me try it. I would put on a Cream or Jimi Hendrix record and try to copy the guitar licks. I loved it! That's how I learned to play violin. I got out of high school in 1970 without graduating and moved straight to Austin, where I lived in a big house full of friends from College Station. We started a band called the Sitting Ducks.

In fact, our first paying gig was where Stubb's Barbecue in Austin is now located, on Eighth and Red River. It was called the One Knite back then. I got paid four dollars.

Then I went down to Mexico for a while and had all kinds of adventures that I barely lived through. When I got back to Texas, I got interested in a guru known as "The Fourteen-Year-Old Perfect Master of Self." He was fourteen years old then. He's not anymore, obviously. So then I went off to India.

CHRIS: This was the same guru that Jimmie Gilmore and Tommy Hancock followed, isn't it? Did you know them?

RICHARD: No, Tommy and Jimmie are both older than me, and they had already been playing music around Lubbock for a long time. I met them after I got back from India.

CHRIS: So how did you end up in Lubbock?

RICHARD: When I came back from India, my dad was teaching economics at State University of New York at Fredonia. They have a good music and recording engineering school, and I was able to get in with a GED.

During summer vacation I hitchhiked out to Denver, where a lot of my guru's followers were living. I met Jimmie Gilmore there in Denver, and I played some music with him. That's when I met his wife Debby and their baby, Colin. The next summer I went back to Denver, and Debby and Jimmie had broken up. Debby and I ended up together. She visited me in New York that fall, got pregnant, and went back to Lubbock. We decided to get married but I finished that semester at SUNY, and then we both moved to Austin.

In Austin I tried to make enough money to support us all. Debby introduced me to Butch Hancock and we played some gigs. But there wasn't enough money to support a family. Those were tough times in Austin.

We would go up to Lubbock sometimes to visit Debby's folks, and there always seemed to be work with Debby's Lubbock friends. I sat in with the Joe Ely Band some. This was about 1976 or '77. I got to know Lloyd Maines through the Joe Ely Band. Lloyd offered me a steady job with the Maines Brothers Band, so we moved to Lubbock.

The Maines Brothers were very professional, a second-generation family band, besides being great people. I always made good money with them. And the Maines Brothers were an awesome band, a powerhouse! They always challenged me musically. I learned a lot from them. It was the Maines Brothers Band that kept me in Lubbock for so many years. I lived in Lubbock until 1986.

CHRIS: How did you find Lubbock while you were living there?

RICHARD: A lot of different ways. There are a lot of good things about Lubbock. Living in Lubbock plugged me into some real basic values, such as loyalty and hard work, good things. It was refreshing, I must admit. But there were a lot of things that made me feel as if I had to get the hell out of there. I was wanting to leave Lubbock for a long time before I actually left. Lubbock is very conservative, and it had gotten too small for me. I missed Austin so much.

But there were a few people in Lubbock, just a handful, who were like the Underground. I would hang out with them, and it was almost like being in Austin, except in a very Lubbock way, if you know what I mean. These were music lovers, freethinkers, some associated with the university, some were independent country folks. This underground community in Lubbock is very rich in culture, but kept hidden away from the general population. In Lubbock you get the feeling that someone is watching you,

VIEW OF DOWNTOWN LUBBOCK

like you can't get away with anything. These people would have me play fiddle at their private house parties, which were frequent. They introduced me to new music. It was a real enlightening experience for me. It kept me alive.

Getting to know Terry Allen was something else that endeared Lubbock to me. I've been playing with Terry since Lloyd got me in on *Lubbock: on everything,* when I first started with the Maines Brothers. I think Terry has had a huge effect on Lubbock music.

I finally did move back to Austin and have been here ever since. I occasionally make it back to Lubbock to play with the Maines Brothers or Cary Swinney. I always enjoy myself in Lubbock.

CHRIS: You mention those basic values you learned from Lubbock. What is it that Lubbock has to teach an artist or a musician living there?

RICHARD: One important thing about being an up-and-coming musician in Lubbock, is you are not a musician in just any old small town. You are in a small town that has produced a lot of successful, well-known musicians. So your sights are much higher than some kid down the road in Abilene or Amarillo. You look at Buddy Holly, or think, "Bobby Keys went to my high school and look at him now! He's playing with the Rolling Stones, and what am I doing here?" The Lubbock music community really makes you set your sights high.

The quality of music in Lubbock has always been really good, compared to almost anywhere. Musicians in Lubbock are serious about the music business, the actual business of it, and serious about playing the music well. You expect everybody to pull their own weight. That was a good experience for me.

People expect the music to be good; I'm talking about the general population in Lubbock. I think their ears are more sophisticated than many other towns. They have been exposed to a lot of good music. And they tend to support weird stuff sometimes. Cary Swinney, for instance; he's pretty radical, for Lubbock especially. But Cary's got a lot of support there. It's strange.

Things were really happening musically in Lubbock when I was there. It has gone like that in Lubbock for a long time, these phases it goes through, strange solar flares that fire up and then die down again.

I think it has something to do with those UFOs they are always spotting in the skies around Lubbock.

LLOYD MAINES grew up playing country and western dance music in Lubbock with his brothers Kenny, Steve, and Donnie in the Maines Brothers Band. Moonlighting as the powerful pedal-steel guitar player for Lubbock rocker Joe Ely and other Texas music icons such as Jerry Jeff Walker, Lloyd has earned a reputation as one of the great pedal-steel innovators and performers. A man known for hard work, Lloyd also earned a reputation as a reliable and successful record producer while working at Lubbock's Caldwell Studio. Since moving to Austin in 1998, Lloyd has been named Producer of the Year at the Austin Music Awards on several occasions.

This interview occurred at South Austin's Cedar Creek Studios, where Lloyd produced several acclaimed albums for artists such as Pat Green, Cory Morrow, Jerry Jeff Walker, Ray Wiley Hubbard, Wilco, and the Dixie Chicks. Coincidentally, the previous evening, Lloyd's daughter Natalie had appeared in her first nationally televised performance with her band the Dixie Chicks. The following year, the Dixie Chicks settled a much publicized lawsuit with their recording label Sony, which earned them considerably more creative freedom in producing their own music. The Chicks then hired the best producer they knew, Natalie's dad Lloyd, to coproduce their third album. They went back to their musical roots for an album of traditional country acoustic instrumentation with progressive lyrics, and they called the record *Home*. Lloyd was on stage alongside the Dixie Chicks when *Home* received the 2002 Grammy Award for Best Country Album of the Year.

Maines

CHRIS: I want your expert opinion on how Lubbock has affected music both globally, from Buddy Holly to Natalie Maines, and then locally, how Lubbock has contributed to Texas music and the "Austin Sound."

LLOYD: I don't think that Buddy Holly got the respect that he deserved in Lubbock until long after his death. Buddy Holly was shunned while he lived in Lubbock. A lot of the dances he would play, he would play rock 'n' roll, and the sponsors of the dances discouraged rock 'n' roll. They were afraid he was going to get the kids riled up, I guess.

To tell you the truth, even though I was born and raised in Lubbock, I didn't really get a grasp on how much Buddy Holly had influenced music worldwide until I started playing with Joe Ely. That was in 1973. Until I heard Joe doing his versions of Buddy Holly music, to tell you the truth, I had never even paid that much attention to Holly's music.

Then I went to England with Joe and toured with the Clash. I hadn't realized what an impact Buddy Holly and the Lubbock music scene had on England. When we landed over there, they treated us like kings, and it was because we were from Lubbock. There were still a lot of Buddy Holly fans over there, and the fact that we were from Lubbock made us part of that scene. So I think that I only started realizing what an impact Buddy Holly had at that point.

When I was a kid, my brothers and I played all around the West Texas area. We would play at a high school gymnasium for a dance on a Friday night and we'd see posters where Bob Wills was going to be there the next night. But at that point, we weren't impressed. We did our gig and went on back home. To us, Bob Wills was just another band on the road. Had I known that I would value the Bob Wills influence as much as I do today, I would have made an effort to hear Bob Wills play live, at least once, which I really regret never doing. Bob Wills had such a tremendous effect on country music worldwide. Every country artist has attempted at least some western swing, and that all started with Bob Wills, from up in Turkey, Texas.

CHRIS: Waylon Jennings was also part of that crowd of Lubbock musicians from Buddy Holly's day. Did you know Waylon while he was in Lubbock?

LLOYD: Waylon was a deejay at KLLL. I remember when I was a kid Waylon Jennings being on the radio. My dad and uncles would do concerts in the park and various music revues, and I remember Waylon Jennings being a part of many of those shows.

CHRIS: Speaking of your dad, tell me about the previous Maines Brothers Band, which consisted of your dad and his brothers.

LLOYD: They didn't do a lot of original material. They did a lot of western swing; a lot of Bob Wills, Hank Thompson, Ray Price. They played the old honky-tonk dance music, and were really good. They had a good pedal-steel player, a good fiddle player. Sort of weekend warriors. They all had other jobs. My brothers and I started singing with them when we were young teenagers. Dad would take us to their gigs to sing for the crowd. That was my first taste of performing music.

At first it was just us four guys. My little sister Latronda started singing with us later on, but when we started she was just a little baby. It was just us four guys all the way through high school. When I graduated, I went to college and got married. Steve went to college; Kenny graduated and went to Las Vegas and started playing with a guy named Kenny Vernon. And Donnie was still in high school. So we all parted ways for a while. Once everybody had gone our separate ways, I settled down in Lubbock and started working at Don Caldwell's studio in 1971. I was still playing music and started playing regularly with Joe Ely in 1973.

Then Kenny eventually came back from Vegas, and he and Steve decided to crank the Maines Brothers Band up again. I was with Ely, so they got the Brownlow brothers, Randy and Jerry. Kenny, Steve, Donnie, and the Brownlow brothers played for a long time, and anytime I was back in town from being out with Ely, I would play with them. About 1980, when Ely started doing so much traveling and was on the road way more than I could be, I started playing with the brothers full-time again.

There was one time in Lubbock where there was music seven nights a week, in the late 1960s and early '70s, when the Maines Brothers were first playing together. Lubbock was hopping then. Lubbock had been dry up until the late 1960s. Anytime anybody in Lubbock wanted to drink, they had to drive all the way to Post, which is about fifty miles away. When Lubbock County voted in liquor by the drink [on April 9, 1972], it was like a feeding frenzy. For a period of about seven or eight years, the Strip south of town on the Tahoka Highway was a really hot spot for clubs, and almost every club had music seven nights a week. The Alamo was the biggest place out on the Strip. There was another bar out there for a long time called the Golden Nugget. Another called the Little Country Inn. It used to be both clubs and liquor stores out on the Strip. These days, you can get liquor by the drink in restaurants and clubs in town; only the package liquor stores are on the Strip now.

Tommy and Charlene Hancock owned the Cotton Club, so they were out there a lot with the Supernatural Family Band. Any touring band traveling from coast to coast had to come through Lubbock, so they would always stop off and play the Cotton Club. Lubbock was a melting pot. Basically, because Lubbock is in the middle of nowhere, it was a good pickup gig for musicians passing through. Seeing those bands had a lot of influence on me. I saw Willie Nelson at the Cotton Club when he still had a crew cut! Learning to play steel when I was seventeen, I got to hear Jimmy Day playing steel for Willie Nelson. Jimmy Day was a tremendous influence on me, the inspiration for me to want to learn how to play.

When I was learning to play, there were no teachers around, as far as taking lessons. I would hear people like Jimmy Day and Frank Carter, who played in my father's band and gave me my first pedal-steel. I would watch them play intently, watch what they were doing, their technique.

There was another guy named Bob Stufflebeme. Bob was a good machinist, and anytime anything would go wrong on my steel, he could fix it. He actually built steels as a sideline. Bob showed me a few steel licks; he was a really good steel player.

I learned from watching people, really paying attention to what was going on. And listening to records. I just taught myself. Consequently, my style is different than your average picker from Nashville, because all the guys from Nashville learned the same approach. My approach is a little different, which actually has paid off for me. It got me a lot of work and a lot of attention that I wouldn't have had.

CHRIS: Perhaps we see so many unique artists coming from Lubbock because, with little outside influence, many of you had to make up your styles mostly on your own. Speaking of unique artists from Lubbock, how did you meet Joe Ely?

LLOYD: I first met Joe through the Flatlanders. My friend Sylvester Rice was playing bass with the Flatlanders when they first started in 1970. Syl told me a couple of times, "You have to hear these guys doing this funky old folk music." I saw them at a place called the Town Pump over on 4th Street, just east of where the bar Fat Dawg's used to be. I thought the music was real interesting, so I went and heard them a bunch of times. Ely and Jimmie Gilmore would come hear the Maines Brothers from time to time.

I started using Ely in the studio playing harmonica on various recording projects at Caldwell's studio. If an album was in progress and we needed a harmonica, I would call Ely because he was as good a harmonica player as I knew. Then I lost track of Ely for a while when he left to join the Ringling Brothers Circus.

Ely came back through Lubbock in 1974 and gave me a call. He said, "I'm trying to raise enough money to leave town and move down to Austin. I'm gathering up some people and I want to play the Main Street Saloon tonight." So he got me, a guy named Rick Hulett on guitar, and a bass player named Greg Wright, just us three guys and Ely. No drums. We were totally winging it. Ely did a few Jimmy Rodgers songs, a few Hank Williams songs, and then he would throw some of his original stuff in. We were all paying attention just enough to where we could follow him pretty well. That first weekend at Main Street was pretty phenomenal. People went nuts over us, and we made fifty bucks each, which was a lot of money for us at that time.

Ely came to us afterwards and said, "This worked great! What about if we do it one more weekend, and then I'll have enough money saved up to move to Austin." We did another show at Main Street Saloon the next weekend. It was standing room only and the line was out the door, all the way out to University Avenue. We made a lot more money that night. That was when the light went on in Ely's head: "Maybe we should do this gig for a little while longer."

We actually called a rehearsal at this point. We went to Joe's house and arranged some songs. The next time we played Main Street Saloon, we charged more money. The word had spread by this time, like a mushroom effect. We were an instant hit, and I mean a *big* hit. Joe pretty much decided then and there that he better stay in Lubbock for a while.

It was strange how it happened, because Joe was all ready to move to Austin. He had nothing going on in Lubbock before that. He was ready to head down because Jimmie Gilmore was already in Austin. But Joe Ely didn't move to Austin until 1980.

We began to tour based out of Lubbock. And man, we toured all over, all across the country. Joe got his MCA record deal in 1976, and the rest is history.

CHRIS: Tell me about meeting your longtime friend Terry Allen.

LLOYD: Terry Allen's *Lubbock: on everything* album was really my first claim to doing a production that I thought was a valid everlasting production. That album will always be around.

In 1977, Terry Allen came into town with a notebook full of songs. We met him one day and started cutting tracks the next. Making *Lubbock: on everything* really got me hooked on recording. I realized then that what I wanted to do with my life is make records. Up to that point, I had enjoyed playing on records and making a living doing it. But the *Lubbock: on everything* record was when I started thinking, "Maybe I have a knack for helping put albums together." I just loved it.

CHRIS: What do you think your production skills are?

LLOYD: I think that my fortes are helping to arrange the music, to coordinate the musicians, and keeping things moving forward. I try to keep everything positive and make the artist comfortable and confident that things are going down on tape correctly. I think a lot of it has to do with a general work ethic, and I attribute that to my parents. They instilled that work ethic in our whole family.

CHRIS: People always say, "Lubbock is a nice place to have a family." Is that fundamentally why you stayed in Lubbock all those years, to raise your kids?

LLOYD: I have two daughters, Kimberly and Natalie. When I was young, I made the decision to be a responsible parent. In 1980, when Ely was touring and Austin was a hotbed for music, I could have made the move to Austin with Ely. But both my kids were in elementary school in 1980. I didn't want to yank them out of school and pull them down to Austin. I thought about their feelings first. I was flying back and forth to Austin and really could do both, juggling music and family.

Then our kids grew up. Natalie joined the Dixie Chicks, and Kim graduated from Tech and moved to Austin to produce the news for KXAN. When I figured my travel expenses for my 1997 taxes, I discovered I had worked in Austin 214 days that year. My wife had been wanting to move for a while, and we liked Austin. We already had a daughter living here. Once we had the empty nest, my wife and I decided that there really was nothing to keep us in Lubbock.

CHRIS: When did you first record with Jerry Jeff Walker?

LLOYD: I met Jerry Jeff in '76, when I was coming down to play with Ely back in the Austin Outlaw music days. Jerry Jeff was a fan of Joe Ely. In fact, Jerry Jeff and his band, Bob Livingston and Gary P. Nunn, were very instrumental in getting Joe his MCA deal. They pretty much turned MCA on to Joe.

I had known Jerry Jeff all of those years but had lost touch with him. He went through a lot of band changes, and he actually dissolved his band in '86. He was just doing solo then. In 1988 Jerry Jeff called me in Lubbock, and he said, "I'm forming a band, just temporarily, in order to do a record called *Live at Gruene Hall*. I'm hand-picking some guys that I've always wanted to play with, so you're the steel guitar player." He put together me and Champ Hood, and he got a piano player from Dallas named Brian Piper and a few other folks. He brought us to Austin; we rehearsed one night and then went and cut *Live at Gruene Hall*. That was an impromptu thing but it turned out great!

After that, I started playing a few gigs with him, and then before I knew it I was back and forth to Austin all the time. I'd come down for recording and playing with Jerry Jeff. So I've produced all of Jerry Jeff's records from that point forward.

My association with Jerry Jeff got me a lot of work in Austin. I did those Lost Gonzo Band records with Bob Livingston and Gary Nunn, and they turned out so good that people began to seek me out for their projects. That connection got me producing Chris Wall's record, and Robert Earl Keen's second live record. At the time, there were a lot of young Texas singer-songwriters coming up out of high school and college that were idolizing Jerry Jeff and Robert Earl Keen. Pat Green and Cory Morrow are among those ranks. Pat and Cory both went to Texas Tech and started out in Lubbock, and they are both making huge strides, selling tons of records and drawing humongous crowds. Those guys hired me to do their records based on the fact that they liked Jerry Jeff's records. It was a domino effect.

CHRIS: Now we can get into Lubbock's influence on Austin music.

LLOYD: There are a few bands that have called tremendous attention to Austin: Jerry Jeff, the Thunderbirds, Stevie Ray Vaughan. Of course Stevie Ray spent a lot of time in Lubbock. Stubb would always let Stevie Ray sleep at his place, and he would feed him barbecue. If you were a traveling musician, you always got a free meal at Stubb's. In the 1980s, Joe Ely brought a lot of attention to Austin, both nationally and internationally. People like Ely would hone their craft in Lubbock, and Austin was the next logical place for getting your music heard. Austin was a little more artist friendly, and more original-music friendly than Lubbock. Until I started playing with Ely in '73, you never even thought about doing original material in Lubbock. You would always play what was on the radio because that's what people want to hear. Joe opened my eyes. He was doing his own music, and people loved it!

CHRIS: Let's talk about your daughter Natalie Maines. What do you think the Dixie Chicks' influence on country music has been?

LLOYD: The Dixie Chicks have changed the whole complexion of country music. Nashville is a very controlled environment and the Dixie Chicks did a lot to wrestle some of that control back to the artists. First of all, Sony tried to get them to change their name right away, thinking the name was politically incorrect and that some women would take offense. But the Chicks said, "No, that's our name. Don't change it." Then Sony tried to convince them not to play their own instruments. They wanted to hire studio musicians, and the girls would just sing. The Chicks, especially the sisters Martie and Emily, said, "No way!" They worked for years learning to play and felt like they had earned it. At that point, Natalie played minimal guitar but now she plays really good rhythms because she's had to keep up with the sisters. But Emily and Martie can stand up and compete with anybody on fiddle and banjo. They are amazing!

Now the Dixie Chicks have had quite a bit of success. They continue to shake up the world of country music, doing things different than most acts are doing it these days.

CHRIS: Do you have any other thoughts or inspirations about why there are so many unique musicians from Lubbock?

LLOYD: It is always asked. There was an exhibit at the Texas Tech Museum about West Texas music called *Nothing Else to Do*. When I answer that question—"Why are there so many musicians from Lubbock?"—I say that there was just nothing else to do. You had to create your own entertainment. You couldn't go to the mountains; there was no water to speak of. You either played sports to entertain yourself or you played music. My answer would be that kids had to create their own entertainment. You could either become a hoodlum, or a football star, or learn to play music.

JAY BOY ADAMS is known for his country rocking West Texas music and consummate guitar playing. In the 1970s, he toured opening for major stadium rock acts such as Joe Cocker, ZZ Top, the Allman Brothers, the Charlie Daniels Band, and Bonnie Raitt. Jackson Browne and David Lindley contribute accompaniment on his Atlantic label albums. Jay Boy retired from performing in 1983, and now operates Roadhouse Coaches, providing custom luxury buses and drivers for major touring acts such as Celine Dion; Shania Twain; Crosby, Stills, and Nash; and Bruce Springsteen.

Boy Adams

JAY BOY: I have got to tell you my greatest Lloyd Maines story. In the 1970s I had a recording contract with Atlantic Records. I was touring, based out of Lubbock. My main gig for a long time was as the opening band for ZZ Top. I had a four-piece band: Lloyd Maines, David Bentley, Paul Culver, and myself. But Lloyd couldn't play all the dates because Lloyd had his Maines Brothers Band gig and he didn't want to leave town as often. Lloyd is married, and Lloyd needed to make a living. Lloyd was always very serious-minded about what he was doing. He wasn't footloose and fancy-free, like a lot of us in those days. He was married and had a house. Lloyd Maines has always been very responsible, very conscientious about everything he does. He still is. So Lloyd had a minimum dollar amount that he needed whenever he left town, because he would have to take a leave of absence from playing with his own band that night. The dates Lloyd could do were great, the ones he couldn't play, we missed him but I still had to do my shows.

Let me tell you, Lloyd was chicken-fried. I mean he was country-boy all the way. Lloyd had seen very little of the country at that time, and Lloyd really kind of had tunnel vision in those days. He knew who Buck Owens was, Merle Haggard, Lefty Frizzell, and Hank Williams; all the great country icons, Lloyd was into. But he knew nothing about Bad Company and the Rolling Stones. The only reason he knew anything about ZZ Top was because of my affiliation with them.

So I'm out on tour with ZZ Top, and Lloyd is flying in to play our next stop, which is the infamous ZZ Top Bar-BQ & Barn Dance at Memorial Stadium in Austin. It was completely sold out. There were eighty thousand people there, the biggest crowd ever at Memorial Stadium.

And Lloyd was just blown away. I remember him saying, "I went out in the crowd to get a barbecue sandwich, and it took me two hours to get it. There were people smoking pot right out there in the open, and girls that didn't have on bras!" Lloyd comes back with his eyes this big and he's thinking, "My God, what is this craziness? I don't know if I like this too much."

We set our gear up and we're getting ready to play. The band that had played prior to us is a band called Bad Company. It was their first U.S. date. And Bad Company's producer was Jimmy Page, so Page was with the band in Austin at this gig. I'm standing to the side of the stage tuning my guitars. I had met Page before, during my years with ZZ Top working for Billy Gibbons as his guitar tech, and Zeppelin was also with Atlantic Records. Page walks over to me and he says in his English accent, "Jay Boy, how you doing? I see you got a pedal-steel player?"

I said, "Yeah, I do. I got a damn good one, too!"

Page said, "Do you think he would mind if I stood alongside him during your set and watched him play?"

And I said, "No, not at all. As a matter of fact, I'll introduce you to him."

He said, "I'll meet him after your set because I want to talk with him awhile."

So we play our set and Jimmy Page is standing there the whole time, watching every move Lloyd is making. I mean, Jimmy Page is standing not ten feet from Lloyd Maines, just eyeing Lloyd like a hawk!

After we finished playing, Lloyd is tearing his steel rig down, and he's got it upside down in the case, taking the rods off and getting ready to pack it up. Page walks over, and I said, "Lloyd, I want to introduce you to someone. Lloyd, this is Jimmy Page; Jimmy Page, Lloyd Maines."

Lloyd stuck his hand out and says, "Nice to meet you."

Page said, "Man, you played really good! I've never seen anyone really play the pedal-steel like that," and they talked about some tunings. Lloyd played a double neck at the time. One of his necks was in C6, which he didn't use with me; he did with Ely a lot, the C6. He used E9 tuning with me, so that's what Page was interested in: the one that really got country sounds, not like a swing or jazz technique.

So they visited awhile and Page said, "Thanks a lot."

And Lloyd says, "Now, are you a picker?" And Page said, "Yeah."

Lloyd says, "Who do you play with?"

And Page said, "I play with Zeppelin." And Lloyd said, "Okay. Wow."

They say their good-byes and Page walks off, and Lloyd turns to me and he said, "Where's that guy from, Jay Boy?" I told him that he was from England, and Lloyd said, "I knew he wasn't from around here with his accent."

And then Lloyd said, "Now what did you say his name was?"

"His name is Jimmy Page, Lloyd," I said.

And Lloyd said, "I never heard of him."

And then he said, "Who's that band he plays with?"

I said, "He plays with Led Zeppelin, Lloyd!"

And Lloyd said, "Never heard of them either." And he just kept packing. He was taking his equipment apart and just never missed a beat.

So that's my Lloyd Maines story, and I challenge someone to come up with a better one than that.

Lloyd is a great example of someone from Lubbock. There is not a pretentious bone in his body. I tell you, what you see is what you get with Lloyd Maines, and what you get is the very best that there is. Lloyd Maines is an incredible man, father, husband, and musician. I mean, he's just an all-around great guy.

DON CALDWELL has lived in Lubbock County his entire life. An accomplished saxophone player, for many years Caldwell owned and operated the only recording studio in Lubbock. Don Caldwell Studios engineered and produced much of the music that made Lubbock famous, including Joe Ely's early records, the Maines Brothers Band, and Terry Allen's *Lubbock: on everything*. Caldwell's protégé Lloyd Maines has gone on to become a nationally recognized music producer.

Caldwell now operates a promotion company with the goal of publicizing Lubbock musicians and performers and bringing attention to music events and venues in Lubbock.

Caldwell

DON: I started playing saxophone in high school because I heard a record by a guy named Sam Butera, who was a honkin', rockin' tenor sax player who played with Louie Prima.

I grew up in Slaton, Texas, in southeast Lubbock County. I had been injured playing football and could no longer do sports, because I had a back injury that inhibited me. I was laid up in bed all summer, and my cousin gave me a record to listen to, which she had bought while she was on vacation at Lake Tahoe. It was a song called "Come Back to Sereno," which was a featured saxophone solo on an album: *Louie Prima, Sam Butera and the Witnesses—Live from Lake Tahoe*. I had never paid one bit of attention to music before. But I heard that saxophone and I thought, "I love the way that sounds!" I got cold chills.

Since my football career was over, I decided to join the high school band and play saxophone. It is amazing to me: I grew up on a farm, and it was just understood that I would be a farmer, but when I heard that saxophone it became my life. That was in 1959.

Here's a weird deal: Bobby Keys and I both grew up in Slaton, two people in a little farm town and both happened to fall in love with the saxophone. In those days, Keys had already quit school and was playing with a band in Lubbock called the Ravens, with Jerry Allison's drum student Ernie Hall. The last time I saw Bobby Keys before he left Lubbock for good was probably 1962. So Keys is older than me and didn't influence my interest in the saxophone at all.

The next time I saw Keys was about a dozen years later in California. I had met Denny Cordell of Shelter Records when I was pitching Joe Ely tapes. Cordell produced Joe Cocker's album *Mad Dogs & Englishmen,* on which Keys was the featured saxophone player. Cordell asked me to come out to L.A., and the first thing he said when I walked in was "Man, you look just like Bobby Keys!" I said, "That's really strange because Keys and I played Little League baseball together." It was real funny. Keys had just gotten back from having done a tour with the Stones. So Denny called Keys up, and we rode around L.A. all night, drinking rum and laughing about old times in Slaton. I'll never forget him saying, "Would people in Lubbock believe that we're out here riding around in L.A.?" It was real strange for me.

I was working at Hi-Fidelity, a music store in Lubbock, when I saw the *Mad Dogs & Englishmen* album, and it said on the album, "Bobby Keys, the ruby-lipped essence of Lubbock, Texas." I always thought, "Man! I wish I would have gone to California like Bobby Keys!"

CHRIS: Tell me about that. Why didn't you leave Lubbock?

DON: I was involved with a girl that I'd grown up with, and we got married and started a family, simple as that. Just taking off for L.A. was something that would have been unheard of. Then I got a little older and with my family ties, I eventually didn't want to leave.

I decided to open a recording studio so I could play saxophone all the time, which was an absolute joke, because when I went into business, I got on the other side of the fence and playing became secondary. Producing records and business-type stuff became my job, doing everything to keep the studio open. From 1971 until '91, about twenty years, I was totally devoted to the recording studio.

CHRIS: Because you didn't leave Lubbock and chose to open the studio, a lot of the better-known music from Lubbock wouldn't have happened without you there.

DON: I guess I was lucky enough to be able to get enough money together to stabilize things. Over the years I've spent a lot of money on projects. I financed all of the original stuff for Ely and worked the deal on the first Maines Brothers albums.

Just staying in business and having a place to record was a pretty hard deal. But my sensitivity has always been to the music instead of how much money I made. There are a lot of people that think that I'm strictly in it for the money, which is a joke. I mean, just last week I literally sold the family farm that I had inherited, just in order to be able to stay in all this crap. It's hard to do.

In my mind, I'm still a musician more than anything else. What makes me feel good is playing saxophone or producing records. Doing music is what I love. The business and money parts are not what I enjoy.

CHRIS: Your studio is one of the factors that convinced Terry Allen to record *Lubbock: on everything* in Lubbock. Tell me about producing that record.

DON: Paul Milosevich is an artist who was teaching at Texas Tech at that time. Paul had met Terry through the visual arts and convinced him to come to Lubbock and record at least one song on his new album in Lubbock, since it was going to be called *Lubbock: on everything.*

My understanding was that Terry was originally going to record it in a studio in northern California. So Paul talked to him and said, "Come down and at least cut one or two songs in Lubbock at this studio where Ely cut his stuff." I thought Terry was one of the funniest people I've ever met in my life. About a month and a half later, when Terry finally left the studio, we had a whole double album cut, because he fell in love with all of the musicians and the whole scene. It was a real labor of love for all of us involved. Terry Allen's music was so different than anything that we had ever heard.

We all said, "No matter what it takes, we're going to make this album as good as we know how to do it." And, in truth, there wasn't any of us that really knew anything, other than we knew how we wanted it to sound.

Our studio was really inferior, compared to major recording studios, so we had to work twice as hard to make it work. We had a tape machine that we couldn't find anybody who knew how to work on it, so there was some of the album that Terry sat with his finger doing back-torque on the reel to make sure that it would run smooth in some of the overdubbing. We'd go up there and stay all night and for days.

But it was such a unique session. For instance: technically speaking, recording Terry Allen would be a challenge if you didn't actually get into who he is. When he played piano, he stomped his foot so hard on the lyre that it just came through all the mikes. Terry told me that when he did his first album, *Juarez,* they made him take his shoes off to keep the noise from coming through. So what we did is, we miked the thing and used it as a present factor in the Terry Allen sound. Terry kicking that lyre became part of the rhythm track.

On the album, the liner notes say, "The album was produced by everybody on the album." That was a real true statement because everybody on the album put in their two cents, a very cooperative deal, as I said, a labor of love.

CHRIS: It seems that because Lubbock is so separated from everywhere else by geography, that there is no real need, or even ability, to do things the same way everybody is doing it in L.A. or New York or Nashville. People in West Texas don't really want other people doing things for them, and don't necessarily want to do things the way everybody else does.

DON: There's a real independent work ethic with people in West Texas, being isolated out here and doing it our own way. Like learning to be an engineer in a recording studio; I learned to engineer by the seat of my pants. There was really not much literature available about what to do. Basically when I got into the recording studio, I was so busy trying to survive that I worked all the time. I didn't have time to sit down and read. We were in the studio working constantly.

When I said we didn't know anything about what we were doing when we cut Terry's album, I mean there was *nothing* we were doing that had ever been validated by major recording studios: the techniques that we used to mike instruments, and the technology. We had a couple of radio-quality boards that were good and clean but they weren't set up for a recording studio. They were radio broadcast boards. We adapted those and turned them into a recording console. We wired it ourselves.

But as time went by, I spent some time with Norman Petty over in Clovis and talked with him. I recorded and engineered in his studio a lot, and I once bought a four-track tape machine from Norman. I learned some stuff from Norman. I feel like one of the greatest privileges I've had was getting to go in Norman Petty's reverb chamber down under the stage at the old theater in Clovis.

CHRIS: I'm glad you mentioned Norman Petty. Buddy Holly was basically doing exactly what he wanted in the studio, and didn't really know how to do anything else. Essentially, they were making it all up over at Norman Petty's place.

DON: You are right. Those amazing drum parts that Jerry Allison played on those records, he had never listened to some drummer before him and said, this is what he would do, and then play it like that. When the Crickets went into Clovis to record, it was what came out of his brain from somewhere. I don't know where all that stuff came from, but Jerry Allison really forged a new path for rock 'n' roll with his drums. There wasn't a way of doing that before him. He made up his own sound and set the standard for everyone else in rock 'n' roll.

CHRIS: Buddy Holly's music was considered outsider music in Lubbock while he was still alive. It was only after he died, when most people really appreciated what Buddy and the Crickets did. When we talk about West Texas musicians, frequently we are not talking about pop music being cranked out by the machine.

DON: West Texas music is spiritual, not by rote. The music here in West Texas is the heart of the people you hear playing. It's not structured by academia or corporations. Musicians who make it to Nashville are turned into just another Nashville product, marketed like the rest and made to sound like everybody else. Nashville will take your heart away. That's showbiz. We don't have any showbiz mentality here in Lubbock, and that's why so much of our music is not directed at a particular market.

You mentioned earlier, how Jesse Taylor had said that Lubbock could have been the recording capital of Texas but didn't. The reason for that was the West Texas rural mentality and the work ethic: "If you play music you're a no-account." Everybody in West Texas has looked at musicians and artists as being not really valid, because music and art had nothing to do with our way of survival in Lubbock. It had nothing to do with beating the Dust Bowl. Music is what you do when you want to have fun. My uncle always told me, "You can play music for fun, but at daybreak you get your lazy little butt out of bed every morning and you drive that tractor." That's why all that great music left Lubbock, that survival mentality. That's the thing that killed the potential for Jesse Taylor and Joe Ely and all of those guys to stay in Lubbock and continue to make a living. There was no tolerance for what was perceived as just messing around.

So in the second phase of my career, I'm trying to change those attitudes and get people appreciating Lubbock music for what it is, how good it is. Now I am putting venues together that heighten public awareness of how great the talent in Lubbock is, and I'm developing a management business to help nurture young local careers.

Generally, we're not good promoters in Lubbock. Our mentality and our way of being raised in West Texas was "You do not toot your own horn. You do not be a braggart. You just shut up and drive that tractor." That was the work ethic. That's why a lot of people around here still don't know how great Buddy Holly is, how great the Holly reputation is. They think, "Nobody from Lubbock who played danged ol' rock 'n' roll music could be that important and renowned throughout the world." You still have that mentality here. I think the philosophy we need is to believe in the inherent quality of the endeavor and believe enough in the music to stay with it. Put your heart completely into it, and good things will happen. I have to believe that.

BOBBY KEYS is one of the premier rock 'n' roll and R&B saxophone session players. Known for his long association with the Rolling Stones, Keys has recorded with George Harrison, John Lennon, Delaney & Bonnie, Eric Clapton, Humble Pie, the Faces, Carly Simon, Harry Nilsson, Joe Cocker, Ringo Starr, Lynyrd Skynyrd, B. B. King, Sheryl Crow, and many others.

Bobby Keys

CHRIS: Tell me some about your background and your folks; who were you as a little kid around Lubbock?

BOBBY: I was a little kid in Slaton actually. I was born December 18, 1943, at the Lubbock Army Air Corps Base, which later turned into Reese Air Force Base. My father was in the Army Air Corps at the time and was in pilot training school there. My mother and my grandparents lived in Slaton, Texas, where my grandfather had worked on the Santa Fe Railroad. I was raised in Slaton by my grandparents, because my mother was fairly young and my father was off defending Lubbock County in World War II.

CHRIS: Being a kid in Slaton, how did you first get hold of a saxophone and get interested in it?

BOBBY: I got hurt playing Little League baseball; I crushed the bone around my eye. So I couldn't play football, and the only way to go to the football games was to join the band. I didn't have an instrument and the only instrument that was left that the school provided was an old baritone saxophone, so that's what I first started playing.

I never really learned to read music; I still don't read music. There wasn't anyone around at the time who really knew how to play saxophone, so I essentially taught myself how to play. Sonny Curtis showed me how to play "Rose of San Antone." At the time, Sonny was playing with Tommy Hancock's band. But mostly I did it by listening, and by trial and error. I could hear sounds real easily. I'd listen to songs on the radio and try to figure our how to play it on my horn. It just came natural to me, for some reason.

CHRIS: How did you meet your friend Sonny Curtis?[1]

BOBBY: Sonny Curtis was from over in Meadow, Texas. But when I first met him, Sonny was living with the principal of Slaton High School, Doc Babbs. Sonny was the State Future Farmers of America Entertainer, which meant he had to go around to the different FFA chapters all over Texas and sing and play guitar at their meetings. Doc Babbs was the FFA district representative, so Sonny lived with him in Slaton since he had to travel a lot of the time.

Sonny first started playing with Buddy Holly when he was living in Slaton. Holly, and J.I., and Joe B, the other guys in the Crickets, would come down to Slaton to hang out with Sonny. That's when I first met Buddy Holly.

The first time I ever heard an electric guitar being played was at the grand opening of N. L. Kress' Humble station in Slaton, Texas. I was fourteen years old, and it was Buddy Holly, Bob Montgomery, Don Guess, and Jerry Allison playing on the back of a flatbed wagon. Sonny had been talking about Buddy Holly and these guys from Lubbock. Sonny had originally played with Buddy but didn't think they were ever going to amount to anything playing rock 'n' roll so Sonny had resigned. But I was attracted to them because of the music, and they were the only guys I had ever heard play rock 'n' roll and who owned real instruments. But I was a lot younger than them; well, I was about four years younger than Holly, so they treated me pretty much like a kid. I'd do things like swipe some change out of my grandmother's purse and go buy cheeseburgers for them. So I'd run various errands for the Crickets, that were designed not only so they could get some free food but to get me out of their hair.

One day, J.I. called me and asked if I could pick up King Curtis at the airport and bring him over to Norman Petty's studio in Clovis, New Mexico, where Buddy was recording and also producing a record for his friend Waylon Jennings. Waylon was Buddy's musical protégé. He was a deejay in Lubbock at the time at KDAV; Waylon and Snuff Garrett, the music producer, were both deejays there.

When J.I. asked me if I could pick up King Curtis at the airport, I said, "You bet

I will!" But in order to do it, I was going to have to miss a basketball game. No one could believe it, that I would miss a ball game just to pick up some black horn player and drive him to New Mexico to record rock 'n' roll, and a lot of guys told me what they thought about it. Things were still very segregated then, and small towns get very enthusiastic about their sports programs. But I had a choice to make and I made it; I wasn't ever going to be a basketball player, so I chose to go into the studio and see how that was done. I knew it was going to blackball me from everybody in Slaton, but I didn't really care. I didn't have any future in Slaton anyway.

That was the first time I was ever in Norman Petty's studio. King Curtis over-dubbed on a Buddy Holly number called "Wait 'til the Sun Shines Nellie" and played on "Reminiscing." He also recorded a solo on a track called "Jolé Blon," which was recorded by Waylon Jennings. That was when I decided I really wanted to get out of town and not come back. Getting to watch King Curtis and Buddy and Waylon record in that studio; that was probably the turning point, when I decided I was committed to playing music.

I lived in Lubbock for a little while longer with Joe B. Mauldin, the bass player for the Crickets. His stepfather gave us a job knocking the mortar off used bricks, and I had a job at a beef processing plant for a week. I didn't really stay in Lubbock that long, didn't have any real jobs. I got my start in Lubbock, but I was gone as soon as I had the opportunity.

But I was very interested in the Lubbock music scene at the time, for what it was worth. There were some really talented musicians around then. There was Glen D. Hardin, the piano player, who was Buddy's cousin. He went on to play with Elvis' band; he played with Roger Miller; he was one of the Shindogs, who played on the *Shindig* TV show back in the '60s. He did all this on his own, independent of Buddy. Glen D didn't ever play with Buddy Holly; they just were cousins. Glen D's mother and Buddy's mother were sisters.

But I really enjoyed working some of the gigs there, in the beginning. Working the Cotton Club was always fun, because you never knew what was going to happen. People got drunk and got into fights. It was a colorful place. There were other places, too: Club 87, the Rendezvous, the Palm Room out on the Amarillo Highway, outside of Lubbock. That was one of those bring-your-own-bottle clubs.

Roy Orbison and the Teen Kings would come to town and play the roller rink on weekends when Holly wasn't playing there. Elvis came through and played the county fair.

CHRIS: Were you at that show?

BOBBY: Yes. Are you kidding? And the first time I saw Jerry Lee Lewis he was playing on the back of a flatbed wagon at the grand opening of the Quinn Connelly Pontiac dealership. There was always music at any "grand opening," because the musicians were cheap and the music was loud.

CHRIS: Did you find the Lubbock music scene to be really exciting and alive at that time?

BOBBY: Yeah, but I was a teenager at the time. What was special to me then was Elvis and acts like that. The reason I got into music was that it was so boring around there. There was nothing else to do in Lubbock. I felt an affinity to the music, and I just happened to fall into several of the right places at the right time. It was not the result of any sort of grand design.

My presence in the Lubbock music scene was probably less than three years, and I was a teenager at the time. I never played with Holly. I did go into J.I.'s studio and record after Buddy was already dead, with J.I., Joe B, Tommy Allsup, and Ernie Hall. At that time, I was in a band with Ernie Hall, Joel Searsey, Lin Bailey, and myself; we were called the Ravens. It was a rock 'n' roll band, we played mostly covers; we had no original stuff. We would play elementary rock 'n' roll, except when we'd get the odd job at the Arthur Murray Dance Studios bimonthly dance, and then we'd play dance music. I did that for about a year.

I could not wait to get out of Lubbock. My welcome had been worn out. I was underage, so it was illegal for me to play in most of the clubs where the music was. I'd play some of these joints, and I'd have to go back to the kitchen area or outside when I wasn't playing. We'd play the Cotton Club in Lubbock on Sunday afternoons. I just wanted to play music, so I sought out every opportunity I could.

My association and friendship with the Crickets led to Jerry Allison getting me a gig with Buddy Knox and the Rhythm Orchids, from up in Happy, Texas. That finally got me out of town and on the road. A lot of things coincided at once to get me out of town. My grandmother died, and she had raised me. School was not working out very well for me and music was. And J.I. got me the job on the road with Buddy Knox. Buddy Knox had a hit song called "Party Doll," so it was a national touring gig. I left Lubbock when I was sixteen years old and didn't go back for many years. I was on the road with Buddy Knox and the Rhythm Orchids for three years.

One of the promoters of a tour we were doing around North and South Dakota and Minnesota, an agent from Sioux Falls, also booked another band from Sioux Falls called Myron Lee and the Caddies. They later became Bobby Vee's road band. But for a while, they worked with Buddy Knox while we were touring together, so we became friends. When Knox decided to stop touring for a while, I ended up with Myron Lee and the Caddies and that's how I started playing with Bobby Vee.

For the record, I recently read another article where a writer said that I was one of the leading horn players in the "Mussel Shoals Horns." Well, there are no Mussel Shoals Horns, as far as I know, and I never played with them in my life if there are. That's something that got out on the Internet and it's a load of shit. The only time I ever recorded in Mussel Shoals, Alabama, was when I did the horn overdubs for the Rolling Stones' "Brown Sugar," when they were finishing up their album *Sticky Fingers* there.

CHRIS: How did you meet the Rolling Stones and come to record on several of their albums?

BOBBY: I was playing with Bobby Vee when I first met the Rolling Stones. We were playing the 1964 Dick Clark Caravan of Stars Tour and were in San Antonio for the Teenage World's Fair that was being sponsored by Dick Clark and Dr Pepper. It was Bobby Vee, George Jones, a couple of other acts, and the Rolling Stones. It was the Stones' first trip over here, real early in their career. The single they had out at the time was "Not Fade Away," which was a Buddy Holly song; it was their first single that got any play over here in the States.

All the acts that were performing were staying together at this motor inn in San Antonio. Keith and Brian were in the room next door to the room I was staying in with the drummer from our band. It was summertime, so everyone was out on their balconies, looking at chicks in the pool. I started talking to Brian, and he found out that I was from Lubbock, and asked if I knew Buddy Holly. I said, yeah, I knew Buddy Holly. So he called Charlie, Mick, and Keith over to meet me. That was the common thread that connected us; that was my introduction to the Stones. Then Keith and I find out that coincidentally we were born on the same day, same month, same year, so Keith Richards and I share the same birthday.

Then we went to perform the gig. They were the first English band I had heard, and they sounded pretty good. They did a good job of playing "Not Fade Away," and I was pretty impressed with them. This was back when all the American bands wore suits and ties and did little dance steps and jazz like that. But the Stones were the first band I had ever seen that didn't do that; I noticed they just wore their own regular clothes, whatever they wanted. That seemed very "un-band-like" to me; we all wore suits and ties. We were playing for several days there, and getting to know each other hanging out backstage together in the common dressing room. Before one show, I remember hearing Keith and Brian talking about how they noticed the other bands all changed clothes before they went on stage for each new show, so they all just traded their shirts before they went out. They were just being funny, entertaining themselves. But I was impressed with their lack of formality. I was bored with the gig and sick and tired of all that dancing; my suit was all wrinkled and funky, so when it was time for our show, I went out on stage in Bermuda shorts and cowboy boots, instead of my black suit and tie. I was trying to make a personal statement. I nearly got fired and only did it that once, but it made a lasting impression on the Stones. They found that amusing and never forgot that.

Then, a few years later, I was recording in a studio in L.A. with Delaney & Bonnie. The Stones were there recording their album *Let It Bleed*. They remembered me from the San Antonio gig and asked me to come over and lay down a horn solo for one of their tracks, called "Live with Me." It was really an impromptu thing. The album came out and it was good, and I was pleased to see that they spelled my name right on the album cover. That was the first time I played with the Rolling Stones and we've been associated ever since.

Then, I met George Harrison in L.A. while the Beatles were mixing one of their albums there. Eric Clapton had told George about Delaney & Bonnie. We were playing at a club in the San Fernando Valley, and George Harrison and some other folks from Apple came out and listened to us. Apple was just being formed at that time and they were looking for a band to record. George and Delaney became good friends so they signed us up to Apple to release our very first album, *Accept No Substitutes*.

Then, I went with Delaney & Bonnie on a tour of England and Europe with George and Eric Clapton. It wasn't that successful because the promoters billed us as Clapton's new band, but all he did was play guitar and that upset some fans. Out of that, though, a lot of other things happened.

The "Mad Dogs & Englishmen" period came about with the demise of the Delaney & Bonnie band. The love was ebbing away in those days, so Jim Keltner, Carl Radle, Jim Price, and I left the band. A week later, Leon Russell called me and Jim Price and said he was in the studio working on an album with Joe Cocker. He wanted us to put some horns on the song "Delta Lady." Then Leon put together this conglomeration of a lot of musicians and we went on the road. That was exciting, playing places like the Fillmore, and all over the country. We were only making $250 a week, but we were getting good experience.

After that, I went back to England because Jim Price and I were originally sup-posed to be part of the Derek and the Dominoes band. So we accepted our plane tickets from Clapton's manager, Robert Stigwood, to fly over to England. Well, some-where between the time we took off in L.A. and when we landed in London, Eric had decided he didn't need or want any horns in the band. But George Harrison was in the studio recording *All Things Must Pass*. So when we landed in London, we were met by people from Apple Records, which seemed unusual. When we got off the plane, we asked, "Where's Eric?" Mal Evans from Apple says, "There's been a little change of plans. You're not going to Eric's house. You're going to George's house." But he didn't tell us what was going on, that we were out of the band. We get to George's house and call up Eric and say, "We're here!" And Eric says, "Stay there!" and let us know he had changed his plans. George then asked Jim and me to do the horns on *All Things Must Pass*.

One night as those sessions were winding down, after a recording one night with George at Apple, I went down to a club in London called the Speakeasy. I ran into Jagger there, and they were recording *Sticky Fingers* at the time. He said, "Bring your horn over to the studio tomorrow." So I did and they were just finishing up *Sticky Fingers*. They were playing the track to "Brown Sugar," and they hadn't even thought about a horn solo. I was listening to it, and I said, "Man, there ought to be a horn in there!" And Mick said, "Well, put one there." It was very much a spur-of-the-moment idea. Since then, I've recorded on a lot of Stones albums: *Exile on Main Street*, *Goats Head Soup*, *Some Girls* . . . I really don't know how many; a whole lot; look it up.

CHRIS: I know that you did quite a bit of work with John Lennon. Tell me about your relationship with John Lennon.

BOBBY: John Lennon was one of the most impressive people I've ever met, man. He was a cool guy, "one of the guys," not eaten up with himself and the publicity sur-rounding him. I was fortunate to run into him and get to know him in London when I was playing with Delaney & Bonnie and Eric Clapton on that tour. John and Yoko were doing some gig that we were involved in, where they were in a laundry bag or something like it, making a statement of some kind, while we were on stage playing.

I just seemed to gravitate to John. He was a wise, very intelligent, funny guy. He had a great sense of humor, very dry. And he wasn't eaten up with the fact that he was a Beatle. He was one of those guys that when I met him, it was just a very special friendship. Keith Richards is like that; there have been a few people in my life like that, where it was just very easy to become friends with them. Harry Nilsson was another good friend of mine. But that time with John Lennon was great. It was very, very fulfilling, let me put it that way.

CHRIS: I first became aware that the saxophone player for the Stones was from Lubbock while watching you play with Danny Raines and the Ace Liquidators at the Texas Spoon Café. What were you doing back in Lubbock in those days?

BOBBY: I didn't make it back to Lubbock until some time in the early '80s. I had met Jay Boy Adams out on the road, and he asked me to come back to Lubbock to play with him at one of those Tornado Jams that Ely put on. That was the first time I had been to Lubbock since about 1964.

My family lived in Albuquerque, New Mexico, although I was raised by my grandparents in Lubbock. So I had gone to New Mexico for Christmas one year and had brought Joe Cocker with me. We went out one night and heard a band that was called the Planets, who were based out of Albuquerque at the time. I enjoyed the band and got to know those guys. The drummer, Davis McLarty, asked me to play on a radio show with them in Dallas and record there on a session.

I was between marriages, I was bored, and there was nothing else I was doing. There wasn't a lot of work at the time; no one I worked with was recording or touring at the time. Then I did some other gigs with Jay Boy Adams in Lubbock. One thing led to another, and I moved in with Davis McLarty, who was back in Lubbock and living there. Several of those guys—Davis, Danny Raines, Joe Don Davidson—were now back in Lubbock. We changed the name of the band to the Ace Liquidators, and I started playing with them. I don't really remember why we decided to do that; maybe we were all drunk. It was just a transitional time for me. I was between gigs. We mostly played at Fat Dawg's and that barbecue joint they called the Spoon.

CHRIS: How long were you in Lubbock playing with the Ace Liquidators?

BOBBY: It seemed like forever; I don't know, probably at least six months. Shortly after that, I began playing some with Joe Ely and recorded on one of his albums. I liked that time, playing with Joe Ely and Davis and David Grissom and Jimmy Pettit. That was a great band.

CHRIS: For me, it was inspiring to learn that someone from my own town, playing right in front of me on that little stage at Fat Dawg's, had gone out into the world and done all these fantastic things, like playing with John Lennon, the Stones, Joe Cocker. But it was fascinating to me also, there you were, walking around pretty much in anonymity at home in Lubbock, playing this little barbecue joint every weekend, like any other local artist.

BOBBY: That's the way I felt when J.I. and Sonny came back to town. I thought, "Wow! These guys were on the *Ed Sullivan Show!*" But I went to Buddy Holly's funeral, and that was no big deal there in Lubbock, just friends and family. Hardly anybody in Lubbock paid any attention when Buddy Holly died. It wasn't even front-page news. Buddy Holly wasn't really acknowledged in Lubbock until later, when the city realized it might be able to make a few bucks off a Buddy Holly Memorial.

CHRIS: Why do you think the community in Lubbock failed to acknowledge Buddy Holly during his life and at the time of his death, despite the fact that he was internationally known?

BOBBY: Lubbock boasted the largest Church of Christ in the world. If you did rock 'n' roll, you were singing the music of the devil and you were going to hell. It wasn't embraced as an honorable profession. I don't know that much about Lubbock now; it may be a great place to live. I only know about what it was like when I was growing up, and I've never been real pro-Lubbock, as far as the government of the city goes.

1. SONNY CURTIS:
   (1) born 1937, Meadow, Texas;
   (2) recorded with Buddy Holly and Don Guess as the Three Tunes 1956;
   (3) first rock 'n' roller to record with a Fender Stratocaster;
   (4) BMI Awards for over a million airplays:
       (a) "I Fought the Law," recorded by Curtis 1959, hit for Bobby Fuller Four 1965, covered by Dead Kennedys, the Clash, Lou Reed, Hank Williams, Jr., and others;
       (b) "I'm No Stranger to the Rain," number-one record for Keith Whitley, Country Music Association Single of the Year 1989;
       (c) "Walk Right Back," Everly Brothers, 1961;
       (d) "More Than I Can Say" (cowritten with J. I. Allison), recorded by Bobby Vee, Leo Sayer; and
       (e) "The Straight Life," recorded by Bobby Goldsboro, 1968;
   (5) wrote and sang theme song for the Mary Tyler Moore Show, "Love Is All Around";
   (6) wrote over five hundred songs, recorded by Buddy Holly, Tom Petty, Bing Crosby, Green Day, Roy Orbison, Chet Atkins, Al Hirt, Lawrence Welk, and others;
   (7) inducted into Nashville Songwriters Association International Hall of Fame 1991.

Tom X

TOMMY HANCOCK is perhaps the most influential personality in the history of Lubbock music. In the 1950s, as the leader of the Roadside Playboys, house band of Lubbock's famed Cotton Club, he was an inspiration and mentor to Buddy Holly, the Crickets, Waylon Jennings, and others. Sonny Curtis has said that Tommy Hancock was "a strong influence on Buddy Holly and us all." Years after Buddy Holly's death, the lake at Lubbock's Yellow House Canyon was drained and Buddy's wallet—lost while he was water skiing a week before his wedding, at the height of his fame—was found. In his wallet was a membership card for "The Club for Under-Appreciated Musicians." Buddy was member number four. The card was issued and signed by Tommy Hancock.

In the 1960s and '70s, Hancock was the central figure in two other Lubbock legends, the Flatlanders and the Supernatural Family Band, which ignited the careers of another generation of well-known Lubbock musicians.

Hancock is retired from performing and now lives in Austin. He remains an avid dancer, frequenting Austin's honky-tonks and dance halls, and is the author of a book entitled *Zen and the Art of the Texas Two-Step*.

Hancock

TOM X: I was half-raised by my grandmother, and she forced me to take fiddle lessons when I was a kid. I was sixteen when I went into the army at the end of World War II, and was beginning to like music, so I took my fiddle with me. I was an MP paratrooper, but the war had ended by the time I got over to Japan. Here's a guy from Texas with a fiddle, and they expect me to play fiddle songs. I had never even heard any fiddle songs. I was trained to play classical violin. The GIs would hum the songs or a guitar player would pick, and they'd teach me the songs that way.

I was eighteen when I got out of the army. When I got back to Texas, I almost immediately got a job playing with a band at the late club called Dance Land, out on the east side of Lubbock. The first night I played, I made five bucks, and I thought, "This is the way for me to go with my life: Have a good time, get drunk, party with girls, and get paid five bucks!" And I kept on doing it for fifty years. Dance music was a good way for a beginner to get into music because you didn't have to be so good. If people could dance to it, the listening quality didn't have to be all that good.

The original Cotton Club was owned by Ralph Lloyd. It was on 50th Street in a gigantic old army Quonset hut, and held a capacity of 1,600 people. My band the Roadside Playboys was the regular house band there. We played a lot of the country hits, Hank Williams and Bob Wills, but we also played a tremendous variety of dance music. As a bandleader I try to make people dance. To me, dancing is the equivalent of applause.

When the original Cotton Club burned down, ages ago, I bought the sign and the name and moved the Cotton Club out on the Post Highway. That's the one most people remember. It held about a thousand people. You get that many young cowboys drunk in a place together, and you're going to have some trouble. There were fights every night and the fighting couldn't be stopped. That was the real dark side of the club.

The Cotton Club was the only club big enough to make any money for a band between Dallas and L.A., so all the big-name bands played there. Elvis played there three times, Little Richard, all the hit bands would play the Cotton Club, including black and Mexican bands. It was the only desegregated club in West Texas.

Later on, I sold the Cotton Club to Joe Ely and Stubb. Joe and Stubb were partners there, but they went broke, and I had to take it back over. Then we closed it for good in about 1984. I believe that building is an X-rated video store now.

CHRIS: Tell me about the development of the Flatlanders. Rather than being a straight country dance band, the Flatlanders seemed to be on more of a mystical journey.

TOM X: Mysticism is so incredible to me, trying to understand the biggest mysteries of life, the idea that there is something out there other than what is obvious. Being born and raised in Lubbock, I never once suspected that anything interesting or beyond the obvious was going on, until I took LSD. Acid showed me that there was something wonderful happening all the time, which I hadn't been conscious of before.

It was the early '60s, before anyone in Lubbock had ever heard of a hippie. At that point of my life I was trying to learn, "What is this thing called Love?" My family and I were living a pretty straight life out in west Lubbock. I was admitted to Texas Tech Law School, in my first year, in hopes of becoming rich and powerful. I had seen a show on PBS about LSD, this drug that makes you act like you're crazy. There was a guy on a table in a hospital, laughing his ass off, with the doctors standing around him with serious faces. The situation was so crazy. I thought, "Anything that makes

TOM X HANCOCK. COURTESY OF THE HANCOCK FAMILY COLLECTION.

it funny to be around a bunch of doctors, I need to try that." I went with a friend of mine out to San Francisco and took some acid, to see what was going on. I had read some holy person had said, "LSD is not the path to heaven but it will show you that heaven is there." That proved to be correct for me. Taking LSD made me realize that we're on this planet to have a good time and to experience the universe. Before that I was just jogging along trying to beat boredom, and studying mysticism damn sure stops the boredom.

At that time, there happened to be several of us in Lubbock who were on similar searches for the Truth. It may have been a coincidence that most of us were musicians. Jimmie Gilmore was the first intelligent person I had ever met who was searching for God. Most of the people around Lubbock were dumb-asses who already thought they had found God. That's the same mentality that nailed Jesus to the cross, so I had always shied away from that element of Lubbock. I was raised around that Christian environment, so I knew enough to know that it wasn't my cup of tea. Although, after I took the LSD, I did go check out several churches. My method for searching for the Truth was to say, "Brother, put your trip on me." I'd do whatever they said to see if it would wake me up to what was really happening.

We had a group called the Lamb's Club. We'd eat at a different Mexican food place every week, and we'd make fun of the Lion's Club by doing the Lamb's Club roar. "Baaaaah!" We would have a lot of fun kicking around what we had learned that week in our search for the Truth. Finally, we discovered that it boiled down to the fact that you can't find the Truth in books, and you can't actively talk about it either. The best way is silence. So that was the end of the Lamb's Club. We broke up after that. But that was the origin of the band that became the Flatlanders, which produced Butch Hancock, Joe Ely, Jimmie Gilmore, Jesse Taylor, Richard Bowden, and Ponty Bone, and launched all their careers.

At that time, I was really the focus of the Lubbock music scene because I had an ongoing dance band. We would get together to play acoustic music around somebody's house, and they would come sit in with me at the Cotton Club. Tony Pearson had the first health food store in Lubbock, called the Supernatural Market. We'd play acoustic music around the depot stove at the store and act like it was a hundred years ago, so we called ourselves the Supernatural Playboys. We weren't really a recording group or a performing band. It was really just for fun. We didn't call ourselves the Flatlanders until we went to Nashville to record the album in '71. Making the original Flatlanders album was a lot of fun but it was way too far out for any kind of commercial venture at the time.

After we had done all the looking for God that we could, we realized that we had to experience things directly. My family and I moved to northern New Mexico, out in an isolated canyon, and lived in teepees. We would follow anybody that was supposed to be an enlightened person or know anything, even just common friends that we'd run into. I'd encourage everybody to put the trip on me because I wanted to know the Truth.

Jimmie Gilmore and I had read that Jeane Dixon had said that a savior is back on Earth and that he was in India and would be in the United States soon. And Guru Maharaj Ji fulfilled that prophecy for us. Jimmie had the experience first and let me know that it was a good one. I took my family and we experienced it, and it proved to be the correct thing for us.

THE SUPERNATURAL FAMILY BAND. COURTESY OF THE HANCOCK FAMILY COLLECTION, 1973.

The words of Jesus that guided me that far said, "The Kingdom of Heaven is within." But when I would go within, all I'd see was blackness and hear my mind rattling nonsense. The thing that sold me on Guru Maharaj Ji is he showed me the heaven within, by teaching me to meditate. The meditation techniques taught me how to get there by myself under any circumstances. That was total freedom. It wiped out any fears anybody would have about losing their mind to a guru, because what the guru, a true Perfect Master, does is he shows you that heaven is there, and he shows you how to get there by yourself under any circumstances.

CHRIS: After the Flatlanders split up to pursue their own various interests, you formed the Supernatural Family Band. How did that come about?

TOM X: The Supernatural Family Band was me, my wife Charlene, and five of our kids, Conni, Traci, Joaquin, Holli, and Louie, and I knew so many professional musicians that I'd get them to sit in when they weren't otherwise working. I was doing it so my kids could play music with the greatest musicians in the world. The whole idea for the Supernatural Family Band for me was for my kids to learn my trade. I wanted them to be able to book a job, get the equipment ready, rehearse songs, play the job, and learn the business end.

The Supernatural Family Band wasn't out to get rich and famous like most bands were, even though I had a really strong commercial band. I had two sons that were nice-looking guys and four beautiful women. But I wasn't doing things like they should be done to make it successful because I wanted to teach my kids to be professional musicians.

We traveled around the Southwest. Our following was mostly countrified hippies. We were damn near the only good-time country party band in the area. We were a big happening when we would come to town. There were a lot of big-money jobs. We were the number-one barbecue band in the state of Colorado. Any big companies would throw a barbecue, they'd hire us to play.

After many years and many good times, I eventually retired from performing. Holli and the boys went on to pursue other interests. Charlene, Conni, and Traci are still performing together as the Texana Dames.

CHRIS: Do you have any other thoughts about Lubbock?

TOM X: I've always had a love-hate relationship with Lubbock. I'm two ways about it. There are a lot of wonderful people in Lubbock and West Texas but that is damn near all there is, as far as any kind of stimulating atmosphere. If you have a circle of friends to be with, that's great. But if you want to take your date out to look at a pretty place or go swimming or anything, you're shit out of luck. I could kick myself sometimes when I think about how long I stayed in Lubbock. I didn't realize how deprived I was in so many areas of life by being there, didn't know what else was out there. But I stayed in Lubbock for forty years, so I can hardly bad-mouth it. After having lived there so long, it would make me look bad. Some people call it the South Plains voodoo, whatever it is that brings you back to Lubbock and often holds you there.

I don't think it's fair to talk about Lubbock as if it had a persona of its own, but if it did, I don't like it. There's a certain mentality that I don't like. When I was a young musician, I got a pretty hard time from the city cops and the newspapers. The cops would come after me, I think, out of boredom because I was the only fun thing happening around there. The cops watched my band real close and hassled us a lot.

When I was at Texas Tech, my competition planted whiskey in the ceiling of the nightclub that I was operating. The county attorney busted me and took me off to jail in one of those big, flashy paddy wagons. It prevented me from making a living and stopped my pursuit of my degree at that time. I was really discouraged by that. A few years later when I was in law school, friends of that same county attorney passed the word to me that he hoped I didn't have any hard feelings. Well, fuck you buddy! I do have hard feelings. It caused me a lot of trouble, and it was a frame-up in the first place. That guy knew it was, but there was an election coming up, he wanted to get publicity, and I was a good way to do it.

I can't actually blame all that on Lubbock. Lubbock is just a physical place. But any town where Dan Quayle and George Bush are the political heroes, that is what I don't like about Lubbock. On the other hand, that side of Lubbock is necessary to produce the side that I enjoy. Reacting against that mentality partly produced many of the wonderful people from Lubbock I know and love. Lubbock is polarized. We all came out of that polarization, that duality. And in Lubbock's defense, it is interesting to note that the three main public statues in Lubbock are memorials to a comedian, a musician, and a cook.[1]

1. The statues to which Hancock refers are: Will Rogers on his horse Soapsuds, by Electra Waggoner Biggs, located on the Texas Tech campus; Buddy Holly, by Grant Speed, located at the West Texas Walk of Fame in front of the Lubbock Civic Center; and C. B. Stubblefield, Barbecue Beyond the Grave, by Terry Allen, located on the site of the former Stubb's Barbecue on East Broadway.

I Ain't Gonna Take the Rap (Gospel Clog)

from the album Dancers Do It on the Floor

I ain't gonna take the rap for Jesus on
the cross.
He knew what he was doing. He knows
who is the Boss.
He wants me to love my life. He saved
me. I was lost.
So I ain't gonna take the rap for Jesus on
the cross.

I ain't a child to suffer for my father's
sins.
I had nothing to do with that. He's just
my next of kin.
And I ain't feeling guilty about no other
race.
I ain't never had a slave or stole
somebody's place.

And I ain't askeered of the Big Bad Wolf
or a landlord at my door.
And I ain't askeered of my concept of
being rich or poor.
This planet Earth is home sweet home.
I'm glad we're welcome here.
The only thing to worry about is hate
and guilt and fear.

Oh, God, You know I love You and I give
my life to You.
You say the word, Lord Jesus, and that's
just what I'll do.
But 'til then . . . I ain't gonna take the
rap for Jesus on the cross.

The Born Again Zenner

from the album Big Band Country & Mystic Music of the Great American Outback

When I die, I wanna be kissed and loved
    to death.
Then I'll try to fly away on the holy
    breath.

You ask me, "Hey, how's it goin'? What
    have you seen?"
I reply, "Every day is Christmas, every
    night is Halloween."
Honesty is the policy of eternity.
I'll tell the truth if you really wanna
    know how it is with me.
I've lived once before.
I reincarnate over and over and over and
    over again.
And I recall two other lives, when I was
    two other men.

AT THE END OF ONE OF THEM . . .
The King said, "Make your last wish for
    your last breath."
I said to him, "I wanna be kissed and
    loved to death."

LATER THAT SAME ETERNITY . . .
General Mackenzie killed this Indian
    boy, a Comanche brave.
I died there at a canyon in West Texas.
    No one saved.
My grandpa said, "Do you wanna go
    back to earth for anything else?"
I said, "Yes! Next time, I wanna be
    kissed and loved to death."

I'm born again, near the place I died.
I'm a white man in this life.
My heaven is a bunch of kids and a
    good-lookin' lovin' wife.
When I die, I wanna be kissed and loved
    to death.
Then I'll try to fly away on the holy
    breath.

Butch

Flatlander BUTCH HANCOCK is known as one of the most talented and prolific Texas songwriters, with a body of songs matched in quality and number perhaps only by Bob Dylan, to whom he is often compared. In one legendary recording project called "No 2 Alike," Butch performed thirty-two consecutive nights of original music in Austin without singing the same song twice. A songwriter's songwriter, his songs have been recorded by Joe Ely, Jimmie Gilmore, Jerry Jeff Walker, Emmylou Harris, and Willie Nelson.

Hancock

BUTCH: My dad[1] was in the earthmoving business around Lubbock, doing leveling and terracing for farmers. He would have me out there after school, on weekends, and all summer driving tractors. The good thing about that job was we got to travel to different farms all around a fifty- or sixty-mile radius of Lubbock, so I wasn't driving a tractor on the same farm every morning to night. There was some variety.

CHRIS: What do you mean? All of those flat cotton fields seem pretty much the same.

BUTCH: That's the amazing thing about it! After doing that for a few months, I remember contemplating that somebody, each farmer, has been over every square inch of that land and knows every bit of dirt out there. They know the subtle differences in density; sometimes the dirt's real sandy and the tractor bogs down a little,

1. Butch Hancock is not directly related by blood to the family of Tom X Hancock, as far as anyone knows.

sometimes it's harder plowing through the drier dirt. That was what made what would have been an otherwise boring task become intensely interesting, watching for the subtle differences in what from a distance might appear to be a plain landscape.

CHRIS: How did that experience move you towards creating music?

BUTCH: I took a harmonica out there and figured out that the key of G was second gear on that ol' tractor. Somewhat exaggerating the speedup and slowdown, you could play any tune you wanted with the tractor. When you're moving through the slow dirt and the fast dirt, then dead-heading between the ends of rows, there obviously are different rhythms of the engine you are listening to for ten hours. Observing those rhythms really affected me.

My theory is that all of the rhythms in your environment imprint a pattern over everything in your unconscious. The rhythms that apply during a day can be compressed down into a two-minute song. Usually it's not going to be an exact one-to-one correspondence; more like a slide rule. The rhythms of cities are amazing things. In a city you get programmed with the hustle, the quick changes, the sudden total reverses of sounds and the spaces you're working through.

I rode a train in Austria one time and had the most amazing revelation, between Innsbruck and Vienna. Passing through the countryside, the hills off in the distance, and the way the farms were detailed and configured, it just blew me away! The correspondence that the landscape had both with the old Viennese architecture and the work of the classical Viennese composers, like Mozart. It's amazing! And I think, "It has to be that way with our West Texas music."

Townes Van Zandt said to me one time, "All you West Texas guys have that High Plains air in your sound. I can't tell whether it's in your voices or in the general feel of the music. But there is something about that West Texas wind in all of your songs." It really is there. You can hear it. We all have a little touch of that West Texas twang. I think Townes nailed it; it's that wind that is blowing through all our ears.

It also must have something to do with the fact that we have a hemisphere of sky! Everywhere else, that hemisphere is broken up by trees and mountains and hills. Even if they are distant, you don't get the full 180-degree frame of vision that you do out in West Texas.

CHRIS: Do you think the lack of external stimulation in the West Texas environment opens your ears to deeper vibrations?

BUTCH: I don't think there is any lack of stimulation. Everybody sees spherically in 360 degrees. We can look down and up and around and behind. There is an equal amount of space surrounding everybody, whether it's crowded or expanded space doesn't make any difference. Each person is looking at the universe from a single point, whether you are in a crowded city or out on the open plains.

The ocean may be the closest thing to the flatness in West Texas, but even on the ocean you get giant waves occasionally. On the ocean, there is the apprehension that the fluid surroundings can change at any time. In the mountains, you go around curves and are surprised by the newness of the view. The great thing about West Texas is that, any idea or stimulation you have out there, you have the opportunity to ponder it awhile. You see something on the horizon thirty miles ahead when you're driving down the highway and it's going to be in your consciousness for at least the next thirty minutes while you get there.

You would think that any theories about the earth being flat would come from out there on the plains. On the other hand, it's also the kind of place where you begin to notice that the earth is round and turning under the skies.

CHRIS: How did growing up in Lubbock lead you toward pursuing a vocation in creating various things?

BUTCH: Sometime in high school, they were expecting us to come up with a theory about what we were going to do with our lives. Architecture was the only thing that appealed to me at the time. I didn't think of music as a profession; I just thought music was music. I still pretty much think that.

I studied architecture at Texas Tech. Architecture is a wonderful way to put together all the mysteries. It is also a great thing to study instead of songwriting in order to write songs. I truly believe that if you have a creative passion in life, you need to study something else as well. Because in doing so, you're going to be measuring this new thing against your passion. Suddenly, you've got a whole new set of ideas, ways and means of accomplishing your goal. It's like binocular vision. That new point of view will then correspond to your chosen field and give you new patterns and ideas, new ways to expand and build and construct.

Studying architecture was perfect for me to learn how to build songs. Instead of building a building, you're simply building a song. You put together all these totally weird, unrelated things that make something new, coherent, useful, and hopefully beautiful, whatever that may mean. For instance, in songwriting, there has to be melody, rhythm, and all the basic elements of design: "balance," "emphasis," "surprise," "sequencing," and "color." See? Color can be both literal color as well as the metaphorical meaning of color. I learned an immense amount studying architecture that has served me in songwriting, and in all other areas. Songwriting and architecture are two examples of what we're here for, which is discovering what the universe is about and our place in it. Songwriting is just something I have done while trying to find out other truths.

CHRIS: Do you believe growing up in Lubbock affected your tendency to seek the Truth through music and art?

BUTCH: The Lubbock environment is a very surreal environment. Nothing looks like it belongs there, because in fact it doesn't. Everything out there is imported. There's not any of that old buffalo grass left, and most of the dirt blew in from the next state. Literally, everything out there is an applied object. The only real things out there are the flatness and the sky. And in the twentieth century, the third basic element is the road.

I made a series of Super-8 movies in cars across West Texas, doing single-frame exposures so that when you speed it up and project it at a normal speed it looks like you're going faster. I did about seven or eight of them, and learned amazing things about the idea of scale. The first one I did was 30 miles from Clarendon to Claude. It played back at a rough speed of about 300 miles an hour. Everything would still be pretty smooth; there'd be a few little jerky movements here and there. The next one I did was from Clarendon to Lubbock, which is 145 miles, with an equivalent speed of about 1,200 miles an hour, and that's when some amazing things would start to happen. The telephone poles would start to wiggle along the side of the road. I'd wait until they were in the same place in the windshield each time before I would snap a picture, so it would make them stand still, then I could control which direction they went. Suddenly the utility poles became an organism, a whole thing, rather than just a line of poles. They weren't all perfectly straight up and down, they became this vibrating thing. They would wiggle around and jump over the crossroads. I began to see that things that were close to the car would disappear first as you got faster and faster; they would blur quicker. The very fastest one I did was about 250 miles in about twenty-nine seconds, roughly the speed of a satellite passing over, but the only things that remain are the earth, the sky, and the road.

The road is always out there in front pointing the way. That became a powerful subconscious pattern for my cosmology of living in America, having cars and traveling down the road. It is the great metaphor of "The Road of Life." That has been a powerful image for all of us.

On the highways we travel, we learn to identify landmarks, destinations, and directions, to get our bearings in that map. Our inner world map is similar. Sometimes we are going too fast to notice the details; sometimes we slow down and can see the basic elements that make up our travels. I think there is a built-in desire, something that humans are always doing, to understand what those motions are and make general sense out of them; finding out what will remain consistent and what are the variations; and why do these variations have a repeating pattern?

I drew a cartoon one time about the first caveman who was looking at the sunrise and said, "It's coming up over here? I saw it go down over there last night!" Now we say, "Well, yeah." But it was the first discovery. Slowly we try to make more consistent sense. At first, you notice the immediate variations, then you get enough data to begin noticing patterns are repeating. We're simply developing a more general idea of our universe. Buckminster Fuller called it Generalized Principles. That is what we are seeking to understand. The great thing that human beings have is this mind that can ascertain these principles at work.

Every time we perceive a system at work, we notice that it is always in relationship to other systems. Everything is transforming, but we can begin to see patterns being made and we can make some amazing generalizations which allow us to understand other systems. Like the system of the English language; we notice that we repeat certain words and hopefully the meanings get conveyed back and forth. We can verify that. And then we are totally surprised when the other person had no clue whatsoever of what we've been talking about for four years. Meaning is a floating, changing thing; it's slow to change, but it does change. When we were kids, there were different meanings for certain words, and there are new words entering the language all the time Obviously, all we're doing with language is trying to describe everything we can.

When I started writing songs, I was describing exactly what I was seeing sitting up there on the tractor: "Oh, the West wind has blowed/Down the dirt road it goes." What you see is what you get, up there on the tractor. Then as I grew and began to explore my own life more, living in the cities, relationships, friends and loves, as all that moved through my life, my songwriting became more of the language of the inner world as related to the outer world.

There has definitely been a development from my beginnings, which were very simple. At first, I played the simplest chords because those were the only ones I knew; the simplest song forms because I hadn't majored in music enough to know how to construct more complicated songs. I began to explore from there.

CHRIS: Did you consciously think, "I want to be a famous songwriter," or was songwriting simply an uncontrollable urge?

BUTCH: I was born in a century where there was a proliferation of billions of cameras and guitars. Those became my two main tools of the trade, my interfaces. Songwriting obviously has been my major output. The camera has been my intake. Photography has helped me train my eye for seeing how things are operating, mainly people. But there is a relationship to them all. It is exploring with the eyes and the mind. "Why am I taking pictures of this? What's going on in that one little moment?" There are those decisive moments of movement from Cartier-Bresson, to the extended moments of Ansel Adams. A mountain doesn't move quite as fast as someone playing catch with a dog, but the light changes in a matter of seconds.

FLATLANDERS IN LUBBOCK, JUNE 2002.

CHRIS: In Lubbock, one doesn't have those moments of watching a mountain, or watching the river flow; more like taking in a square acre of dirt in your backyard. Does that stimulate the desire for that creative process in an unusual way?

BUTCH: Growing up in Lubbock, we got our hearts tied to looking for the Question Mark, the Great Mystery of the Universe. It's like the old Tom T. Hall observation "Some people can fly around the world and not see anything, and some people can walk around the block and see everything."

Sitting up on the tractor, watching each little clod made up of grains of sand getting turned by the plow and becoming a row of dirt a mile long, suddenly you are into the scope of the universe. The whole scale of everything is right there in a pile of dirt. It is the universe in a grain of sand. Everything is everywhere, at all times.

You've got your physics and your metaphysics. Once you figure out the difference between physics and metaphysics, the rest of your life is just comparing them to learn how things operate; exploring, pushing, and testing all the conclusions we have drawn while seeking the whole truth.

Look for the exceptions. It is finding the exceptions to conclusions that shows us the next level of conclusions. In other words, conclusions are steps for getting further down the road. Conclusions are temporary.

Seeking those exceptions and how they fit with the whole allows you to develop a more accurate generalized principle, a more accurate understanding. The human race may not be making that much progress, but here and there progress is made. And we've been able to record a tremendous amount of understanding. You can either embrace all that knowledge or ignore it. If you ignore what so many people have spent much of their lives discovering and understanding, you are cutting yourself off from opportunity for greater understanding. There is a theory that too much specialization is what causes extinction, because the environment changes. If you are not adaptable you perish. Humans don't have any physical features that make them specially adapted for changing situations, but they do have that ability to collect useful information and pass it on. Seeking God or complete truth, whatever that wholeness is, should be our passion, instead of our aversion.

CHRIS: Growing up in Lubbock, I think people there are very aware of the duality between good and bad. There is a right way and wrong way to have your hair, to pray, et cetera. Where I'm going with this is I want you to comment on a quote attributed to you: "We all grew up in Lubbock with two things pounded into our brains from the day we were born. One is 'God loves you and he's going to send you to hell.' The other is 'Sex is dirty, evil, nasty, filthy, sinful, bad, and awful, and you should save it for the one you truly love.'"

BUTCH: Duality is part of the universe. Contrast exists in everything; otherwise you wouldn't be able to differentiate anything. We only learn by contrast. In a place where contrast is strongest, where enforcement of one side is heavy-handed, perhaps there is huge opportunity for growth on the opposite end of the spectrum.

Counterbalance is the word I'm looking for. When everybody else goes to one side of the ship, I am going over to the other side that is above water. I think how a lot of the musicians wound up coming together in that community was the process of being pushed out. Humans have an incredible tendency to go in the wrong direction from what they are looking for. Often, if you watch where everybody is headed and go the opposite direction, you may find what they are all seeking.

CHRIS: I believe it was C. S. Lewis who said, "It is not progress to continue to go forward if you are going in the wrong direction."

BUTCH: Direction does have something to do with it. Aim or purpose is an essential part of what we are about. Without that reference, you may measure things on whims. Your stomach may determine everything for you for a day or two. If your aim is clear, you can go literally weeks without eating.

It is like a magnetization process. Once you detect a glimpse of that place which lies behind the Question Mark, you want everything to apply to revealing that glimpse again, so only what is magnetized toward that goal can stick to you. That process applies to songwriting. The closest I've been able to describe songwriting is you tune into some little vibe and amplify that magnetization. All the words and phrases that don't fit, won't stick to it.

I think the wonderful thing is that our minds have the ability to intuit all of what we have been talking about. It doesn't have to be spelled out precisely. Every once in a while it is nice to make it obvious to yourself and try to delineate it better; but you don't have to do that all the time every day. You need to move back into the world to get some work done, scrape your knuckles a bit, and work your muscles.

Wind's Dominion

from the album The Wind's Dominion

Like a fallin' moon—like a risin' mountain
All the days are numbered—but nobody's
    countin'
Another man's god—one man's opinion
They're blown apart—in THE WIND'S
    DOMINION

High waters cover—wide open spaces
The queen's daughter's lover—has a mil-
    lion faces
But the king succumbs—to the crown's
    opinion
And his power fades—in THE WIND'S
    DOMINION

At the Three Mile Island—there's an un-
    known factor
In the NRC—everyone's an actor
It's a risky business—based on opinion
But it can't hold water—in THE WIND'S
    DOMINION

From the high and mighty—to the low and
    lonely
From your archest enemies—to your one
    and only
One more companion—one more opinion
They're lost forever—in THE WIND'S
    DOMINION

When a man of the cloth—and a man of
    science
Meet a man who stands—in full defiance
The chain of command—the wheel of
    opinion
Will come full circle—in THE WIND'S
    DOMINION

Baby don't despair—if the road gets longer
If you keep on movin'—it'll make you
    stronger
Just don't depend on—public opinion
That blows away in—THE WIND'S DOMINION

You're the smoothest—little operator
I'm the lowest common—denominator
But there ain't no hard proof—just this
    opinion
Love lives under—THE WIND'S DOMINION

Dry Land Farm

from the album West Texas Waltzes & Dust-Blown Tractor Tunes

There's thunderstorms building up
Over on the county line
All the neighboring farms get rain
But I never get a drop on mine
You might think a little ol' summer breeze
Couldn't do nobody harm
But it burns like a blazing blowtorch
When you're livin' on a dry land farm

When the west wind comes blowin'
Well, the sand comes blowin' too
And I must say a mouthful
Is more than I can chew
I've swallowed a gallon for every acre
And God knows it hurt
But it ain't as bad as the trouble I've had
Breaking up that dry land dirt

Now the politician says to the farmer,
"You're the backbone of this land."
The irrigatin' farmer says, "Thank you, sir,
I'll eat right out of your hand."
And your average automobile
Has air conditioning when it's warm
Yeah, things are cool for everybody
But the man on the dry land farm

Now if I had my wicked way
In this equally wicked world
I'd make a Garden of Eden
For every boy and girl
But I'd take our two-faced president
And I'd grab him by the arm
Stick him out in the middle of the desert
And make him work a dry land farm

Firewater (Seeks Its Own Level)

from the album Firewater Seeks Its Own Level

Life is a cyclone--death is but a breeze
Will you die on your feet—or live on
    your knees?
Guitar strummin'—wine's overflowin'
They say you have it coming if you never
    got it goin'
You blame it on your baby that your
    heart was broke in half
But I can see you just been crying—so
    you don't have to laugh
There ain't nothing sacred you can beg
    or steal or borrow
When you're swimming in self-pity—
    you'll be drowning in your sorrow

Chorus:
You got drunk last night and you swear
    you saw the devil
Don't you know firewater seeks its own
    level?

Your clothes fit fine and your hair looks
    great
You got time you can waste but no time
    to wait
You're drowning me in the waves your
    brain sent
It ain't love anymore
It's just entertainment
If the devil made you do it, then go for
    it, honey
Just be sure you give him a run for his
    money
You can kill the bottle
There ain't no murder mystery
There's a little bit left but the rest is
    natural history

Chorus repeats

Perched on your back was a loud-
    mouthed vulture
Y'all were talking back and forth about
    the counter-counter-culture
Smoke was hanging heavy—everybody
    had to breathe it
Your hands were on the table but your
    thoughts were underneath it
Everybody got stoned and when the
    night was over
The wildest one there was coldest sober
But you and all the rest
Well, your eyes were getting muddy
'Cause the bartender knows
He's gotta serve somebody.

Chorus repeats

Lord of the Highway

recorded by Joe Ely on the album Lord of the Highway

With your fan belt slippin' and your bare
    tires squealin'
Every time you hit the road you think
    you're rich.
You're Lord of the Highway but the way
    you been drivin'
Sends them hitch-hikers divin' for the
    ditch.

Well the law's on your trail and there's
    another law to lead you
And yet another law to let you down
And the laws of the game they're the
    very same that freed you
The Lord of the Highway gets around.

You weren't the only one who saw the
    dark days a comin'
And you weren't the only one who shut
    'em out.
It was nothin' like your pride; it was
    somethin' deep inside
That saw the Shimmer felt the Shake
    and heard the Shout.

So lay it on thick if you lay it on at all
If you're gonna do the job, do it right
If you gotta hit the road, leave your
    burdens behind you
The Lord of the Highway travels light.

With your air cleaner hissin' and your
    radiator steamin'
And the sun burnin' bugs to the glass
You're Lord of the Highway, you're livin'
    you're not dreamin'
And if time really wants to, let it pass.

You'll be miles down the road when the
    toll bridge is burnin'
And your mirrors face forward at last.
You got what it takes to be Lord of the
    Highway
The Lord of the Highway travels fast.

Boxcars

recorded by Joe Ely on the album Live Shots

I gave all my money to the banker this
    month.
And I got no more money to spend.
She smiled when she saw me comin'
    through the door,
When I left, she said: "Come back
    again."
Well, I watched them lonesome boxcar
    wheels,
Turnin' down the tracks out of town.
An' it's on that lonesome railroad track,
I'm gonna lay my burden down.

I looked for my little lady in the lost an'
    found,
But she had already been claimed.
Now I'm gonna find me a ticket to ride,
To a town that never had no name.
Nobody may care where I go tonight,
But they may, the truth be told.
I'm goin' down to the railroad tracks,
To watch them lonesome boxcars roll.

I was raised on a farm the first years of
    my life.
And life was pretty good, they say.
And I'll probably live to be some ripe
    ol' age,
If death will stay out of my way.
This world can take my money and my
    time,
But it sure can't take my soul.
And I'm goin' down to the railroad
    tracks,
Watch them lonesome boxcars roll.

There's some big ol' Buicks by the
    Baptist church,
Cadillacs at the Church of Christ.
I parked my camel by an ol' haystack:
I'll be lookin' for that needle all night.
Well, there ain't gonna be no radial tires,
Turnin' down the streets of gold.
And I'm goin' down to the railroad
    tracks,
Watch them lonesome boxcars roll.

If you ever heard the whistle on a fast
    freight train,
Beatin' out a beautiful tune,
If you ever seen the cold blue railroad
    tracks,
Shinin' by the light of the moon,
And if you ever felt the locomotive
    shake the ground,
I know you don't need to be told,
Why I'm goin' down to the railroad
    tracks,
Watch them lonesome boxcars roll.

ANGELA STREHLI is known as the First Lady of Texas Blues. One of the original members of the Austin blues scene, Strehli helped spur the national revival of blues music. Angela was Stevie Ray Vaughan's featured vocalist for his 1984 Carnegie Hall performance, one of the watershed marks for modern blues music. She was voted Austin's best female vocalist five times. Now living in Marin County, California, Angela and her husband operate Rancho Nicasio, a historic roadhouse restaurant famous for its live music.

Strehli

ANGELA: I was born in Lubbock, but neither of my folks were native Texans. My father ended up in Lubbock as a professor in the Romance Languages department at Texas Tech, where he mainly taught Spanish. My mom was born in Puerto Rico and was raised for several years in Panama. Her grandparents had come from Spain to Puerto Rico as educators and her father was also an educator, and he was sent to Panama by the U.S. government to establish public schools in the Canal Zone. My parents eventually met when they were at Middlebury College in Vermont. My mother's father was born in New England.

After my father settled in at Tech, my mother established a very successful preschool in Lubbock. In addition to getting basic numbers down and that kind of thing, she would also teach French and Spanish because she and my dad were always crusaders to have languages taught earlier in the schooling process, because it's much easier to learn that way. It was a wonderful background to be raised among educators, and to be around the university faculty atmosphere.

CHRIS: How did you get interested in music as a youngster? Were your parents musical?

ANGELA: They did appreciate music, especially my dad. He played piano a little bit, and we were exposed to good music by our parents. Both my brothers, Chuck and Al, played instruments in school. I really think, of all of us, Al is certainly the most talented musically.

CHRIS: Was Al the one who was most interested in music when you were kids? Was he perhaps the driving musical force in the Strehli household?

ANGELA: I sort of think so, yeah. But I apparently did fool around on the piano some and could play it by ear; I even have a recording to back it up. I did have a lot of fun with piano until I started taking lessons, and soon quit. Now I really do wish I would have pursued the piano, because it certainly would have assisted my song-writing and translating the music to the band. I did play cello at Hutchinson Junior High.

Our connection to Spanish culture was a great musical inspiration for us. Al and I got to spend two months in Argentina in the summer of 1962, because Dad was there teaching other teachers this new method of teaching Spanish which he was advocating. They were residing with native speakers and learning this new method intensely. Before, they would teach grammar first, then reading and writing, and finally speaking the other language, and they were trying to reverse that process. So Al and I were lucky enough to be immersed in this other culture. When we came back, we fooled around with playing guitars and singing the Argentine folk songs we had learned.

About that time there was a folk club that got started in Lubbock by a guy named Stinson Belen, who lived in Slaton. He made dulcimers and other instruments by hand, and was into European folk music. He inspired this folk club that would meet to play music every so often, once a month or so. There weren't really any other connections as far as getting together with others to actually play folk music. Al didn't participate in that group so much, but I definitely remember Jimmie Gilmore and Joe Ely, when he was around. And even Johnny Deutschendorf, who happened to be in Lubbock going to Tech for a time. He later changed his name to John Denver and made it big.

CHRIS: So at this time you're playing Spanish folk music; I want you to talk about how you began your interest in blues music. You have written and recorded a song called "Two Bit Texas Town," and it sounds rather autobiographical. In that song there's a line that says, "The first time I heard the blues was on the radio. It scared me half to death." Tell me how you first heard the blues and came to develop the intense love for this music for which you are known.

ANGELA: I had a little Zenith shortwave radio. The local stations would mainly play country and western and normal pop music of the day. None of that grabbed my attention particularly, although I loved listening to the radio and everything on it. When I got old enough to stay up later, I discovered my radio could get these powerful late-night clear channel stations from all over the country. There was XERB out of Del Rio, which was the Wolfman Jack show that came on late at night. Then there was another one out of Shreveport [KWKH], which played blues and gospel. All that just blew my mind. There was another from Nashville, station WLAC with two deejays named John R and the Hossman.

CHRIS: Do you really remember that moment, the first time you heard the blues? How did it make you feel?

ANGELA: Intense intrigue. What is this music that is so different from what I'm hearing locally? What do you even call it? I didn't even know for a long time that you called it the blues.

CHRIS: So, really, the first time you discovered the blues was spinning that radio dial. There's another line in "Two Bit Texas Town" that says, ". . . back when radio could turn your life around." Please comment on what you meant by that. How could radio turn your life around?

ANGELA: I think radio then was so much more wide open than it is now, as far as what disc jockeys played. They played whatever they thought was good, and they didn't necessarily care if it was pigeonholed in a style or format. Radio back then opened up a different world for people just like I was, out in the middle of the country somewhere. I think that was much more true for people who didn't live in big, urban areas. When they would hear something that was so out of their local element, then music could change their life, if it made them curious enough to find out what the deal was, which is what I did. I started going to record stores and I didn't even know what to ask for. I would just ask if they had a record by Howlin' Wolf, or whoever I heard on the late-night radio.

CHRIS: What would the record store clerks think when they would see a little white girl come in asking for a record like that?

ANGELA: Of course, that's the ironic part of my whole career. The question is, "Why would this middle-class white girl want to pursue a career in blues music?" But there's no explaining it. If you really have it in your heart and want to do it, then you just do it and ignore the people who question you. And believe me, they certainly did question me back then.

CHRIS: At what point did you decide you really wanted to pursue the blues as a career?

ANGELA: It took a long time. I was really mainly a huge fan, and I still consider myself primarily of fan of music. At that time, I just collected records. I didn't have any intention of pursuing music at that time. I eventually took up playing the bass and harmonica when I really got into the blues but that was after I had graduated high school and left Lubbock.

One reason I kind of lost my connection with a lot of the other musicians from Lubbock is because when I graduated from Monterey High School in 1964, I went to Northfield, Minnesota, to attend Carleton College. I just wanted to get out of Lubbock and into a different atmosphere and broaden my horizons. I was lucky enough to get into this school, which is pretty academically demanding. I was just barely up to that part, but the school felt like it needed people who were a little more well-rounded than just scholastically brilliant people, so because I had traveled a lot with my parents and had traveled not only in Argentina but also Mexico a couple of times, that definitely was an important factor.

In college, I was exposed to more and more music, blues and jazz. I was probably equally influenced by jazz at the time because I got to hear some really heavy folks while I was up there, even right on campus. I got to hear Thelonious Monk, Art Blakey and the Jazz Messengers, people like that. Jazz was much more accessible up there. I'm sure my collection of jazz records is just as large as my blues collection. Jazz has influenced my singing quite a bit; now, I'm talking about instrumental jazz, not vocalists. My phrasing and tone are very much influenced by jazz music.

I was a sociology and psychology major in college; like I said, I was just a record collector and fan. I went to Carleton for two years but didn't graduate from there. For one thing, it made me realize how wonderfully rich the culture is in Texas, because of black folks and Mexicans who are in such large numbers in Texas. When I went up north, I noticed, "Wait a minute! Where are the Mexicans and black folks?" They simply weren't there.

CHRIS: Did you have a lot of interaction between whites and blacks and Mexicans when you were growing up in Lubbock?

ANGELA: Not a lot. But because of my dad and mother speaking Spanish, I did have contact with many Mexicans. Then, when I started hearing blues and was old enough to drive, I started going on my own over to the east side of Lubbock, where the black folks all lived, just out of curiosity, and looking for record stores. I've always been adventurous in that way, and I have always been treated so well and welcomed by people, because they see a person who legitimately wants to learn about their culture. I've had many nice adventures that way.

After being at Carleton for two years, I took a summer job in San Antonio as a social worker for the YWCA. I lived on the west side of San Antonio, which was about half black and half Mexican and just a sprinkling of Anglos. I attended a black Baptist church there, and that's when I got a real heavy dose of gospel, which is another aspect of American music, which is essentially black music. Other than country music, the music which originated in the United States is primarily gospel, jazz, and blues, and those are what caught my imagination. And the gospel music at this black Baptist church I was attending really did inspire me vocally to think about singing.

Then, at the end of 1966, I went back up to Chicago as a student representative to the YWCA national convention. It was a perfect excuse to hear my blues heroes. I would go to the YWCA convention during the day, and at night I would go hear Muddy Waters, Howlin' Wolf, and Buddy Guy, people like that. So I got that heavy dose of hearing the masters of Chicago blues.

I moved to Austin and ended up graduating from the University of Texas in 1968. By my senior year, I was fooling around with music, playing with other folks around campus who were knowledgeable of the blues and other musical renegades around town. I sort of got pushed into singing; I really started out wanting to play bass guitar. It's so much fun to be backing the band, and I'm pretty rhythmical.

CHRIS: When you say you got pushed into singing, do you mean that the bands just thought it would be cooler to have a woman singer out front?

ANGELA: Exactly. There were plenty of bass players around Austin, but not that many female blues singers. I had a pretty neat band called the Fabulous Rockets. We were probably one of the first integrated bands in Texas at the time. We'd play almost exclusively at black clubs on the east side of Austin. When I started, the blues was completely out of fashion, even in the black community. The blues was no longer being played on the radio. Disco was taking over, even in the music clubs. It was the worst time you could imagine for the blues, but we had so much fun and the older black folks were tickled to see us take up this music that they loved, because the young black kids were definitely not going to take it up. We had a ball playing these little clubs and meeting the regional musicians who had been playing the blues for years. But there was so little going on in Austin as far as clubs and recording studios that were available to us at the time. I ended up going out to Los Angeles with some of the guys in the Rockets, and we changed our name to Sunnyland Special. I was out there for a couple of years, getting to know the record business. I had a couple of chances to record then, but I knew I was not ready. I knew that I didn't have the vocal chops or the life experience to be putting out blues in a credible way. I was still studying it and just getting away with performing. I didn't take myself seriously for probably a good fifteen years after that.

I came back to Austin and joined a rhythm and blues band called James Polk and the Brothers. James Polk is an amazing musician and teacher. He led Ray Charles' band for a number of years. That was a learning experience. I don't really consider myself a soul singer, but it's all relatively in the same spectrum of music. We mainly played at black clubs all over Texas. You wouldn't even imagine this world exists; you'd go out into the middle of nowhere and there'd be some nice, big club. People would come from a hundred miles around to go to these places, because the entertainment would be so good. The audiences were very demanding. You had to really put out to get any sort of response. That was a wonderful experience for me, but it was mainly kind of a weekend band. During the week, I worked as a substitute teacher and I ended up with sort of a semipermanent job at one school, for a while.

Then I had a band with W. C. Clark called Southern Feeling, and that was a very popular band in Austin. That band lasted two or three years, and now W. C. Clark is fairly well known in the blues world. That was a really fun band, but I was working all the time and didn't feel like I was contributing anything. I was just singing cover songs and not writing anything myself, and I was getting a little antsy about all that. When the musicians start changing around more than once, to me, that's when a band is no longer a band so it was time to go do something else.

About that time, Clifford Antone started noticing that we folks who were trying to perform blues were not being successful because we didn't have too many good places to play. Clifford understood this was simply because people didn't know about the music and therefore didn't know what they were missing. He was a huge music fan, coming from Beaumont. That whole Louisiana-Texas border area was just teeming with good rhythm and blues. He ended up in Austin running a family business there, but he was so into music that he had dreams that, if he could just open a place and have the real masters come through and play, he could get the college students and everybody else turned on to that music. Then people like me would benefit from it, because we would be seen in the right conditions.

Southern Feeling had kind of defaulted by then, and I felt like I needed a break from singing five nights a week and trying to book the next gig. I thought I would do something more on the practical side, which was working at Antone's club. Once Clifford got the club open, I did it all; I was the stage manager and I ran the sound. I was one of the founders of Antone's, who helped get that place off the ground. That version of Antone's club was wonderful. It was right in the middle of downtown on Sixth Street, which was a typical dead downtown at the time, with winos lying around the sidewalk. Nobody gave a darn about Sixth Street at that time; it has become this whole other scene since then, of course. Because it was right in the middle of town, black folks would come out there. It was natural for them to know about the place. There was enough room for a lot of tables and chairs, so we could present big names like Bobby Bland and B. B. King.

That era was incredible for me because I got to see just about everybody I could ever care to and I didn't have to go to Chicago. We had nothing but blues seven days a week. That's a crazy thing to try to do, but somehow Clifford just kept at it doggedly. When he'd have someone big come through town, he'd have them play at least three or four days so it would give more opportunity for people to come out to see them, and it gave the artists an opportunity for us all to relax and get to be friends. It was like blues college. Stevie Ray Vaughan would hang out all day long in the place, just hoping to talk music and the blues with his heroes.

I was getting to know many of the blues greats working there, and not only getting to open for them but actually getting on stage and performing with them. That's the real education, getting up on stage and doing it live. I really got the picture of what they were doing for the audience.

CHRIS: At what point did you start moving from being a blues enthusiast to a full-time performer and recording artist?

ANGELA: I established the original Angela Strehli Band, which consisted mainly of

George Raines on drums, Sarah Brown on bass, Denny Freeman and Derek O'Brien on guitars, and Denny also played the keyboards, and Mark Kasanoff on horns and harmonica. Clifford had started to record some people live when they came through the club. He thought people would want to come in and record these historic shows, but no one ever did so he started to have it done himself. No record companies came forth and offered to put any of this out. I started wondering what was going to happen to all of us and this music in the future? Were we going to just keep playing clubs the rest of our lives? I had been to the West Coast and seen the recording situation out there, which was pretty cold. They would want you to use studio musicians, which is inappropriate for blues. So it just made sense to start our own record label, to put this historic material out and to give the opportunity to artists like me and my friends to learn studio skills, the technical skills, for producing our own records. Then we could have a future in music, not just going out playing until two in the morning every night.

That was the birth of Antone's Records. Clifford was glad to sacrifice his personal resources to make it happen and get it off the ground. So that was my opportunity to start recording. You do have to start somewhere. It is not easy to record. It is just different from playing live, and you have to learn these skills in the studio. I now really enjoy working on other people's projects, as a producer, or mixing sound, getting good performances out of people.

Soul Shake was my first full-length album, although we had released an EP before called *Stranger Blues*, which was later incorporated into *Soul Shake*, when we converted it from vinyl and cassette to CD.

CHRIS: So where did your career go from there and where are you now?

ANGELA: I'm still in the same position of working to have original material that is good enough to warrant going into the studio and recording. It is daunting and expensive. I feel so privileged to have recorded as many times as I have, which hasn't been that many records, considering how long I've been doing it. But I have taken my time with my recording career, waiting until I'm ready to contribute something before I try to record. I've tried to do it my own way, because I've seen many other artists who were taken in a different direction by a producer, and some of those experiences left them bitter because they felt like their recordings didn't really represent them. So I feel fortunate because Antone's Records gave me the opportunity to record and have the time to do it the way I wanted. Nowadays people can do it much more easily.

People have studios in their homes, and digital technology has opened up a whole other world, and I think that is wonderful. But I still think it is a privilege to record and have a distributor.

Of course, since I've left Texas and come out here to California, various situations have changed, including the setup at Antone's Records. Now, when I finish recording, it just depends on what record label is ready, willing, and able to put it out at the time. It's an ideal way for me to record, to do the whole album myself and then just offer it up to the regular labels to see who is interested, to have that control from the beginning. It's a very fortunate situation to be in.

CHRIS: I believe that is one of the things that have made music from Lubbock unique. Many artists from Lubbock seem to have this dedication to being independent and shirking labels, at times when maybe that wasn't quite as popular a career choice to make. Joe Ely is a good example of that.

ANGELA: I agree. Because my husband's son is a chef, we ended up buying this historic roadhouse here in Marin County, and we have live music as well. One of the most fun things has been to have the Flatlanders come out and play. It's really been fun to get to catch up with Joe and Jimmie and Butch. When we lived in Austin, not

COTTON FIELD AND POWER LINES.

many people knew we were connected from back in Lubbock, because we were in different musical worlds. Your genre of music has so many people in it, you don't really get to interact much with people from other genres, which is a shame. When your nose is to the grindstone, and you're playing all the time, you don't get to hear other people you'd like to hear. But Joe Ely was always one of the exceptions to the rule at Antone's. Even though it was a "blues club—period," Joe Ely has always been a welcome performer at Antone's.

CHRIS: Do you have any final insights about how growing up in Lubbock, Texas, may have affected your decision to pursue a career in music?

ANGELA: Obviously, the history of Buddy Holly is pretty heavy. To know of someone who grew up in your own neighborhood to have hit records on the radio, that was pretty jaw-dropping amazing. And of course Roy Orbison was from the area. That was inspiring of a certain confidence.

And it was like I was saying earlier about listening to the radio: seeking out the mystery of music, where it comes from and why. It is so "normal" in Lubbock, that it is amazing to think that there is this whole other world out there.

When I say Lubbock was "normal," I mean Lubbock was so pleasant, a wonderful place to grow up. The people in Lubbock are extremely friendly and open; it gave you a feeling of being carefree and safe. And they are very independent, as we were saying. I think that independence is a wonderful trait of those West Texas families, having their own minds and beliefs, not just following whatever trend is going around. I'm talking about the legacy of these pioneers who had enough strength and nerve to get out there on their own and go to this godforsaken place. You gotta like that.

Two Bit Texas Town

from the album Blonde and Blue

Well, I never will forget
When I heard the big Wolf howl
It scared me half to death
To know he was on the prowl
Back when radio
Could turn your life around
I know what it did to me
In that two bit Texas town

I remember Muddy Waters'
"Hoochie Coochie Man"
And I know I heard Lightnin' Hopkins
Talk about a mojo hand
Jimmy Reed and Eddy Taylor
Putting the big beat down
Made us want to dance
In that two bit Texas town

Now, these were mighty, mighty men
But they rocked it out so cool
Made us want to learn
What they weren't teaching in school
Back when radio

Could turn your life around
I know what it did to me
In that two bit Texas town

Late at night
On the radio
Del Rio, Texas
Shreveport
WLAC
John R and the Hossman
In Nashville, Tennessee
The first time I heard the Blues
Was on the radio
It scared me half to death
In that two bit Texas town

Jesse "Gui

Lubbock native JESSE TAYLOR became internationally famous as the blistering lead guitar player for the Joe Ely Band. He has toured with many recording legends, including Bob Dylan, the Rolling Stones, the Clash, Tom Petty, Bruce Springsteen, and Billy Joe Shaver. A chance encounter between Jesse and his longtime friend C. B. Stubblefield, better known as Stubb, was the birth of the legendary Stubb's Barbecue Sunday Night Jams in East Lubbock, a seminal event in Lubbock's musical heritage.

tar" Taylor

JESSE: At the time I first met Stubb, I was living in Lubbock and playing my guitar around there. I had been living in California awhile but had recently come back to Lubbock. Like all the other musicians in Lubbock of my era, we used to go back and forth between California and Austin and Lubbock all the time, with some diversions to Colorado. I was just back in Lubbock from one of those trips, and I happened to be living on East Broadway.

Stubb's Barbecue was also on East Broadway, at the top of maybe the only hill in Lubbock, the one closest to Avenue A. Or I guess it was more of a valley than a hill. You went down this big draw by Mackenzie Park, and where I was staying was the top of the other side of the draw from Stubb's.

I would go to my friends' houses to jam, over to Ely's house or Jimmie Gilmore's. Of course, I was a poor, broke musician hippie, like we all were. I didn't have a car or nothing, so I would just hitchhike whenever I needed to go anywhere. This one day, I was standing there hitchhiking and this big Cadillac pulls up. I look into the car, and it was Stubb driving this Cadillac.

CHRIS: Did you know who he was when he stopped?

JESSE: No, not at all. But I had walked by his barbecue place quite often. Because I lived on that street and had to walk by Stubb's all the time. Every once in a while, I would walk by there and the door would happen to open, I would see this smoky little room and hear blues music coming out. I would think, "I want to go in that place so bad!" But it was really unthinkable to me, I guess. It was all black people in there. I never saw any white people go in there at all, so even I was a little intimidated to go in there. And normally I am not real easily intimidated.

As it turns out, I never should have been. Stubb and Cuz and Little Pete would have loved it if I had just walked in the door and begun visiting with them.

So that day, it was amazing. Stubb picked me up on one side of that Mackenzie canyon, got up to the top of the hill on the other side, and he stops his car in front of Stubb's Barbecue. He said, "Well, this is where I'm going," and he started to let me off.

I said to Stubb, "I've walked by this place so many times and have never been in here. Do you go in here very much?" Because I wanted to know what was going on in there, what this place was all about.

Stubb said, "Sir, I own this place!"

I said, "Really? I've always wanted to go in there."

Then Stubb said to me, his exact words, "I'll tell you what, I got a barbecue sandwich and a cold beer that's got your name on it in there." That was our first meeting, right there. As far as I know, that was the first any of us musicians, in our group of friends in Lubbock, had even been in Stubb's Barbecue.

After that, I would go in there almost every day. We would sit around listening to the jukebox and visiting, but there wasn't very much going on there. Stubb said to me one time, "What we need is some live music in here."

I knew all the musicians in town, so I said, "Let me get on the phone. I'll bring you some live music!" After that we had Ely, Ponty Bone, and all the local guys playing there. But pretty soon, it was Stevie Ray Vaughan, Townes Van Zandt, George Thorogood, Tom T. Hall, Muddy Waters, and a whole lot of other folks that played live music at Stubb's on East Broadway in Lubbock. Stubb really loved live, real music.

But all this was before Stubb ever moved to Austin. There are a lot of folks right there in Lubbock who never even knew that was all going on over there. A lot of people just know Stubb's as the great place down here in Austin. But that little place on East Broadway was something else.

There was a sign in the old Stubb's that said, "THERE WILL BE NO BAD TALK OR

LOUD TALK IN THIS PLACE." I had been hanging around Stubb's for about five years when I suddenly noticed that there were three words in the sign stenciled in red and all the rest of the words were stenciled in black. The three words in red were "bad," "loud," and "place." From that day on, I could not see that sign where it didn't say to me, "Bad Loud Place." That's what that sign said to me: "This is a bad loud place."

That is pretty much how that whole deal got started. What started out as a ride ended up being friendships that lasted half a lifetime.

CHRISTOPHER B. "STUBB" STUBBLEFIELD, SR.
Cook, Poet, Philosopher & Texas Legend
Born 3/7/34 Navasota, TX Died 5/27/95 Austin TX

This is the original site of STUBB'S BAR-B-QUE. From 1968 until 1984, 108 E. Broadway was the Heart and Soul of Lubbock, Texas... and maybe the whole planet. People of every age, race and background gathered at this spot to eat the food, jump to the music and hang-out with STUBB's big grin and hear him "DISSER-RATE" on the meanings of it all.

Nearly everything he said was a poem of some kind or another.

As the reputation of STUBB and his cafe grew (locally and around the world), hundreds of musicians... the famous, not-yet-famous and people who just wanted to make some music... played on STUBB's stage and ate at his table.

To it all, STUBB simply said "LADIES AND GENTLEMEN, I'M JUST A COOK" (then proceeded to sing SUMMERTIME) and, if pushed to reveal the ingredients of his famous secret sauce, he just smiled and said "LOVE AND HAPPINESS"... which also sums up exactly what he made happen right here.

The Lubbock Arts Alliance has joined with all those who loved STUBB to commemorate a remarkable man and an important time and place in the musical legacy of West Texas. The bronze statue of STUBB was made by artist/songwriter Terry Allen, who played here as a young musician.

This site was dedicated to STUBB and his life August 29, 1999.

LUBBOCK ARTS ALLIANCE, 1999

STUBB'S MEMORIAL PLAQUE.

PONTY BONE was the fiery squeezebox player in the original Joe Ely Band in the 1980s. He is now the leader of the popular Texas zydeco band Ponty Bone and the Squeezetones.

PONTY BONE AND CONNI HANCOCK.

Ponty Bone

PONTY: A lot of people think I grew up in Lubbock, but I really grew up in San Antonio. The first time I ever went out to that part of the world was to go to Texas Tech. On the way up there, somewhere north of Midland, we encountered these migrating hordes of tarantulas, bigger than a man's head, the body about as big as a fist. Horrible! They were walking across the highway in broad daylight, and there was nothing to do but run over a few. When your tires rolled over them, they went plkkcrrssstd. It was like the biggest omen.

From day one in Lubbock, I immediately began meeting larger-than-life characters. I immediately met a black bluesman who would come to my house on 14th and Avenue S and play with me and my brother. This guy could play like Lightnin' Hopkins. He was a yardman who lived in the alley of some apartments. He loved us because we always had wine. I met gamblers. I met graduate students who were geniuses, who would go on to become well known in their fields of literature and art, like Grover Lewis. When I first met Grover Lewis he was a graduate student in English. He was well known on campus for being an intellectual with a circle of friends that partied. Immediately, little naïve undergraduate me is hanging with him and a bunch of guys like that.

CHRIS: What would we know Grover Lewis for now? What did he go on to do?

PONTY: He went on to be a writer. He lived in Los Angeles and was on everybody's list in the '70s. He passed on early from a life-threatening disease he had all his life. He was almost blind. He wore real thick glasses but could hardly see. He wrote quite a few interesting things in *Rolling Stone* in the early '70s.

I agree with your thinking about Lubbock being unusual. Although skeptics will say, "You read other authors, and it's the same wherever they grew up. What you are really celebrating is your passage, the things you know. Every town is the same." Well, I don't think so! People who think that is true weren't ever in Lubbock. It is true that there are a lot of other towns that have amazing music scenes. But you know what? A lot of the people in their amazing music scenes, they lived in Lubbock at some point.

I am always amazed when I mention Lubbock to other musicians I work with. They say, "Oh, did you live in Lubbock? I used to live in Lubbock. I worked for Jay Boy Adams," or, "I was working with the Traveling Salesmen." They were two brothers, a cover band. They wore suits and ties, and they were on the road constantly. Their mother was their booking agent, and she was smart as a whip. She made money with that band. They played all the right parties.

Lubbock has always been a lucrative market. A lot of great bands came out of Lubbock, and a lot of great musicians came to Lubbock to live. A lot of them were there because of something more on the intellectual side of the equation. Like being in a band, or going to Texas Tech, or having some kind of a connection to the arts. Lubbock has got uniqueness about it, I agree.

I spent fifteen years in Lubbock, on two separate stretches. Six years the first time, a very interesting six years. I was in college the first three. Then I married a Lubbock girl and settled into life in Lubbock. My wife and I had twins after about two years. I had a day job, a car, a TV.

However, I thought of myself as some sort of artist long after college. I have thought of myself as a character in a novel all my life. I just knew I was different. I knew that it wasn't right to tell people that I was a surveyor or a draftsman, because I didn't feel connected to that. That was like saying I work crossword puzzles.

My dad was real technical and retentive, and I inherited that as a mirror image of my artistic side. I'm a Libra, and I've had this lifelong fascination with the entire spectrum, both ends of the poles. I think my father realized right off that I was an artist, and he didn't want to encourage it. But he did want me to learn music as a discipline. He basically wanted me to be well rounded. My dad started me on the accordion when I was five years old. The accordion is a very technical instrument to learn, but if you learn it when you're five years old, it's not a problem because you're just a machine at that age, soaking up information.

CHRIS: Did your dad play accordion?

PONTY: No, Dad did not play the accordion. In fact, Dad never told me when he was alive, but his father and his two uncles were musicians. They had a band in north Texas called the Bone Brothers. I found out from my Aunt Inez. She produced a clipping from the newspaper where they'd interviewed ol' A. P. Bone about his early days as a musician. The point of this article was that sometimes they wouldn't agree on a certain harmony note, they'd go outside and fight over it and whoever won was the way they played it.

It was only very much towards the end of my father's life that he encouraged me musically. After he died was when I really began to pursue music as a career.

About that time is when I met Joe Ely and Jimmie Gilmore and everybody. My wife and I moved to Phoenix and became the midway point for all the Lubbock bunch who were constantly trekking back and forth to California. While we were living in Phoenix, we took trips constantly. We would visit her folks in Lubbock, or come hear our friends play in Austin. Any excuse to come back to Texas, we would do it. We started a band called New Moan Hey, and the first thing we did was come to Austin and play the Vulcan Gas Company.

On one of those cross-country trips, I came to Austin and saw Lewis Cowdrey, who also had lived in Lubbock. Lewis had just met Jimmie Vaughan, who had just come down from Dallas, and they were starting a band called the Storm, and Lewis wanted me to be in it. He said, "How many nights a week do you feel like working?" I said, "Well, I don't know. I have to run to Lubbock to visit my mother-in-law and father-in-law, and I'll be back on Monday."

And I never got back. I went to Lubbock, and next thing I know, I'm sitting there at my old job again, same damn job as a surveyor, where I had been six years earlier. I had run into one of the guys I used to work with and he said, "We're needing somebody right now, and you'd be great."

I had done some surveying in Phoenix, because I had these twins. Obviously, we all had to eat. As a matter of fact, we had to have a little extra money because we were in a band. You think you'd be making some extra money because you're in a band. But every musician knows, in fact, it takes money to have a band.

So it was 1971, and I've got my old job back. We moved to Slaton, outside of Lubbock, because it was so cheap to live out there. We commenced to start having these wonderful jam sessions on Sundays out there with Tommy Hancock and all of his family, Joe Ely, Jesse Taylor, Jimmie Gilmore, lots more that I could name. I began to play the Cotton Club with Tommy Hancock and his country band the Roadside Playboys, with his wife Charlene.

CHRIS: Tell me about the Supernatural Family Band.

PONTY: The Supernatural Family Band was a grand idea. The Supernatural Family Band was more than a band; it was Lubbock's own little version of Ken Kesey's Merry Pranksters. I have a short list of bandleaders I know who are successful, and Tommy Hancock is right up there. He's great on keeping business going. It's a hard thing to make a band actually pay your bills, and Tommy has done it for a long time.

In 1976, my first marriage went on the rocks. I'm out in the front yard playing Frisbee with my twins. Joe Ely rides up on his bicycle and says, "Hey Ponty, it looks like MCA is gonna do my first album. We're getting together tonight over at my house on 9th Street. Get your accordion and come over and jam with us. I got some songs I want you to play on the album." Don Caldwell was in the band but was leaving, so Joe asked me to take Don's place on his first album for MCA.

The next six and a half years are history because I took the job. I quit my day job, and we started touring. I was about to buy the surveying company, and, to make a long story short, I went on the road with Joe Ely instead.

I was on the road with Joe Ely until New Year's Eve of 1983, when the Joe Ely Band broke up. The Joe Ely Band had kicked some serious booty for a number of years, and it gave me credibility. As a musician, I felt unchallenged living in Lubbock. Then it dawned on me, I had been in Lubbock from 1971 until 1980 and had been saying that I was on my way to Austin for nine years. I moved to Austin and started Ponty Bone and the Squeezetones, which is what I have been doing for some time now. I might still be in Lubbock owning a surveying company if I hadn't taken that chance with Joe Ely. I feel like taking that chance is now being repaid. It's clear to me now that I've been on the right path.

CHRIS: Do you have any more observations about Lubbock? Or great stories about things that happened in Lubbock?

PONTY: Up until I was about thirty-six years old, I was just following the path of least resistance. I wasn't thinking much before then. About that time, I began keeping a journal contemplating whether I had any real control over my life or not. One of the first things I noticed was Lubbock. Lubbock is a wonderful place to live, once you begin to notice the special things about it. As a guy who was traveling all over the United States and Europe, and then in his time off is riding his bicycle around Lubbock, it's real illuminating.

Once you open up your eyes to it, you start noticing all these, what individually might seem like coincidences, but which, over the long haul, "coincidence" just doesn't explain them. It's a strange thing to me that so many of the people I hung out with in Lubbock, at the very least, are subject matter for tons of literature and theatrical productions. And those are the ones who aren't in the limelight themselves.

I'm starting to take this devil's advocate position now toward people saying, "That would be the same anywhere else." But a lot of people who weren't originally from Lubbock, like Michael Ventura and Grover Lewis, immediately noticed it once they got there. Michael Ventura wasn't originally from Lubbock but he immediately noticed, "Whoa! This is way cool!"

I remember, for instance, when we had Linda Ronstadt hanging out in Lubbock with us at the Tornado Jam. And we had the Clash hanging out in Lubbock with us. I mean, give me a break! The Clash didn't hang out anywhere else on their whole American tour that was any more bizarre, any more full of coincidences and crazy stuff. That gig at the Rox-Z, the place was packed, and the Clash wasn't playing any towns anywhere near that small at the time. It was a magic night!

Stubb was with us all the time. Anybody who came to town, we always took them to Stubb's. One thing Stubb liked to do was produce concerts, and he produced some great ones. At the old Stubb's on East Broadway, he brought Stevie Ray Vaughan in there frequently. Stubb also booked the Cotton Club. I'll never forget the night that Muddy Waters played the Cotton Club. It just doesn't get any better than that!

Stubb is a good argument that Lubbock has produced totally unique characters. Did you see Stubb on the *Letterman Show* that night? Of course, Letterman's famous at that point in his career for these interviews with people where there's a demonstration, especially cooking. The first thing he asks Stubb is, "What are the ingredients that go into your barbecue sauce that I've heard so much about?" Stubb looks out at the audience and says, "Love and Happiness." The audience cracks up, and Letterman and Schaefer were just dumbfounded, dead silence. Stubb was totally the "Real Deal." Everybody who knew Stubb loved him.

Bruce

BRUCE JAGGERS was the cofounder of the Main Street Saloon and the owner of Fat Dawg's; both were legendary Lubbock live music venues during the 1970s and '80s.

Jaggers

BRUCE: Main Street Saloon was a real interesting place. It was across the street from the College Inn, which was an off-campus dorm. There was an international community living there, a lot of Africans and people from South America and Puerto Rico. Being right across the street, we had an interesting mix of folks at the Main Street Saloon.

Jay Boy Adams was our regular house band at that time. Jay Boy played a three-day weekend gig at Main Street, two or three weeks a month. This particular week, however, Jay Boy was doing a show out of town and couldn't do his regular gig.

It was 1974, and Texas Tech's football team was ranked fourth in the nation at the time. Tech was playing the University of Texas in Lubbock that weekend, so it was going to be a big party weekend with a lot of people in town.

Earlier that week we noticed this guy we had never seen come into the bar. He

THE STRIP, LUBBOCK'S ALCOHOL SOURCE.

was noticeable because he was wearing a Barnum & Bailey Ringling Brothers Circus jumpsuit. He comes up to us and says, "I'm a musician. I can put together a band for you this weekend." My partner John Kenyon and I did not know this guy at all. I didn't grow up in Lubbock and had never heard of the Flatlanders. I moved to Lubbock only after liquor by the drink became legal,[1] to go into the bar business. Kenyon and I decided what the hell; we didn't have anybody else to play that weekend. It turns out that guy was Joe Ely. But it was Joey Ely then. I've got a poster somewhere that says "The Joey Ely Band."

That weekend, Texas Tech beat Texas in the football game and the whole town of Lubbock just goes berserk! So there happened to be this tremendous energy around the town. Main Street is just a couple of blocks from the stadium, so we always got a lot of business after games, and here was this new band playing that everybody thought was tremendous! The place was packed and the word got out fast. The next

1. Liquor by the drink became legal in Lubbock on April 9, 1972.

DUST STORM. COURTESY OF ELIZABETH OGLESBY.

week, we booked him again and the line to get in was around the corner. Main Street was not a very big place; it had a capacity of around five hundred people.

It was a real positive thing for Joe Ely and a real positive thing for Main Street Saloon. Not long after the first few shows, Johnny Hughes came in and started managing Joe. Johnny Hughes is a character. He is a professor at Tech and not a professional promoter at all. There was this scene around Broadway Drug Store on University, and you'd see Johnny Hughes in there a lot. Johnny took a liking to Joe and certainly did a lot for promoting Joe Ely; there is no doubt about it. Joe took off like wildfire shortly after. It wasn't long before he was touring Europe and making albums. But I'll never forget that first Joe Ely show. What a powerhouse!

JOE ELY is internationally known for his unique brand of roadhouse country-rock. He has recorded over a dozen albums with his own bands, and three more with the beloved Texas supergroup the Flatlanders. Ely has earned a Grammy Award for his participation in Los Super Seven, featuring Freddy Fender, Rick Trevino, and members of Los Lobos. Ely has recorded with the Clash, Bruce Springsteen, Uncle Tupelo, and Dwight Yoakam. He has toured with the Rolling Stones, Merle Haggard, Carl Perkins, Tom Petty, and the Kinks.

Joe Ely

JOE: When I was fourteen years old, I washed dishes every day after school at the Chicken Box on 34th Street. I was getting my first band together at that time. I would go out at night after washing dishes and play. Pretty soon it became obvious that music was a damn sight more fun than washing dishes at the Chicken Box. Chicken Box Johnny used to go over every night and lose all his money gambling to Tom and Bingo at their barbecue place across the street. Lubbock was like that. It was a hard-hit-on place. Living there, you just thought it was normal, but when you look back on it, for people to eke out a living there, it was damn impossible, this ol' place on the prairie that had not really meant for a town to be there. Lubbock just accidentally opened up.

CHRIS: Did you leave Lubbock right after getting out of Monterey High School, or were you trying to do your music in Lubbock?

JOE: I was doing music in Lubbock. I was playing at the Koko Palace and the old sleazy clubs out on the Strip: the Rendezvous, the Music Box, the Linger Longer. They were horrible old places, those rock 'n' roll clubs where kids went, but that's where we played.

CHRIS: What was your relationship with Lubbock while you were living there?

JOE: I had a bumpy relationship with Lubbock. I was always getting in trouble. I ran around with all the motorcycle guys and the hot-rodders. All the hot-rodders would circle the Hi-D-Ho drive-in, and Raymond Beadle and Kenny Bernstein were archenemies. I used to watch Kenny Bernstein and Raymond Beadle drag race their '55 Chevies every Saturday night out on 82nd Street. In fact, they're still at it. They became the world's fastest guys. Kenny Bernstein is the fastest dragster in the world. He just ran 330 miles an hour in the quarter mile. And Raymond Beadle set the world record in funny car. He was the first guy to turn over 300 miles an hour in funny car. Lubbock is the perfect society to breed rebels because it's a closed society. It's separated from the rest of the world, not on the beaten path. Lubbock is an island.

If people in Lubbock want any culture or anything from the outside world, they cannot just half-assed want it. They have to really want it bad because you have to look deep and hard in order to find music there. Hardly any concerts ever came to town. Some big shows would play at the honky-tonks or at the fair, but it wasn't like Dallas or Houston where major acts came through all the time. You had to go out and search on your own and find sources that were invisible to you there.

Being in Lubbock means having to make up what you are doing, because you're not in L.A. or New York or Nashville, and nobody's really there to show you how to do things. Or else somebody is always telling you what to do, and you're always saying, "Go fuck yourself." There are a lot of totally ridiculous rules in Lubbock. I used to get in trouble a lot for vagrancy. And I never ever understood the charge. There was this one cop named Sergeant Aycock . . .

CHRIS: You have to be kidding!

JOE: That was actually his name. He used to bust me for vagrancy all the time, and I'd ask him, "What exactly is vagrancy?" He'd say, "You got five dollars in your pocket?" I said, "Of course not, that's a lot of money, man." And he'd say, "Then you have no visible means of support." And he'd explain all these ridiculous things. Then he'd take me down to the police station.

One time he was bragging how Texas had the greatest vagrancy laws; he said,

"If we want to, we can take a preacher out of a pulpit or a pilot out of a cockpit and book him on vagrancy." And I said, "Real nice, Mr. Aycock. Anybody that looks like they need to be put away, you can just put them away. Is that just your excuse to have something to do?" Of course, being a musician and running around with all the hell-raisers, we were big targets for the police. I was always in the jail for vagrancy or some silly form of it. That made me even madder.

CHRIS: It obviously made you want to get out of town. How long did it take for you to get out of Lubbock?

JOE: My early band was called the Twilights and then it became the Rox. But bookings around Lubbock were real sporadic. When I was about seventeen, I took off one summer, went to Dallas, and got a gig in the Cellar Club, this horrible little place in downtown Ft. Worth but real famous around that period of time. Then they transferred my band to Houston, where they were opening up another Cellar. We'd play from six in the evening to six in the morning. We'd play an hour and then the other band would play an hour. And it turned out the other band was ZZ Top. So that got me out of town the first time. But I always came back to Lubbock after wandering far and wide.

Things happened in my life because I was out looking for that well which people draw from. I followed Woody Guthrie's tracks across the West and followed the old blues guys down through the South, was out on the West Coast during the big hippie days, the Summer of Love. All of my travels were about getting out of Lubbock to see where things that I was interested in came from, like how songs got written and why Henry Miller wrote about New York City and Paris.

Eddie Beethoven was a real amazing cat. I don't know where exactly he came from. He came to Lubbock to go to school. We started hanging out, getting in the same trouble. I met him around the time the Flatlanders were getting together. He was just a free-form poet who wrote all the time. Eddie Beethoven was one of those guys where everything he said kind of put a kink in your head; he twisted everything to where you just wondered where he got it. He's really a totally brilliant guy. He started making up songs with the rest of us. "Shaking Tonight," "Don't Put a Lock on My Heart" are Eddie Beethoven songs; we cowrote "Cool Rockin' Loretta." I've recorded three or four of his songs.

After the Flatlanders made that first record in Nashville and then fell apart, I had been out jumping freight trains around the country. Eddie Beethoven and I were sitting at the International House of Pancakes on University Avenue one night and decided over a cup of coffee that we wanted to watch the leaves change color in New England. We had like five dollars between us and not a care in the world, and our only goal was to get to New England to watch the leaves change. So this gal gave us a ride to Amarillo the next day. We jumped the train to Texarkana the next day. While we tried to figure out how to get from there on up to New England, a big cold front came through. It got so freezing cold that we decided to hell with New England and we headed south to Shreveport and waited out the cold.

We had no money but we were just traveling, seeing the world. We were homeless. I tried to play a few shows, a few pass-the- hat things in cafés, bowling alleys, tittie bars. But we had no money, not a penny. It was like a mission, like a Jack Kerouac book. We started heading north from Vicksburg, up through Memphis, Toledo, Pittsburgh, and it just got colder and colder and we ended up realizing about the time we got up to Ohio that the leaves had already fallen off the trees. So Eddie Beethoven and I ended up just going to New York together.

Eddie stayed up there in New York for about three months and came back to Lubbock a little sooner than I did. I stayed in New York about six months, living in Greenwich Village. Never really got anything going there, no paying gigs, but I had a lot of fun just learning. I was doing a lot of writing then. I wrote a lot of songs on the first album at that time, ones like "Johnny's Blues" and "Gambler's Bride."

I wasn't back in Lubbock two days when the Ringling Brothers Circus came through, and I joined the circus. I talked them into giving me a job as the wrangler for the World's Smallest Horse. So I was off again.

I had to go out and really see the world, because I knew that when I got back to Lubbock, I would be coming back to that same desolate emptiness. I realize now that desolation and emptiness was important to me. Some of the best stuff I ever wrote was in Lubbock, when I'd get back from my travels, because there is this empty desolation that I could fill if I picked up a pen and wrote, or picked up a guitar and played. Those were the things that helped me fill the emptiness. Otherwise, I would have just gone off the deep end.

Anybody that ever came from there knows that feeling: that big ol' sky and that lunatic desolation; what the wind does to you the way it rubs the branch against the screen all night long and grates on your nerves; the way the dust blows and the static electricity makes the hair stick up on your arms and the back of your neck. You get pissed off because it's blowing all the time and you're eating all this dust! It's almost a Zen thing. It would make you crazy but at the same time you knew you had to deal with it, so you dealt with it in whatever way you could.

After quitting the circus, I had decided it was time to stop rambling and take all of my rambles and put them into context. I was sick of sleeping under bridges and on couches and anywhere I could. I was ready to put it all into a form. And for me, Lubbock was the place to do it because I always knew that the greatest musicians were in

JOE ELY ON STAGE.

Lubbock. I went back there and rounded up a band. I got Ricky Bob Hulett, a guitar player, and Lloyd Maines, and a bass player named Greg Wright, and we started putting these songs into a form; songs that I had written on the road and songs of Butch's from the old Flatlander days, songs I had written traveling around Europe. We put together a set of probably twenty-five songs, went down to Main Street Saloon, and started playing every weekend. Within about three weekends, we had about five hundred people packed in there as tight as they could, every night we played.

The band started rehearsing more, learning more songs. We added a drummer and experimented with different kinds of musicians. Pretty soon we got it to where we could play the big honky-tonks and pack them in. Literally within a year from the time I decided to go put that band together, I had a recording contract with MCA Records.

It was funny, that decision process of leaving and becoming a homeless hobo out there in America, and then coming back to Lubbock and sitting down at the Broadway Drug Store, having a cup of coffee, and all of a sudden I just realized it was time to start putting this stuff together. That was the beginning of moving from traveling and rambling into what I have been doing now for quite a few years. I look back and I see all these distinct pieces of time of losing myself, finding myself, still always on a search, looking to see where things came from, how they were made, all the shit you had to put up with in order to do all the things you really wanted to do. And running into guys like Terry Allen and seeing that he put up with the same shit, only he went in a different direction. He went to L.A. following more art than music, and I went off following more music than art. But we both had the same interests and just developed in different ways.

It was leaving Lubbock and coming back to Lubbock, that process of tearing away from the mother ship and at the same time being attracted back there for some insane reason. Almost like you had to go back because you couldn't believe that it was really still there.

CHRIS: Tell me about meeting the Clash in England and bringing them to Lubbock.

JOE: The Clash asked me to record with them for "Should I Stay or Should I Go." It was like a shotgun thing. I went down to the studio in New York, Jimi Hendrix's studio Electric Ladyland, and me and Strummer wrote all the Spanish in our bastardized version of Strummer's European Spanish and my Tex-Mex, and there was a Puerto Rican engineer who helped us out on it. My daughter was real impressed when she found that out. She thinks of the Clash as like a modern-day band.

I met them on our first tour of England. They came to a show we did at the Venue in London. We had gotten the band together and we recorded an album in Nashville, the first one, with the picture on the cover that Paul Milosevich did of me in the cowboy hat. We had played some horrible shows around America. We had a Nashville booking agent that booked us at county fairs and little honky-tonk dives. That was terrible. We didn't go over. Then we got this offer to go over to England and we thought, "Yes! Let's jump on it!" We went over there and we were like pop stars! The record was in the top ten on the charts and played everywhere. We were doing TV shows and big, huge venues.

I'll never forget it; the Clash and Pete Townshend came to see us one night. The Clash were real amazed with our music, Lloyd's steel and Jesse Taylor's guitar. They asked us all about Texas and said, "We're going to do a U.S. tour and we want y'all to bring us into Texas."

We brought them into Lubbock. They wanted to see where Buddy Holly went to school. It's funny that Lubbock is so blind to all that. I guess they're finally realizing that they're known more by Buddy Holly than anything the Chamber of Commerce could ever dream up. I moved to Lubbock from Amarillo right after Buddy Holly died, but it was several years before I knew Buddy Holly was from Lubbock. In fact, the first place where I learned to play electric guitar was in a house on 28th Street that the Holleys lived in for less than a year when Buddy went to Hutchinson Junior High. But I didn't find that out until years later. It's like all these coincidences were always constantly happening to me in Lubbock. Lubbock is truly a big mystery.

All That You Need

from the album Streets of Sin

I been workin' on the farm
Just me and my brother Jack
Choppin' a sea of cotton
Till I thought I'd break my back
Everything changed
When my daddy got hurt
Our lives were so connected
to that brown ol' flatland dirt

When the government man from Austin
Come sniffin' around our land
Askin' a bunch of questions
That we did not understand
There's more to farming cotton
Than just tendin' to your seed
The ones who set the policy
Don't give a damn about our needs

Chorus:
Sow the seed in the ground below
Fall to your knees and pray real slow
That rain will come and kiss the seed
And bless you with all that you need

Mama says to Jackie
Would she bring the car around?
She's wearing her finest dress
That's how I know she's goin' to town
I wish I'd never seen that letter
That I found there in her room
They're selling the farm on the courthouse
    step
This Saturday afternoon

Me and Jack moved into town
To a shack by the train depot
Jack got a job as a bouncer
At a bar on Paradise Row
Mama got a job in the cotton gin
Grading cotton by the bale
She cried when a trailer full of cotton come
    in
From the farm we had to sell

Chorus repeats

Me, I ended up in jail
Sick of livin' on welfare
And the hardest thing ever happened to me
Is when Mama come to visit me there
Don't you worry your pretty little head
I said as I buttoned my shirt
When I get out of this Iron Hotel
I'm goin' back to that Dryland dirt

For some it's just a livin'
But for us it's our whole life
If it kills me I'm gonna rake that dirt
And make a livin' out of toil and strife
The ways of the cities makes no sense
Strapped to dependency
I'd rather be sweatin' 'neath a clear blue sky
Plantin' cotton with my family

Chorus repeats

I Got to Find Ol' Joe

from the album Streets of Sin

Smoke from a downshift blows across the
    grain
And the blackbirds are flyin' across the
    golden plain
I'm goin' back to where it was I came
I got to find ol' Joe before he loses it all

Last night in the café I wanted to hold your
    hand
So I told you with my eyes that I under-
    stand
That life sure ain't easy here in this no-
    man's-land
I got to find ol' Joe before he loses it all

Chorus:
Somewhere I believe there's a place for me
Down the road to destiny
Can you hear that eagle call?
I got to find ol' Joe before he loses it all

The dogs go to barkin' at the risin' of the
    moon
And the highway's a-callin' and I'll be
    listening soon
Another weary rambler crazy as a loon
I got to find ol' Joe before he loses it all

The motel up ahead has a vacancy sign
But I'm travelin' too hard to pay it any
    mind
There's a rainbow in the clouds down ol'
    Highway 99
I gotta find ol' Joe before he loses it all

Chorus repeats

The Wild West was made with the blood of
    the brave
Where there was little to take and even less
    to save
Where they buried their heroes in un-
    marked graves
I got to find ol' Joe before he loses it all

You work all your life to get where you are
Then you throw it all away to chase some
    crazy star
While the prophet on the radio slings his
    guitar
I got to find ol' Joe before he loses it all

The Wild West was made from the blood of
    the brave
Dry as the creek bed, cracked with age
Where they buried their heroes in un-
    marked graves
I got to find ol' Joe before he loses it all

SHARON ELY is a fashion stylist, actress, dancer, and model from Lubbock. Her fashions have been seen in popular magazines, including *British Vogue*. She now lives in Austin with her husband, rocker Joe Ely.

Sharon Ely

SHARON: This is a little story that goes with what I'm fixing to say: I was cooking the other day, chopping carrots to sauté, and a carrot fell off and rolled underneath the icebox. If I left it there, that carrot could attract a whole new world of insects or even a little mouse. That's like a theory of how the world began. I think that's how Lubbock began: Somebody's covered wagon broke down there and they could never get out. I think Lubbock is where it is because someone got stuck out in the middle of nowhere and a town grew up around them.

I have a four-volume history of Lubbock, and it says that Lubbock was set up to be real protective from the beginning. It is a harsh landscape; food and water were not very available. It was really difficult. So the people who settled Lubbock wanted it to be very protected from all outside elements and people. To me, Lubbock always felt like a fort. I always felt safe inside Loop 289. People go out into the world and come back to Lubbock, because it is safe and protected there.

CHRIS: It seems that a lot of Lubbock people have a knack for creating events and fun situations out of nothing. I have heard stories about fun events you have organized. That creative process is what I'm curious about; what causes somebody to get those juices flowing?

SHARON: I've thought about this. The thing that was important in Lubbock was the group of friends. Without that group, I don't think anybody really would have done anything that they did.

For instance, Stubb and Paul Milosevich; Paul was a very close friend of Stubb's. Together they attracted groups of artists. Paul's wife Debbie Milosevich knew Terry Allen through her brother, and Debbie introduced Terry to Stubb and Paul. Terry and Jo Harvey had been out in California, and they came back into this whole circle of musicians that were gathering around Stubb's Barbecue. Then these musicians attracted many girls, needless to say. There was much love and romance which attracted all these girls, and all of their families and friends.

I think people forget this, but we were all nineteen, twenty, twenty-one years old and there was a spiritual quest going on through all the music. Butch and Jimmie and Tommy Hancock and Joe and all of us one time jumped in a van, drove over to the Lama Foundation in New Mexico to learn how to Sufi dance. Steve Wesson played the saw and we'd all do this spinning Sufi dancing in Tech Terrace Park, in front of where Paul Milosevich lived.

Everybody was falling in love with everybody else. It was the 1970s when this group of people was coming together in Lubbock, from 1967 on. I can't call it an Underground because it is very difficult to be underground in Lubbock. Everything is pretty much in plain sight in Lubbock. The only things underground are the prairie dogs. But there was this group of wonderful people involved. Everybody was attracted to each other and amazed at each other's musical ability or character or personality. We all really liked each other. The spiritual quest aspect of the whole scene was very real. A lot of people overlook that.

From the first time I met Joe I was in love. When I met Joe, he had come back from L.A. and his hair was down below his waist. I heard him play at Alice's Restaurant, in the alley off Broadway, across from the university. That property is called Mesquite's now. He was playing a solo concert with his drums, harmonica, and guitar. Truly, my life changed after that. I fell madly in love with him. From that point on, everything that I did and created was focused towards my love for Joe Ely. That is why I am in Austin today.

CHRIS: Tommy Hancock has said that you are one of the most creative, artistic women he knows, and that sometimes you may not get enough credit because you are with Joe. What are some of your artistic endeavors?

SHARON: I like to conjure fun things up in my head. For instance, here's one. All my group of friends had left Lubbock to go different places when I was about twenty-one. I was in Lubbock, and I was all alone. I was living for a very short time at my parents' house, and I suddenly realized that I had to make my own friends. So I made five human-sized dolls. They were my dancing dolls, because I love to dance. I didn't have a lot of money, so I found some sparkly satin material in the alley. I put it on these life-sized dolls, and they became my friends. They became my five Muses. I had little cocktail parties with them. Before I knew it, by making these dolls and accepting that they were my friends, all of a sudden everybody returned to Lubbock. I had so many friends, and they all loved my dolls. They thought they were wonderful, and we started having parties together. Before I knew it, I didn't have any time to sew anymore and make dolls because we had all these friends.

You can make your dreams happen. Instead of just going out and killing myself, I decided to do something. Because loneliness is a horrible feeling and if you let it get to you, it will kill you. I think that's another thing in Lubbock: People become lonely there, and that's why so many people attracted each other, because they didn't want to be lonely. If you look at this from a psychological point of view, we were all just trying to be happy, which is essentially what we are trying to do today. And we want everybody else to be happy.

I would do things to get Joe's attention, because in the 1970s he had attracted about fifty-five girlfriends. To be attracted to somebody like Joe was a big commitment on my part. I either had to be totally nuts or truly in love with this guy to put up with it. I would try to do things to keep his attention. One of them was at a photo shoot at Stubb's Barbecue for one of Joe's album covers. All the girls came and the musicians were there, and I thought, "I'll just blend in with the wallpaper if I don't do anything." So I wore my roller skates and played pool. Because I had roller skates on, I got my picture taken. I am tall anyway but I was really tall when I walked in on those skates! But it also got Joe's attention, which was the goal.

CHRIS: Weren't you the cause of Tom T. Hall writing the song "The Great East Broadway Onion Championship of 1978"? Please tell your version of that story.

SHARON: There was a large group of people that had gathered at Stubb's because they heard that Tom T. Hall was there. The boys were in the back room, playing pool, where not very many people could go. Everybody else was out in the front, listening to the jukebox, waiting for something to happen. So I went to the back room and thought, "I'm just gonna get that white ball and hide it in my back pocket. Then they won't be able to play pool, and they'll have to come out and play music." I snuck the cue ball, put it in my back pocket, and sashayed out into the front, thinking that they would come out once they couldn't play pool anymore. They never did come out. When I went back to see what was keeping them, they had the onion sack open and they were playing pool with the onions. I asked Stubb, "Why are they playing pool with these onions?" And Stubb said, "I don't know. They couldn't find the cue ball so they just used an onion." I realized that trick didn't work. I was very cocky back then. I guess it caused them to write a song and have a big fun tournament, so that was fine.

CHRIS: Let's continue to talk about Stubb. Tell me about getting Stubb's barbecue sauce company started.

SHARON: First of all, Stubb was not healthy. He had a complicated problem with his heart and diabetes. When they would give him medicine for his diabetes it would screw up his heart, and his heart medicine would screw up his diabetes.

Stubb was really having a difficult time after he moved from Lubbock down to Austin in '84. He had rats in his restaurant over on Interstate 35, and his rent was like $1,200 a month. For years, Stubb would come over almost every week asking for money, because Joe was his close friend. Of course we would come up with it and give it to him. But we had been audited by the IRS and were trying to keep aboveground. So I thought maybe we could figure out a way for Stubb to make money and not feel so defeated all the time by his health and his financial situation.

I knew from way back that Stubb's barbecue sauce was good. You know when you taste something good and think, "They should bottle this." I had always thought that about Stubb's sauce. I kept telling Stubb he should bottle his sauce to sell. He made big batches for parties, so I knew that he could make big tubs of it.

It was near Christmas and he didn't have any Christmas money. I said, "Let's get some bottles. You come out, and we'll set the whole thing up in our kitchen. My friend Kimmie Rhodes knows how to can, so we can make it safe." Kimmie came out and we bottled up these mason jars. Apple computers had just come out, so Joe was experimenting with graphics. Joe made a label, and we printed it out. Joe's a genius on that computer. We printed the labels up, cut them out with little scissors, and glued them on the mason jars. Kimmie and I got on the phone and got some customers for Stubb, to buy his barbecue sauce for Christmas gifts. Kimmie and I would deliver the sauce to their doorstep, and Stubb would drive us in his Cadillac. Kimmie and I dressed in matching white lace formals and cowboy hats that we put corsages on. Kimmie is about five feet tall and I'm about six feet tall, so we looked very funny. We would walk in looking like this, with the barbecue sauce and our boom box playing "The Chipmunk Song."

We were having a great time, and Stubb was happy. That day, I think we must have brought in two hundred dollars selling barbecue sauce. I gave the money to Stubb and I said, "Stubb, look! This is just one day! This is what you can do with your barbecue sauce. People love it!" He understood that. Because he had this handful of money, he could see the reality of it. We worked all week and pretty soon had made over a thousand dollars.

Then he got the idea to open his own little factory and rented a place in South Austin on Ben White. He started collecting Jack Daniel's and Crown Royal whiskey bottles because he didn't want to buy the mason jars. He said, "We got all these free whiskey bottles!" Also, they were prettier bottles; Stubb was a very artistic person. I gave him a desk for his business. It was half-assed being done, but it was being done. He was selling his sauce to all kinds of people. He gave a lot away.

Then suddenly John Scott appears. We were going to have a business meeting in our backyard, and John Scott showed up with his briefcase. Stubb says, "This is our new president of my barbecue!" I knew then that this was going to take a whole different avenue and would become successful. I was happy to let go of whatever we had started. John Scott knew what he was doing. John and his partners Eddy Patterson and Scott Jensen took Stubb's barbecue sauce company to the highest limit.

The whole thing made me so happy. Stubb was very sick. He passed out at a grocery store while doing a demonstration. But when he got to see that barbecue sauce on those shelves, it was like his dream come true.

CHRIS: Stubb's Barbecue Sauce is available all around the world. It is the number-one-selling barbecue sauce around.

SHARON: Stubb always said, "I wants to feed the world!" It would make him happy. In the sense of Buddhism, Stubb was a true bodhisattva, because he truly cared for other people. We learned a lot from him. I think everybody learned many lessons from him. People were attracted to him, and something would happen. Suddenly the whole group of people would become involved in solving some problem and we would all learn huge lessons from it.

CHRIS: Talk a little about the Cotton Club. I'm sure you spent some time out there.

SHARON: I have the fondest memories of the Cotton Club because there was a dance floor there. It was *the best* dance floor! The wood was so smooth, and they would take care of it by putting this sawdust on it and clean it. It was perfect sized. It was *perfect*.

Joe and his band would play out there. My dear friend Charlie Sanders, who is not living anymore, was my dance partner. I don't know if you have ever had a really good dance partner. They might not be your romantic intention but they are your best dance partner. Charlie was my best dance partner, and we would dance on this incredible dance floor to this incredible music that Joe would play with Lloyd Maines, Ponty Bone, and Jesse Taylor. It was some of the most exquisite music ever played! Charlie Sanders was this strong, rhythmic guy, and we would pretend to be Fred Astaire and Ginger Rogers, or Ann Margaret and Elvis. I would run and jump into his arms, he would swing me around and people would stand back. It was heaven!

That was in a time where everybody danced. You could get really high dancing. We would dance every dance. Truly, I have to say that was what I would call getting pretty close to what they call bliss.

Every time Joe played, I would be there. Sometimes I'd even wear a formal dress. It was so funny! I would wear a formal to the Cotton Club because it was my dancing dress.

CHRIS: And some people say Lubbock is boring. It's not boring at all, is it?

SHARON: Here is a theory I have about the Cotton Club. During the '50s, when those flying saucers they called the Lubbock Lights were discovered, all over West Texas there were honky-tonks. Everybody would dance in circles on the dance floor. Think of the explosive energy put out on that dance floor! I felt that energy from dancing and I know other people did, too. So it's Saturday night; here you are in this flying saucer and you look down on the Cotton Club. The sensors pick up all these circles of energy. Red-heat circles is what I call them. The UFOs were trying to figure out what the hell the energy circles were, and they came down low. What do you think?

CHRIS: I think that's a good theory. Native Americans believe that dancing in circles can bring down those higher elemental intelligences. Do you have any other fond memories of fun times in Lubbock?

SHARON: I did a tour service when the Buddy Holly fans started coming to Lubbock. I got a Cadillac convertible with steer horns on the front, and I would take people on tours of Lubbock. I took the Clash on a tour of Lubbock. Joe had brought them to Lubbock. Can you imagine what they thought of Lubbock, coming straight from London, England, never been to Texas? They knew Buddy Holly was from Lubbock, so they wanted to come. I took them to the Cotton Club, to Buddy Holly's grave, Prairie Dog Town, Lubbock High School—you know, all the tourist attractions of Lubbock. There's at least four or five.

I knew I was fixing to leave Lubbock because Joe was moving to Austin. Needless to say I wasn't about to stay in Lubbock without Joe there. But that was about the time I got the idea to take people on tours of Lubbock. That was sort of my way of saying good-bye to Lubbock. My parents still live in Lubbock, and I go there about once every month or so. I enjoy going back to Lubbock to visit because I know that I don't have to stay there.

LUBBOCK HIGH SCHOOL.

The Great East Broadway Onion Championship of 1978
from the album Places I've Done Time *(RCA APL-13018), 1979*

Chorus:
The Great East Broadway Onion Cham-
    pionship of 1978

In Lubbock, Texas, the other night
Drinkin' beer and about half-tight
Me and Paul and Jim and a guy named
    Al
We were drawing pictures and writing
    songs
Sitting there talking, before too long,
Paul said, "We oughta' move this party
    over to Stubb's."

The smoke was hangin' low and thick
And the guitar-man was huntin' licks
And Joe Ely was in the backroom
    shootin' pool
We all went back there to check it out
And Joe says, "Well, now, shut my
    mouth!
I hear the old storyteller knows how to
    handle a stick."
I said, "I've had chalk on better clothes."
And y'all know how that stuff goes
Pretty soon we were shootin' pool and
    raisin' hell

Chorus repeats

Joe and me kind of drew a crowd
The place got drunk and the place got
    loud
And Joe reached over in a sack and
    pulled out a big onion
He placed that onion on the felt
And said, "Here's where you're gonna
    need some help.
We're gonna use that hamburger helper
    for a cue ball."
Then Joe picked up a big ol' broom
And he waved it all around the room
He said, "I'm gonna play that onion cue
    ball with a broomstick."

We battled back and forth all night
Tears were streaming from our eyes
And I had that onion for an eight-ball in
    the corner pocket
Now the place got quiet as a mouse
And we told the guitar-man to lay out
And I could barely see that onion for all
    that grass
But I sipped a beer and fought back
    tears
And watched that eight-ball disappear
And the whole damn town of Lubbock,
    Texas, went wild!

Amidst the yelling and the tears
Joe said, "Y'all wait until next year."
And that's how I won the Broadway
    Onion Championship of 1978

I want to thank all the small people that
    made me what I am today: The Great
    East Broadway Onion Champion of
    1978!

KIMMIE RHODES is another successful songwriter from Lubbock, and an accomplished playwright. Now based in Austin, she has made several appearances performing on *Austin City Limits*. Kimmie is also the author of the mystical cookbook *The Amazing Afterlife of Zimmerman Fees*.

Rhodes

KIMMIE: I sat down to write a song one day, called "Small Town Girl," and it turned into a play. I ended up roping all my friends into performing it with me and Joe Sears, the actor from *Greater Tuna*. We did a workshop out at Willie Nelson's Western town. We set up the scenes around the town and actually moved the audience from set to set. The play incorporates the audience; pretty soon everybody is in the play. Governor Ann Richards was there and said she felt like she had been part of a West Texas Fellini movie. It was really magic and fun.

I realized I had written this play from my unconscious. It incorporated my family and my early childhood experience growing up in Lubbock. It is an avant-garde piece which takes place on two levels: West Texas Heaven, where angels are punching through to the earthly plane, and the real earthly West Texas.

At the beginning a little girl gets her assignment from an angel, played by Joe Sears. He tells her that she has to be born in West Texas to take care of this pool-hustling rounder, to be his daughter and help him find his place in life. Her job is to help him fulfill his dream. He is actually a very talented man but living a dull life and not getting anywhere. Joe Ely played the dad. The mom, played by Sharon Ely, dies soon after the girl is born. The story is about how the girl helps her father fulfill his dream. The last thing the angel says to the girl as she is leaving West Texas Heaven is "I'll be with you. I'll always be with you." He shows up throughout the play as an angel-unaware, in the forms of Old Tom the Wino and a magic doll.

I think some of the best pieces you write are when you don't know why you are doing it and just start. You are trying to work something out personally through doing it, and there's a message involved. Usually it's a good message because you're trying to make a communication.

Joe Sears and I later did another play called *Hillbilly Heaven* in his theater that he built in Cody, Wyoming. I've actually written several musical plays.

CHRIS: It seems like everything you write is set in heaven or has to do with angels somehow.

KIMMIE: Yeah, and I don't know why that is. I don't really attribute my spirituality to going to church in Lubbock. Churchgoing was very sporadic in my family, dependent on the climate in the family at the time. My experience going to church in Lubbock was sort of contrary to my spiritual beliefs. Nothing bad against it, I didn't really enjoy going to church when I was a kid. I never liked the sermons. I found church boring, and it always seemed like they were trying to collect money.

But church is how I got started singing. I didn't mind going to choir practice at all. I think it was the musical relief, where everybody would get the hymnal and sing together. We always went to church for the music more than anything. My best memory of church was at Christmas when we would do the Christmas recital. I was totally in it for the showbiz aspect. I would sing, and I got to be the page-turner for the lady who played the piano.

CHRIS: Did you know early on that you wanted to be a professional singer and songwriter?

KIMMIE: I have this theory. I think when you are born you come to the party already knowing who you are, and you grow up to be that as quickly as you can. I started singing and making up songs when I was really young. I didn't have any idea what I was going to do with my life; I was just a little kid singing. My dad noticed that I was always singing, and he cultivated that in me. He owned a car dealership, and he would take me to the car lots to sing for people.

I didn't aspire to growing up to be a singer. What I really wanted to do when I grew up was to be a florist. I would go to the flower shop and spend my lunch money so I could watch the ladies make the bouquets of flowers.

Music sort of snuck up on me. There was never this big plan to grow up and be a performer. I didn't think of myself as a writer. I got a guitar and started to play some chords, for something to pass the time. It was during the back-to-nature, earth-mama hippie days, and I had moved to this peaceful country setting on a family farm outside of Sunset, Texas, near Wichita Falls. I was writing songs before I even realized what I was doing, unconsciously making up melodies and tunes. I believe I started writing songs just because I had something to say.

Then I moved to Austin and met Joe Gracey, who years later became my husband. Gracey had worked at KOKE-FM in Austin, which was a very progressive radio station that played everything from Lightnin' Hopkins to Asleep at the Wheel. Gracey had lost his voice to cancer when I met him, and he had decided to produce records. He produced Stevie Ray Vaughan's first record. I had written several songs by then, so we formed a group called Kimmie Rhodes and the Jackalope Brothers. The Jackalope Brothers were Joe Gracey and Bobbie Earl Smith. That was in 1979.

Soon after, Bobbie Earl and Gracey introduced me to Lana Nelson, Willie Nelson's daughter, who has been a dear friend of mine now for years. We were all out on her dad's golf course when Lana introduced me to Willie. Willie asked how long I had been a singer, and I said since I was a child. He asked if I write songs, and I said yes. Gracey and Bobbie Earl and I had been joking earlier with Lana, saying how God was our record distributor and laughing about it. So Willie asked me, "Who's your record distributor?" And we all just blurted out laughing. Lana said, "Tell him!" I told him, "God is my distributor," and we all laughed about that.

Willie said, "Why don't you come out here and make a record?" I went out to Willie's studio a couple of weeks later and recorded my first album called *Kimmie Rhodes and the Jackalope Brothers*.

My next record was called *Angels Get the Blues*. I think that was when I started to come into my own as a songwriter. One song on that record called "I Just Drove By" ended up being a really good song for me. Wynonna Judd and Willie Nelson both recorded that one.

A few years went by, and I made my album *West Texas Heaven*, a concept that eventually ended up being part of the play *Small Town Girl*. The concept is that if heaven turns out to be the best version of what you knew while you were alive, and all you had ever known was West Texas, then heaven would look like a beautiful version of West Texas.

CHRIS: Waylon Jennings recorded a couple of songs with you on that album. How did you meet Waylon?

KIMMIE: Waylon had cut a song by my very dear friend Beth Nielsen Chapman, "Old Church Hymns and Nursery Rhymes." He liked it and asked to hear more of Beth's songs. Beth gave Waylon a tape of her songs, but she hid one of my songs in the middle. That's the kind of friend Beth is, the big sister type. Waylon called her and said, "Who wrote this song? This is not you singing it. I want to cut this song." Beth said, "The one song you pick on the tape, I didn't write," and she gave him my phone number. I came home one day and there was a message on my answering machine from Waylon Jennings! I played it about five times. I was thrilled! He said, "Send me everything you've got. I love you. I love your writing, and I love your voice."

CHRIS: Did y'all make a connection about both being from Lubbock?

KIMMIE: We had that conversation early on. He didn't know anything about me when he called me. But we figured it out, after we started talking. He took to calling me at ungodly hours, like seven o'clock in the morning. When I started recording *West Texas Heaven*, I asked Waylon if he wanted to record a song with me, and he said yes. I had written a song years before called "Maybe We'll Just Disappear" that I knew was a great song for Waylon. But the first person I ever played that song for laughed, so I never played it again. It is kind of a funny song, but it was supposed to be a protest song and I was so sensitive. I sent Waylon a bunch of songs and I thought, "I'll just slip this one on there and he'll barely even notice it, but that way I'll find out if it really was a good song for Waylon Jennings."

That was the song he picked, the one he really wanted to do. Also, he really liked a song called "Be Mine" that I wrote. We ended up doing both of those songs for my album.

We later went on to write a song together called "Lines," which Waylon recorded. It's a song about writing songs, everything you go through in the process of writing music. Honestly, writing "Lines" with Waylon Jennings, sharing for hours what it means for both of us to write songs, has been one of my most cherished and memorable songwriting experiences.

CHRIS: I saw the *Austin City Limits* episode where you played with four of my all-time favorite songwriters: Waylon, Billy Joe Shaver, Kris Kristofferson, and Willie Nelson. There was one woman on that stage, and it was Kimmie Rhodes.

KIMMIE: We were all on the same record label at that point, Justice Records. I also did an *Austin City Limits* with Willie, Rodney Crowell, and Emmylou Harris, two of my very favorite songwriters, and another hosted by Waylon, with Lyle Lovett and Bobby Bare and Beth and a lot of different songwriters.

CHRIS: Tell me about meeting fellow songwriter Jim Rushing.

KIMMIE: I was with Almo/Irving Music Publishing in Nashville and they asked me if I would write with a songwriter named Jim Rushing. I hadn't done much cowriting at that time, and I didn't trust that process much, but I knew Jim Rushing had written hits for Don Williams and Charley Pride, and I loved his songs. He is a great songwriter. I thought, "Okay, I'll go over there and try."

When the day arrived I was having second thoughts. But I was trying to be open-minded, so I went over to Jim's house and said, "Look, I write all my songs by myself. I had started to make excuses why I couldn't come over here, to tell you any number of lies. But I decided that I would meet you in person to tell you I'm not comfortable writing songs with someone I don't know. What would we write about? We would just make stuff up, and it wouldn't mean anything."

Jim said okay, he understood that, and offered to make me a cup of coffee. When he was putting the water in the coffeepot, he asked where I was from.

I told him I was from Lubbock, and he said, "I'm from Lubbock, too!" He asked what street I grew up on, and I said 27th and Avenue Q. Jim said, "I grew up on 26th and Avenue Q!" We had lived right across the alley from each other! He was older than me, driving around in Chevies when I was a punk kid playing with dolls.

Jim asked my mother's name, and I told him. He asked where she worked, and I told him the telephone company. He told me his mother's name and that she worked for the telephone company, too! At this point, I had been at Jim's house for only about ten minutes. The coffee is still brewing, and I'm on the phone to my mother asking if she remembers Jim's mom, and she did.

Jim and I immediately bonded. We ended up spontaneously writing a song, called "Long Distance Operator." We wrote it for our mothers, about how they were unsung heroes, helping people make connections and getting together. We wrote another song the next day called "Separate Lives on Parallel Streets" about two people who live across the alley from each other and are living their separate lives. We ended up writing several other songs together. I love all the songs I wrote with Jim. I don't think anybody has ever recorded them, but they are great songs, nonetheless. That's my story about Jim Rushing.

I've been very happy with my career. I have had amazing experiences and gotten to travel places I would have never gotten to go. It was never about being famous for me. I have stumbled through my whole life, following whatever dream I had at the time. I wanted to travel, so I got to by singing.

I have had a rich life, many fabulous nights with talented people, playing music because we loved each other and we loved the songs. I never compromised what I wanted to do. I always got to do exactly what I wanted, to play any song I wanted, anytime I wanted. I have had every size audience you can imagine, anywhere from five people to eighty thousand people. I have done every size television show you can do. There isn't anything I didn't get.

Maybe I didn't get a huge amount of record sales. But it is not really about selling records. I feel like I have been successful, because I have had an incredible life. That is what success has come to mean to me. Having said that, the one thing that will always be sad to me is the fact that I have written many more songs than I will ever be able to record. I heard Paul McCartney say one time, "Your songs are like your children and you want the best for them." I love every song I have ever written, because they are the journal of my days, what was going on in my life at the time. I have written and cowritten hundreds of songs now. But you can only put twelve or so songs on a record. I have so many songs that will never be on a record and nobody else will ever hear them; even I am forgetting some of the songs I have written. But that's a good problem.

West Texas Heaven

from the album West Texas Heaven

I left West Texas heaven
It was the only one I've ever known
I've been on the road down here
Driving with my blinders on.
All life was to me was like a truck stop
    where you want to stay.
I never even saw it when you built your
    dream right in my way.
No, I just passed on through it like a
    lonely town.

Playing in my head I heard this music
    like a radio
In another town somebody turned on
    somewhere down the road.
Everywhere I turned I tuned in some-
    thing that you had to say.
Your signal never cleared.
I guess it matters that you're so far away.
So, I just passed on through like a lonely
    town.

I left West Texas heaven.
No, I guess I'm never going back that
    way.
Did your love get lost, Babe, or did your
    love just get misplaced?
Everywhere I go, the ghost of you just
    follows me.
Everywhere I go, I hear you whisper
    down my empty streets.
Everywhere I go looks like a lonely town.

Jo Harvey

JO HARVEY ALLEN is an accomplished playwright and stage and film actress who has costarred in many unique character roles, including "the Lying Woman" in David Byrne's paean to West Texas, *True Stories,* and "the Sex Therapist" in the Southern fried classic *Fried Green Tomatoes.* She has written and starred in numerous plays performed throughout the United States and Europe. Her solo off-Broadway productions include *Counter Angel, As It Is in Texas,* and *Hally Lou.* She is a recipient of National Endowment for the Arts fellowships and Art Matters grants.

Allen

JO HARVEY: I have thought about Thomas Wolfe's *You Can't Go Home Again* in rela-
tion to talking about Lubbock, and it occurred to me that you do go home over and
over again. Because it is your heart, and it is everything that made you and set you up
for this fantastic adventure of life. For me, Lubbock was a magic world. I had a glori-
ous childhood full of love. And Lubbock was the town where I met the love of my life
and we danced all night long, or at least until nine o'clock, when I had to go home.
We were only eleven at the time. When Terry and I were seventeen, we flipped a coin
to decide, New York or L.A.? And I ran away with Terry forever. Right before we got
married, Terry said to me, "I don't know what I'm going to do but I can promise you
it'll be different than anybody else in this town." And I laugh now and say, "You're
nuts! You do exactly what everybody else from Lubbock does. A lot of our friends
from Lubbock are artists, musicians, and writers!"

But we are always returning, for better or for worse, to Lubbock. I have a love-hate relationship with Lubbock now, and vice versa; the same love-hate relationship I think Lubbock has with all of its many musicians and writers, actors, and artists.

Seems to me there was never any encouragement for artistic behavior, and that is probably the exact reason so many of us rebelled. And yet I can honestly say the exact opposite, too. I was encouraged and inspired a lot by Lubbock. It's just that I don't think anyone meant to do it, certainly never dreamed you might actually leave town and head out in the directions of art or music or theater. God forbid! Where's the money? And what about the scary lifestyle and the scary places you might end up, like New York City with all those rats running in the streets, or Paris, France, where we had heard women let their underarm hairs grow long and hang out of their clothes.

My parents did make me very proud, though, when they were the only ones to stand up in the middle of church and admit that they had cocktails on Saturday nights delivered by the bootlegger right up to the front door, to my great excitement I might add, and that they probably would continue to carry on like that. I admired that courage and truthfulness. My parents also stood out in my mind as great examples and odd ducks for telling me to love all people, even if they were different. Come to think of it, we also learned that song in Sunday school, "Yellow, red, black, or white, they are precious in His sight." That's why, when Terry and I graduated and got married, I was eager to pack up my Monterey High School annual with "Nigger Lover" scrawled all over it and head out for L.A., where I hoped to actually meet one or two of them. Remember, Terry and I grew up in the '40s and '50s in Lubbock. They tried to outlaw Halloween one year because of so many devils, and I think that was the year all the little devil suits in Lubbock got sold out.

I was raised with such paradox growing up in Lubbock. There were only three books on the bookshelf in our house: Emily Post etiquette, the Bible, and the *Girl Scout Handbook*. But *Lady Chatterley's Lover* was in the cedar chest, and it was the most read and most worn out.

In my play *Home Run* I said, "Lubbock is like India," and I really believe that. The paradoxes in Lubbock are that extreme. One time, my son Bukka was sitting on the commode when he was a little boy, and he asked me what paradox is. And I said, "Sugar, paradox means if your soccer coach says the word 'nigger' one more time, we are gonna get his ass fired, but your granddaddy says that word every day and we still love him." In reality, my daddy was very generous and kind, but you wouldn't know it by hearing him talk. I certainly credit knowing about paradox because I was raised in Lubbock.

I am still trying to understand Lubbock. I am always trying to get home, and always trying to run away. It's like I said in my play *Home Run,* "You get all the way to third base where you are safe and yet you still want to risk it all and get to home base."

CHRIS: Tell me about *Home Run.*

JO HARVEY: It was such an unbelievable experience for me to go back to Lubbock and perform it. It was the first autobiographical piece I had done in over twenty-five years. It was a lot about Lubbock. I had had good success with it in other cities, but the producer in Lubbock got so scared of what I might say, at one point he tried to pay me not to do it! He didn't make a dime on it but he did end up liking the play. Some of my own aunts and uncles and cousins wouldn't come. I was stunned. Here I am doing a ninety-minute one-woman show I had worked on for three years; half of it is about my family whom I love and they love me back. But they don't show up! I think it was more than them thinking, "Maybe I'll hate it, so I won't go." I believe it never occurred to them to go, or that it wouldn't matter to me one way or the other if they saw it or not. Making a play was just that, "play." I doubt they thought I had put much time into it. And why would you? We could all sit for hours on end telling each other great lies and stories, laugh and cry and carry on and love every minute of it. That was all we ever used to do, our favorite pastime, sitting on the front porch telling stories, making up stuff, lying out on a pallet underneath a blanket of stars looking for flying saucers, pretending those little green people were trying to get us. But a play, that was different, maybe even threatening.

My mother saw both of the plays I did in Lubbock. The first one was called *The Beautiful Waitress,* about an angel in a truck stop who cussed a blue streak. It got a standing ovation from everybody but the mayor and my mother. She called me up a few years ago and said that I could have made millions if I had just sold real estate.

When Terry and I came back to Lubbock for about six months in 1969, one of my uncles asked, "Have you finally come back to get a real job?" Terry was making art, writing songs and theater pieces, and we were doing a radio show out in L.A. Not many people we ran into in Lubbock thought of that as real work and seemed to be hoping that we had come to our senses and moved back to Lubbock to get busy. I remember that someone asked me, and I'll never forget this, was Terry a queer? Just because he was an artist. I went, "A what?" I didn't even know what that meant.

JO HARVEY ALLEN IN *COUNTER ANGEL*, NEW YORK CITY.

I had been very unhappy in Los Angeles. I lived there ten years and always thought I would never be happy unless I could get home to Lubbock. I didn't feel accepted in L.A. because I was scared to death of L.A. I was very much a small-town girl with a small-town mentality. Then I sort of got obsessed with it all when I was about twenty-seven years old. I had been asked to be in a movie. I had a popular radio program called *Rawhide and Roses*. Terry programmed the music, and I did all the talking on the air, told stories. I believe I was the first woman country deejay anywhere. The show was a big hit because it was on KPPC, the first underground rock station in L.A., and everybody was glued to that, because you could say anything. It wasn't censored like it is now.

But the L.A. lifestyle scared me so much. Everything was going great at the time, but I demanded that we leave. I put up an ultimatum to Terry that we had to go to Lubbock and were going to leave in two weeks. Terry did it because I was so nuts. I remember my next-door neighbor saying, "Good God! What do you want in life?" I said, "I want Little League baseball games." She was totally shocked when I said that. Even though I wanted all that other stuff, that is how I wanted to raise my family. I wanted to go back home to Lubbock. That was in 1969.

CHRIS: What did y'all do when you went back to Lubbock?

JO HARVEY: We almost starved to death. I was supposed to do the local weather on TV to earn our living. Terry was going to do his art, and I was going to work as a weather reporter. But when I got to Lubbock, they told me I couldn't do it because they couldn't get anyone to sponsor a woman. "Nobody would believe her," they said. Now that was in 1969! Can you believe that? I said, "Well, I could do it real straight." Also, I had sold the *Rawhide and Roses* syndication to the Armed Forces Network and to several other stations in cities around the country. I was going to record my radio program in Lubbock and send it out to the various stations every week. The deal fell through because there was only one stereo station in Lubbock. They heard a demo tape for the radio program I had done in L.A., where I was telling a story, talking about the drinking laws in Lubbock, and said Lubbock was the wettest "dry" town in the country, which is true.[1] The radio station wouldn't let me use their equipment because I said that about Lubbock. But it was true, and besides it's only with great affection that I talked about Lubbock. I absolutely *loved* Lubbock.

Terry had rented a building for an art studio out on the highway in the black part of Lubbock, between a pool hall and a soul food restaurant. We were hosing it down and painting it, getting it all fixed, and the cops came up and tried to get us to not go through with it. We were sitting out in front on the curb having a Coke, and the cops told us we didn't belong there, that we certainly would be killed. Of course, all the neighbors around there fed us every day, and Terry shot pool with everybody and

1. Since April 9, 1972, liquor, beer, and wine may be served by the drink in restaurants and bars, but package liquor sales in retail stores remain forbidden.

we had a great time there. We were back in Lubbock for about six months, and we realized that we just couldn't survive there doing what we were doing. We did almost starve to death.

But once again, the paradox is that I really did have such a rich storytelling heritage growing up in Lubbock. I wasn't studying literature; I was living it. The very essence of what I do, I got from that storytelling tradition. Everyone was a character. My great-grandfather Pa was a flamboyant Flannery O'Connor preacher-type character who could stop bleeding. Doctors would call him while people were bleeding to death on the operating table. He would say, "It will be okay," and the bleeding would stop. He could stop a calf stuck in barbed wire from bleeding. When I was a little girl, Pa would put me behind the draperies and operate the drawstring for most of the afternoon. Every time he opened the draw-drapes, I would come out with a different act.

Everything I did as a kid propelled me into what I do now. All the kids on our block would decide on a theme for a show at the beginning of every summer. We would make fabulous costumes, and send out invitations. We would raise money for the show, selling cloverine salve door-to-door with pictures of Jesus and 8 x 10 glossies of the disciples. We would learn to walk the tightrope. We would always make some poor kid be the dog. Our stilts were as tall as the shed. We were terrified of Zenda Buck, who ran the show, because she had a real hypodermic needle and would threaten to kill anybody by giving them an air bubble with this needle if they didn't do what she said. I loved being a kid in Lubbock.

Childhood in Lubbock was a magic adventure. The weather is so harsh. When it would turn ugly, the teachers would pull the blinds down and turn on all the lights so we couldn't see outside and get scared. It would be so bad we had to put bandanas over our mouth and nose to go outside. I would stay out all day long, forging through the wind and sand, dig a hole by the railroad tracks and put a potato in and cook it all day in the sandstorm by myself, pretending I was a hobo on the lam.

All those things are what make you. I would wait for the sky-writing plane to fly by. It was such a major event when you would see in cursive "Coca-Cola" up in the sky. There was so much magic to that stark Lubbock landscape and what you did in it, a great canvas for a bunch of budding artists and writers and a great stage for musicians and actors.

Everybody would sit out on the porch with my granddaddy, and you had to keep up, to prove yourself by telling the best joke. My relatives were all great storytellers.

We would tell stories constantly at dinner, and nothing was censored. We never ate without discussing topics like murder. Yet we went to church and Sunday school every Sunday. When I was growing up, my friends and I would get drunk and have a ball on Friday night. But on Saturdays, we would go to brunches at people's homes, with floral arrangements, white gloves, and receiving lines.

My whole family was a paradox. My parents had been raised poor, and I was raised rich. My daddy was a carpenter and they worked hard for everything we had. There was nothing I ever wanted that I didn't get, including massive heaps of love. My mother sold ready-to-wear at Hemphill Wells Department Store and managed a dress shop called Sweetbriar, so she wore beautiful clothes, was pretty and fancy-looking. My two grandmothers lived catty-corner from each other. I loved them both and they loved each other. One was skinny and lived in a big two-story house. The other one was fat and lived across the street in a two-room shack. They were really good friends. I was forbidden to listen to country music by the skinny one, who was so proud in this two-story house, because it reminded her of her poor roots. Also, she was immaculate; you could eat off the skinny one's bathroom floor. But the fat one was filthy. This is absolutely true: I watched her wring a chicken's neck out in the backyard, throw it in the sink to pluck its feathers out, and mash cockroaches around her own sink with the same open bloody hand. Of course, she loved country music. There was my mother, right in the middle, dressed up in these beautiful suits. So there were these three totally different types of women who raised me.

One grandmother, the fat one in the shack, taught me to sing "Peace in the Valley" for the Second Baptist Church and always said, "You can stand in front of the church when you are six and sing for everybody." I never got to do it, but I remembered the idea. I remember my fourth grade teacher Mrs. Breedlove had a huge influence because she let me come to school in my tooled-net formal for two days, while all the other kids wore their normal clothes, and sing with the pump organ in every room. I would screech "Tennessee Waltz" real high soprano, and think of myself as a singer like Patti Page. Therein lies the paradox; maybe they didn't realize what they were helping to create.

Those events gave me such confidence. They propelled me to do something out of the ordinary in a place that is so ordinary and stark. You thought you could go anywhere, do anything. What it did was it gave me this incredible gift that I felt comfortable in so many different situations.

CHRIS: Do you think that has anything to do with the unique environment in Lubbock?

JO HARVEY: I think when you are raised with that much love and security it makes you feel that confidence. Lubbock was a nurturing environment. There is a basic family value structure which exists there in Lubbock that seems a little archaic now, and I think that is too bad.

CHRIS: Lubbock definitely gives you a moral point of reference when you are defining yourself. It forces you to evaluate the rules. There are many values that you get there in Lubbock that make people strong and successful. But if you are a thinking person at all, you are forced to evaluate, "Is this a good rule just because it is a rule?" Molly Ivins once wrote that she felt sorry for the kids in San Francisco because their parents are so permissive that they don't have anything to rebel against.

JO HARVEY: It is all of those paradoxes that I find staggering about the place! Elvis played at Terry's daddy's place, the Fair Park Coliseum, so when Elvis first came to Lubbock, he came to eat at Terry's house, which I think is so incredible! But my mother wouldn't even let me go to the Elvis show. I went with Terry to the first mixed dance in Lubbock at Fair Park Coliseum. It was Ray Charles. By mixed, I mean it had

JO HARVEY ALLEN.

Mexicans, blacks, and whites all together in the audience. We double-dated, and my friend that I was with was so afraid that she threw up.

I will never forget things like this: We all had been out one afternoon at somebody's house dancing. And then, right at sunset, we drove our cars way out Slide Road somewhere to a cotton field. We did not plan it. It was like it happened as a vision. We all got out of the car, and picked a furrow and walked toward the sunset. I bet there was twenty-five or thirty of us. We walked real slow down these furrows until the sun completely set and then we all sat down, a line of us in the furrows, all facing the sun. Simple things like that you love.

It's about the freedom. It's about the space. When you stand on that horizon and you see all around you in every direction, you could feel like a minute speck of absolute nothing, and at the same time feel like you are all of it—the center of the universe. When you see the whole world around you, you realize you are nothing in the scheme of things under that vast, big sky, and yet you are in the center of it all.

Also, my mother always told me something when I was a kid, "Never forget that you are no better and no worse than anybody else." People in Lubbock are proud of who they are. It's like: "If you don't like me, to hell with you. This is who I am!" You go out to California, and everybody is trying to be something else. In Lubbock, people are being who they really are. They are not trying to be something else. You would want to be different. You were sort of applauded for being different, in a way, and also shunned in another.

I see Lubbock as a town of massive contradiction. I said in my play *Home Run,* "Everything has its opposite. Everybody in Lubbock knows that there are horrible times and fantastic times, real good and real evil, total right and total wrong and not much else in between worth mentioning."

JO CAROL PIERCE is as much performance artist as she is a songwriter. Several prominent Austin musicians, including Troy Campbell, Darden Smith, David Halley, Kris McKay, Alejandro Escovedo, Joe Ely, Jimmie Gilmore, and Michael Hall of the Wild Seeds, recorded her songs on the 1993 tribute album *Across the Great Divide: The Songs of Jo Carol Pierce.* Jo Carol has written and starred in several dramatic performance pieces, including *In the West,* performed at the Kennedy Center in 1991, *New World Tango,* scored by Joe Ely, and her musical comedy *Bad Girls Upset by the Truth,* which was made into a record album in 1996. Jo Carol was fifty-one years old at the time of her recording debut.

Bad Girls Upset by the Truth is a somewhat autobiographical fantasy that takes place in Lubbock, a world of dreams and arcane biblical and mythological symbols. In short, it is the story of a young West Texas woman who has a spiritual revelation that, because all boys are merely one aspect of the completeness that is Jesus, in order to know Jesus more fully she must experience every one of those boys. She is guided by the voice of Jesus, played by Robbie Jacks, best known for his portrayal of Leatherface in *The Texas Chainsaw Massacre.* In the play, Jo Carol reveals why bad girls are justifiably upset by the truth and why they must commit suicide every morning first thing to start each new day. She also manages to give birth to the second coming of little baby Jesus, who happens to be a girl.

Jo Carol was featured in the motion picture *Deep in the Heart of Texas* (1998). She is married to Austin graphic artist Guy Juke, aka musician Blackie White, who is with South Austin's Cornell Hurd Band.

Carol Pierce

JO CAROL: Because Lubbock was a town where there was not anything else to do, one thing that influenced all the writers in Lubbock is that the main social event was church. The whole place was overshadowed by that one book, the Bible. Whether we wanted to or not, whether we went to church or not, we were all influenced by this long and violent poem with beautiful, old-fashioned language. I noticed that people from Lubbock talk like that, words like "beholden," only around Lubbock. It took me a long time to be out of Lubbock to realize that people don't talk the way that we all grew up talking.

There were lots of fascinating people in Lubbock. One of the best things about Lubbock was the set of friends and the loyalty. We were held together by people like Sharon Ely, who was the hostess for the whole group and made sure that we were together all of the time. There were real magic people like Al and Angela Strehli.

I remember one time we were at a party at some little bitty house stuffed with people. We were in the backyard and it was really hot. Al Strehli came through that party and all of a sudden the energy caught fire, things started happening. We ended up doing this protest against the National Guard, who was having a show that day. This little jug band I was in played extemporaneously. It was real exciting. But I swear, if Al Strehli had not walked through that party then none of that would have happened.

Sharon Ely always knew where to find any foreign people coming through Lubbock, anybody from any other culture, because she was hungry for anything from outside. She met Swiss watchmakers and Japanese businessmen; if any dance troupe was coming in from out of town, Sharon would go down to the rehearsal, get to know them and carry them around Lubbock.

Tommy Hancock always seemed to know about all the interesting, dark little places. Tommy Hancock was like a real thug back then. He always dressed in black. He always drove interesting cars. I had a huge crush on him. He gave me rides home occasionally. He was always really nice and never even knew that I had a crush on him. I liked Tommy because he always seemed to know about the underbelly of Lubbock. He seemed like he knew about places I had never gone into. One place that was intriguing was called TV's. It was a bootlegger place out east of Lubbock, an all-night club. It had TV sets lining the driveway, for what reason I never found out. There was always a big bonfire, and you could see the lights of downtown. All the musicians would play there. There were pool tables. You could get anything you wanted there.

There was a feeling of the oneness of the group that I think was important to all of us. It was like centrifugal force. This bunch of people all could go out further because we had a center core that held us together. I had to have the friends around. It was an essential situation to me. Even though I had friends, we were all just clinging together. The friendships became so strong because it was like living in some alien place, and yet we grew up there, the loneliness that arises in that really geometric space. Lubbock is so patterned and angular. It is inescapable.

Always for us, life in Lubbock depended on being in some sort of hidden place. At night, we could be out because that was ours, but in the daytime it was not a friendly place to be. Our group of friends used to call ourselves the Alley Society because we all lived in alleys in those little garage apartments. A lot of the houses in Lubbock had great little alley apartments. We would move every time the house got dirty because you could get another thirty-five-dollars-a-month, furnished, bills-paid garage apartment, so why not?

When I was growing up, I had a mother who said things like, "You really can't survive unless you get married," and in the same breath say, "Marriage is no way for a woman to live." I was stuck in childhood for many years, playing kick-the-can when my friends were dating and sun-tanning their boyfriends' initials on their back. I did not want to grow up to be any of the things I saw around me. Like a drill-press operator or run a beauty shop? All that stuff just seemed so dreary. I would rather be a child than grow into that sort of life. But I bought into it for a long time, until I left Lubbock. In high school, I took an interest and ability test and my results were, in order of what I should do: (1) musician; (2) writer; (3) psychiatrist. I thought, "I guess I have to be a psychiatrist." The others never occurred to me at the time as something you could really do. I did eventually get a degree in psychology from Texas Tech.

It was hard to conceive of life down the road from Lubbock, to imagine anything I wanted to do. When I got out of Lubbock, it was easier to think about other things, to think about doing what I wanted.

I was married to Jimmie Gilmore in 1964, and we went to California with our five-month-old baby Elyse, sixty dollars, and an old Rambler. We lived in Watts and would go down to Venice Beach, where Jimmie would play music in coffeehouses.

CHRIS: Would you play or sing with him?

JO CAROL: No, I didn't ever play music with Jimmie. I didn't start playing music in public until I was forty-seven years old. I had always written songs. I would write one when it came to me, but I did not start writing seriously until I was more in my forties. There were a few before.

When we were in California, I was just supporting Jimmie and the baby. I think there were lots of creative girls that really didn't express their creativity. Instead we married musicians and artists, people we wanted to be like, to express the creativity that way, which is not a real satisfying thing. However, by the age of forty, most of us girls grew up and started doing something on our own with our talents.

CHRIS: Did you know Guy Juke from college at Texas Tech?

JO CAROL: I did not. The first time I knew Juke and got a crush on him was from seeing the posters that he was doing for Butch Hancock here in Austin in 1971 or '72. Juke did a series of posters that illustrated each of Butch's songs. I saw his work on a telephone pole and I just could not believe it! People were tearing the posters off the telephone poles as fast as they could. Everybody was keeping them because they were so cool-looking. I looked at those qualities that were represented there, the joy and the naughtiness, and I really wanted to meet the guy that did that. So before I ever met my husband I had formed a relationship to his work.

CHRIS: What were you doing in Austin in those days?

JO CAROL: I had moved to Austin with Jesse Taylor. After Jimmie and I broke up, Jesse and I lived together for several years. We moved down here so Jesse would have a better place to do music than in California. Jesse never found a band he really wanted to play with in California. I went first from Lubbock to California with Jimmie, and then back to Lubbock, then to California again with Jesse, then I came to Austin where I am now with Juke. That's my whole life history.

It seems like in our twenties, we were all living each other's lives and we were all in each other's living rooms constantly. Even though we don't live each other's lives as much as we did, I have a feeling that as we get old, it might go back to being that close again. Everybody went off and pursued their own deal, and we interconnected with each other as much as we could along the way.

Vaginal Angel

from the album Bad Girls Upset by the Truth

Vaginal Angel fell down into your
    dancehall
She was upset by the truth
and the Tender Tarts in their trumped up
    dirty rainbows
were upset by tattoos that were trying to
    come through.

There's a snake in their rock pile
and he was upset, too.
Scream for mercy, but those tombstones
just scream back at you.

They were upset by the truth
Upset by the truth
Upset by the truth.

Under her blouse were many naked
    cowboys
driving round and round her Hi-D-Ho
and electromagnetic music that was
    playing
from some secret station on the radio.

On her windshield was a sticker
that had expired so long ago
In her flame, though,

was a flicker
That remained so she could know
what the good girls never show, no
the good girls never show
what the good girls never show.

They're afraid that their husbands
will find their secret dog teeth
in an empty playhouse somewhere
And Jesus is afraid of where
the nightclubs and the day meet
but everybody's got to be somewhere.

Prepare a place for another bad girl
She's on her way down here
for communion in this dark hall
with the bright flesh of despair
the bright flesh of despair
the bright flesh of despair.

For God so loved the world
that he gives his only daughter
to be upset by the truth.
He put her in a bag
to be delivered like a letter
to grow up and do what bad girls do.

They give their bodies to the music
cause the music knows what to do
for the bad girl who has forgotten
who she is and who to give it to
the music knows what to do
the music knows what to do
the music knows what to do.

Goodbye and good luck
little baby Jesus
I know you think we're leaving you
but remember, we're just
a song and a dance away
If there's anything
that we can do.

You're just here
for a little while
Just to let your light shine through
In this dark place,
you will be all right
If you let the beat keep you
If you let the beat keep you
dancing in the street
when you're upset by the truth,
won't you let the beat keep you.

I Blame God

from the album Bad Girls Upset
by the Truth

I can't blame you for leaving me
especially since I drove you to
Can you blame me for my part,
which was just to be born too stupid to
　　know my own heart?
If we tell the truth, can't the blame be laid
with the creator who made
this world without end
His original sin,
this world in which you and I live, Apart?

I blame God
He's the only one original enough to make
　　a mess like this
even he can't clean up
I blame God
I didn't do this by myself, I had Divine
　　Assistance, yes I did
and I blame God.

I know you're tore up by all of those things
Jesus Christ told me to do.
I don't blame you for blaming me for all
　　this pain,
but the things that I did tore me up too.
I know we were meant to be together
　　eternally
and we would be if weren't for Him
and his world without end
His original sin,
this world in which you and I live, Apart.

I blame God
He's the only one original enough to make
　　a mess like this
even he can't clean up
I blame God,
You'd have to be a Deity to be this mean,
and you know that's just not me.
No, I blame God!

Apocalyptic Horses
from the album Bad Girls Upset by the Truth

Once in two thousand years
I get an invitation to ride
Apocalyptic horses across the Great Divide
and my RSVP will ever be
Are you crazy?
Do you think I like to be crucified?

I'd lay down my life
make a blood sacrifice,
for just one more chance
to go dancing on the other side.

I want to move
in mysterious ways.
This earth is flawed like a diamond
but something makes me want to stay.

Mother Mary won't you meet me out under
    the stars?
You know they're burning just like we are.
Did that secret burning in your heart
keep you apart from this world?

Virgin Mary Magdalene,
girl you sure know how to dream.
Suspend your disbelief over all Eternity
Be the road my horses ride forever,
Across the Great Divide.

I'd lay down my life
make a blood sacrifice,
for just one more chance
to go dancing on the other side.

*Throngs of people showed up in Lubbock
from all over creation to see the Blessed
Virgin Mary, and they were all asking the
same question: "Why Lubbock?" Although
many questions remained unanswered,
when it was all over with, we never did find
out the answer to that one, neither.*[1]

EXCERPT FROM
BAD GIRLS UPSET BY THE TRUTH

1. On August 15, 1988, hundreds of pilgrims celebrating the Feast of the Assumption at St. John
Neumann Parish in Lubbock claimed to witness
an image of the Virgin Mary in the clouds. Others say they saw the miracle of the sun, similar
to the event reported in Fatima, Portugal, in
1917. The Holy See of the Catholic Church has
never made a final ruling whether the phenom-
ena in Lubbock were miracles or not.

GUY JUKE is a graphic artist in Austin, Texas, known for his album covers, poster art, and paintings of musical artists. He is married to songwriter and playwright Jo Carol Pierce. While attending college at Texas Tech University in Lubbock, Juke cultivated friendships with many Lubbock icons such as Joe Ely, Eddie Beethoven, and the Supernatural Family Band.

Guy Juke

JUKE: There was a lot of performance art going on in the streets of Lubbock. To create any type of incident through which you could get a laugh was just a great success.

One night, Joe Ely and I were at the Tower of Pizza, which was a little pizza place near Texas Tech University. We were sitting in there drawing pictures on napkins, and somehow Joe got his driver's license out on the table. I was drawing a picture of Groucho Marx and said to Joey, "You'd make a pretty good Groucho Marx yourself. Give me your driver's license." So he gave me his license, and I drew a Groucho Marx mustache and glasses and eyebrows on his picture.

Joey said, "Hey! That is pretty good." We went over to his place, went through Sharon's makeup and pulled out eyebrow pencils. I made him up to look like Groucho. He put on a dark suit and pulled his hair back and tied it real tight. We got a cigar and some glasses. Then we went out again for the rest of the night with Joe dressed like Groucho Marx. He was trying to talk and act like Groucho all night long. It wasn't even Halloween. This was just an everyday occurrence.

BUDDY HOLLY AVENUE SIGN.

That is amusing enough, right? But then on the way home, we got pulled over by a policeman, and Joey was driving. Of course, by this time we had forgotten about how this all got started. Joey gets out of the car and the cop said, "Oh, I see. We got Groucho Marx here, huh?"

"Yeah, officer. We've been to a masquerade party." We were making up excuses. The cop says to Joey, "Let me see your license." Joe pulls out his driver's license, and the cop starts cracking up. He said, "I have to give you credit for being thorough!" It was then that Joe remembered my drawing of Groucho on his driver's license.

We all had a big laugh about it. No one had to go to jail. I think he had pulled us over for having a taillight out. The cop said, "The guys down at the station aren't going to believe this! You young kids are okay. Whatever you're on, I want some of it."

DAVID HALLEY is acknowledged among the Austin and Nashville music communities as one of the most talented songwriters from Lubbock. Halley has appeared twice on *Austin City Limits* and recorded two albums of original music. His song "Hard Livin'," recorded by Keith Whitley, reached the Top Ten on *Billboard*'s Country Music chart in 1985.

Halley

DAVID: I loved music and had a sense that I wanted to do it professionally as soon as I knew that you could. I was seven years old in 1957 when I saw Elvis Presley on the *Ed Sullivan Show*. It was then that I knew I wanted to do something like that. I started bugging my parents, asking about guitars and being a musician.

CHRIS: That brings up an interesting question: Buddy Holly was still living in Lubbock at the time you were growing up. Did you recognize the Buddy Holly phenomenon when you were a kid?

DAVID: Kind of not. I was really too young. The very first record I ever bought was "Peggy Sue," but my older sisters really convinced me into buying it. At the time it was a hit on the charts, so it was cool among teenagers that Buddy Holly was from Lubbock. But among the regular middle-class people, he was almost beneath notice and considered kind of ridiculous. There were plenty of people in Lubbock who were oblivious to Buddy Holly's existence.

In the atmosphere I grew up in, there were not any musicians or people doing entertainment for a living. We were not unlike the old *Donna Reed Show*. There was a model of American family life, and we did not miss it by much. We were the kind of family that belonged to a country club and drank; there was a lot of drinking going on.

I got a guitar for Christmas when I was twelve. I had never seen any live music as a child but there had always been music in my family. My mom grew up playing the piano, popular songs from her generation. There was a baby grand piano. Kids didn't have hi-fis in their rooms; there was usually a family stereo center in the living room. Our family record collection included popular folk music like Harry Belafonte, the Kingston Trio, the Chad Mitchell Trio, and the New Christy Minstrels. We had sound tracks from every musical ever made, and dad would buy records like *Twenty Favorites from the '40s* played by some generic big band.

I was in a folk music combo at Coronado High School. I don't think we really ever had a name. It was a couple of cheerleader girls and a football star, my best friend Gary Madison. All these people but me were popular A-types. They had been elected to something in most cases. I was the one who was musical, who was passionate about guitar. Even though I went through this very nerdy stage with thick glasses, I was recognized as somebody who was deeply into music.

I wanted to be in bands but I had trouble getting motivated to perform in front of an audience. At the time when a lot of people in Lubbock were in rock bands, I managed to miss a lot of fun opportunities. I just drifted around for a long time. I played guitar some with Bob Livingston and his brother Don.

At that time, I was just somebody who liked music. I was in school at Texas Tech for a while, but I realized that I did not know what I wanted to do. I did not want to be a businessman or a lawyer or anything like that. I started as a general liberal arts major, trying some music courses, and eventually ended up in the Fine Arts department. I quit school as soon as I was no longer in danger of being drafted. If it hadn't been for the Vietnam War, I wouldn't have been in school at all. After twelve years of public school, in college I felt like I was in prison.

I had a longtime girlfriend, and we went through the death throes of our relationship before I could leave Lubbock. It was ending that relationship that put me in the frame of mind to get lost. I hitchhiked up to western Massachusetts to a yoga ashram.

Another artist friend of mine from Lubbock had lived at a similar ashram in Espanola, New Mexico. He had received a scholarship with the Chicago Institute of Art, then lost his mind over a girl, similar to me. I told him I was miserable and maybe I would come to New Mexico, and he said to go to Montague, Massachusetts, because that ashram focused on music.

On the way there, I started having some unusual experiences that were spiritual in nature. After the ordeal of my first couple of days of hitchhiking, I was scared of sleeping out on the road, and every little discomfort was new to me, a few weird rides, and I was still heartbroken over this girl. I was trying to catch a ride on Highway 40 east of Oklahoma City. I walked off the road into the woods, and I tried to pray for the first time in memory.

At the time, I thought of myself as an atheist. But I was really up against the world and down on myself, so I went off the road and tried to pray. When nothing seemed to be different, I went back to the highway, and almost immediately this guy stopped for me. That was the beginning of a series of real synchronistic encounters with people.

CHRIS: Do you think there was some sort of connection between your prayer and getting this ride?

DAVID: Well, yeah, I was completely convinced there was a connection at the time. I was with that guy for more than twenty-four hours. His name was Hollis Etheridge, and he seemed to be who I needed to talk to right then. He picked me up because he saw my guitar. Hollis was a collector of valuable guitars and accordions and played in a gospel band in Arkansas. He was an electrician by trade. He was very religious but unconventionally so. He had been a rake and rambling man, an alcoholic, and he had gotten religion after a lot of fairly unhappy adventures.

I wasn't much for volunteering things at the time. But Hollis started talking, telling me about his life. When he got religion, he had started going to church but he was not happy in his congregation. They never talked about the things which he thought were important, and the church did not speak to him like when he first had gotten excited about religion. He was very curious about things from the beyond, things that didn't get talked about. He had read an article about a woman who had died in a Las Vegas nursing home and came back to life and was now a preacher on the West Coast; she was Jewish and had been transformed into a Christian by this experience.

His curiosity was so piqued by that he drove out there to meet her. He confirmed with the hospital her terminal illness, death, and coming back to life without any apparent symptoms. He met her and became convinced, and went back to his church and tried to tell people about it. That and similar other incidents eventually got him thrown out of his church. It was not their style, apparently.

CHRIS: You said you had considered yourself an atheist at that time. Did this conversation make you feel like there was something more to think about?

DAVID: When I prayed that day, I was not fooling around. I had thought a lot about what I was going to say before I said it out loud. And it was not a long prayer either, so it was still fresh in my mind. That night we were driving through the Ozarks. I was already deep in a trance from this spooky stuff he was telling me about, him talking lit up by the light of the dash, his old craggy face with the lines and crevices defined by the shadows. It was almost like around a campfire. In paraphrasing something Jesus is supposed to have said in the Bible, Hollis said a two- or three-word phrase that was a phrase that I had used when I was praying. To myself, I went, "That's interesting!" Then another two minutes later, he managed to say a whole sentence that I had said when I was praying. Then he said about ten words, verbatim, exact words that I had used. Each word felt like a nail in the coffin of my agnosticism. It had an effect on me. It is not any use to try to make it have that effect on anybody else by telling the story, but that's what happened to me. It completely blew my mind. I was willing to believe anything, at that point. Everything he said I felt was aimed right at me from a power greater than him.

It was the beginning of a summer of being a different person than I had ever been before. A whole new dimension opened up as worthy of serious investigation. I met a lot of people in Massachusetts for whom that inquiry was not new. I felt like I had a lot to learn, like meditation and the zeitgeist, the whole worldview.

CHRIS: This sounds like simply a process of seeking and finding. You were looking for answers and meeting these people.

DAVID: Very much so. Because I was so aware of how much I did not know compared to what there was to know.

CHRIS: You were learning about yourself and opening up to all these new ideas; why did you go back to Lubbock?

DAVID: I was going to try to make a food co-op in Lubbock. One of the things I got into in Massachusetts was natural foods. I had come to rest at a place called New England Center for Gestalt Psychology, run by this hip young couple who had workshops and invited authors in, and they served this great natural food.

CHRIS: You thought this would go over well in Lubbock somehow?

DAVID: I just all of a sudden knew that there was such a thing. I returned to Lubbock with this idea, but just to make a little money and then hitchhike again. At this point, hitchhiking seemed to me like the spiritual path; so many cool things happened when I hitchhiked. Hitchhiking seems to keep one on the edge of the moment.

I put a flier up at what had been the Supernatural Food Store. Tony Pearson didn't own the food store anymore, but he had sold it to this guy named Paul who played mandolin and guitar, so there was still music around that place. I met a new crowd of people in Lubbock because I had put this flier up for people who were interested in a food co-op. One of them turned out to be my future ex-wife, Linda Haverstock. But I finally realized that if I didn't keep pushing the co-op along it wasn't going anywhere.

During that time I met the guys from the Flatlanders, but I was only twenty-three years old and they were already not-a-band anymore by the time I met them. I had seen them perform one time five years earlier.

I had heard about Maharaj Ji from a guy in Massachusetts. When I came home to Lubbock, I met all these people who were already into that experience. Jimmie Gilmore and Linda and several others had already been initiated. I was skeptical for a while because, compared to the yoga ashram people who I had hung around with, this Lubbock crowd was a very self-indulgent, undisciplined, hedonistic bunch. Their spiritual angle was a lot more like Jack Kerouac than this serious crowd that I had just left in Massachusetts.

My wife was friends with Jimmie and Jesse Taylor and Ponty Bone. We would get together on Sundays at Tommy and Charlene Hancock's house. The whole hipster community would show up, and there would be food and music. Tommy and Charlene Hancock were so friendly. They wanted to be friends with everybody that came along. Everyone was interesting, and they all had strong opinions about things. Tommy had gone back to law school with the intention of eventually running for public office someday, largely because he didn't like the way things were going around Lubbock. When these people would talk, I always felt like I was gratified in my intellectual curiosity. They were smart, and they had a lot of the same kind of experiences as I did. There was a lot of healthy skepticism.

Jimmie Gilmore really engaged me at that time. Like many people, I felt very charmed by Jimmie. He asked me to play guitar with him some, and I was looking for any opportunities I could have to play music. They were the most interesting thing going on around Lubbock, but it wasn't what I thought I was looking for at the time.

I came to feel Lubbock was a hard place to leave, hard to actually get away from. You could move to another town, but when the money started running low or malaise clicked in, there would always be something magnetic about going back to Lubbock. I had a circle of friends, familiarity, my folks. Maybe there wasn't really anything. It was just safe. It was easy. It was cheap. It was something I knew how to do.

My wife and I eventually separated, and she went to Denver in the same caravan as the Hancocks. Over the next eight months or a year, I would go to Denver and stay at the International Headquarters for Divine Light Mission for a month at a time. I got to have a detached outsider's view of that, still trying to decide if it was for me. After a couple of years, I was convinced that I did want to get involved, but that is a whole other story.

Somewhere during that time, around 1975, I wrote the song "Rain Just Falls." That was the first song I had written that everybody seemed to like. Jimmie recorded it, and Jerry Jeff Walker recorded it. That was the first time I really thought I had a keeper. It gave me some validation. Within a few months after that, I wrote "Hard Livin'." Up to that time, I may have thought of myself as a songwriter, but nobody else did. This was the beginning of other people thinking maybe I could do something good.

Keith Whitley and Joe Ely both recorded "Hard Livin'." Keith Whitley's version of it went to number 10 on the country charts. I made some real good money off that one. Jerry Jeff recorded "Hard Livin'," too. It also got recorded by others. "If Ever You Need Me" was recorded by Kris McKay on Arista Records. I have had songs in movies and television shows, one in a soap opera.

Now that I had written a couple of songs, suddenly people were friends of mine who didn't used to be, people from that 14th Street Flatlanders crowd suddenly were talking to me, without me even talking to them first.

People still ask me, "What were the Flatlanders like?" As if they think I was in the band. But the reality is I was not actually in the Flatlanders. I did play with Butch and Jimmie, some with Joe, and the four of us played together on occasion. For probably a year, I was called the bandleader for the Jimmie Gilmore Band, mostly because I had to do the things nobody else wanted to do, like fire an occasional musician. The title song on Jimmie's first record *Fair and Square* is one of my songs. But when we got to the end of that project, I felt like I didn't have an excuse not to move on and make my own record.

After Keith Whitley recorded "Hard Livin'," I had a lot of open doors for me in Nashville. Suddenly I had money for the first time in my life. I bought a house out by the lake in Austin, a new car.

I was consciously looking for a new bunch of people to relate to, because I felt like I had been on other people's coattails for a long time. I enlisted bassist J. D. Foster, and we got to work on my record *Stray Dog Talk*. When the album was released in Austin, a number of the music writers at the *Austin American-Statesman* and the *Austin Chronicle* embraced me. I discovered that I had a lot of friends who I had not thought about before. I was getting a lot of support from people like Alejandro Escovedo and a whole crowd of artists who were not from Lubbock. I started consciously trying to shake the label of being from Lubbock, because I was not a Flatlander. My friendship with all those people was not based on that experience.

There was a big buzz going on about me. I played the very first South by Southwest festival in a band that included Rich Brotherton and J. D. Foster. That was my dream band, my favorite band experience ever. We played at the Hole in the Wall, and right after the show, two friends of mine from Nashville BMG told me they wanted us for a record deal. The next day we got together, and they told me the offer, and I felt like I could not say yes to it. It was not what I wanted. I would not have been allowed to write the songs or even choose the songs on the record. I basically would have to be the singer on this project and the producers did everything else, made every decision. I think my friend felt betrayed that I didn't say yes because, after all, that is the way it is done in Nashville. It was as good as it gets. There are probably a lot of people in Nashville who would kill for what they were trying to do for me. But that was not what I wanted. Besides, I thought I was going to be a big star doing what I did want to do, at that point. I was really seduced by my own press, which was considerable.

At the next South by Southwest festival there was even more buzz, and I got another offer, from RCA this time; same deal, and I turned it down. I had produced *Stray Dog Talk* myself, and we had sold it to Elvis Costello's label for more than they had ever paid for a record before. That turned out well for me, and things looked pretty rosy.

Then a few years later I made my record *Broken Spell*. But J.D. had left town, and he was really a touchstone for me. I felt like I could really relate to his musical language, more so than with anybody I've played with. Clubs that had been good venues for us to play, where we could count on making eight hundred or a thousand dollars on a Saturday night, started going south for one reason or another.

CHRIS: That was a common experience for a lot of people in Austin at that time. Recently I heard you were doing a songwriters show at Austin's Paramount Theater with Bruce Robison, Shawn Colvin, Billy Joe Shaver. Have you been getting out more lately?

DAVID: That was an isolated event for me, like coming out of the closet. But that was a great night. It was a benefit for Lance Armstrong's Cancer Foundation at the Paramount, which is a great place to play. It was what they call in Nashville a guitar pull, where one person sings a song, then the next person sings a song, and every once in a while somebody will try to sing harmony.

CHRIS: I want to go back and talk specifically about Lubbock. Can you talk about how your environment growing up has affected your songwriting?

DAVID: Being how I am, I feel like there is some higher reason that we were all in that same town at the same time. It's something that I am willing to believe; I could never prove it.

Also, I have never seen such a celebration of collective sense of humor as I have between musicians from Lubbock. There was a group of us who were acutely aware of the aesthetic poverty in Lubbock. Joe Ely has always celebrated Lubbock, and Terry Allen's songs celebrate the redneck backwardness. But I think there is a bitterness about life in Lubbock, broken dreams passed down from generation to generation. It is something that cannot be talked about because it is so ubiquitous: how people emulate the values of Dallas; how everybody is a Republican and nobody can tell you why; a dread that is pervasive. There is nothing much you can do but drink and smoke pot. It is a nameless, existential bleakness in this farming community. But it also produces that humor, like Butch Hancock's indomitable humor.

CHRIS: Tell me about that humor. How would you describe it?

DAVID: There just seemed to be some jokes that were definitely like "Lubbock humor" to us. The joke that I can remember as being demonstrative of what I'm talking about is this one about two farmers. The joke always takes about five minutes, but I'll make it short. One farmer mentions he can fly, and the other says, "I didn't know you had a pilot's license." The farmer says, "No, not like that. I mean I can fly. Let me show you." He puts tar all over the arms of his shirt and dives into his chicken coop and gets feathers all over him. He starts flapping his arms and running around in circles in the barnyard, and eventually he actually does take off and gets some loft and flies around. When he finally comes back down to the ground, his friend says, "Oh. Like that. Well, sure, anybody can fly like that."

In a crowded room, the people that laugh at that joke are usually the ones from Lubbock, and the ones who aren't, don't, generally.

Born in Lubbock and educated at Texas Tech, CARY SWINNEY has earned a worldwide audience with his brand of musical satire, putting songs on the charts in Europe and Australia. Swinney was named Americana Songwriter of the Year in 2000 by the Freeform American Roots chart. His third album of original music, *Big Shots*, reached number one on the Euro-Americana chart in October 2005.

Cary Swinney's lyrics are characterized by straightforward honesty and a critical search for the truth. If Cary Swinney's songs don't get a rise out of a certain portion of the population, then he isn't doing his job. Following a Good Friday performance of his apocalyptic "Jesus Christ Is Coming to Town" (sung to the tune of the one about Santa Claus), an old friend of Cary's remarked, "That boy just raised the bar on smart-ass."

Swinney

CHRIS: Many well-known artists have moved away from Lubbock, but you are making a living as a musician while living in Lubbock. How do you feel about working and writing in Lubbock?

CARY: When I turn on the news in Lubbock and look at the attitudes, I do feel kind of like the enemy, a bit more liberal than a lot of people. Then I come to Austin and realize that I am not liberal at all, whatever that term means. It seems like everybody in Austin is striving so hard to be different that they all end up being the same, so they have not really accomplished anything. I always feel good about going home to Lubbock if I have been gone for a while. Because there is an underground subculture in Lubbock that exists; it has always existed. Everyone that has ever played music in Lubbock becomes aware of this subculture pretty quickly.

CHRIS: Tell me about that first time you played music in public, on the Burks' back-porch stage.

CARY: I had become friends with a guy named Paul Bullock. Paul had invited me out to this house north of town that belonged to Mike and Jack Burk. You might call them old hippies, but they are more or less just countrified freethinkers. I pulled up with Paul to a ratty old white stucco house in the middle of a cotton field. There was a band playing on the front porch, with people standing around listening to music. I noticed Jesse Taylor and Richard Bowden. I knew who all these people were. They didn't know me but I had been watching Richard Bowden play with the Maines Brothers for years, and I damn sure knew who Jesse Taylor was.

I thought, "What the hell is going on here?" You have longhairs and you have professor types standing next to this rundown stucco house out in a cotton field. All of a sudden, there was a piece of Lubbock that I never even knew existed. I had lived in Lubbock for quite some time and was just playing my guitar at home basically. This would have been in 1988. I had my degree and a job and did everything like I was supposed to do, before I ever met any of these people.

I was coaxed onto the stage by Paul Bullock. He said to the crowd, "We have this songwriter here. I've heard him, and he is really good." I get on stage, that porch, and nobody clapped. They all looked at me like, "Who is this jackass?" Then I did my first song. They had a pickup truck pulled up next to that porch, and Richard Bowden was sitting there with his fiddle. He wasn't playing it; just looking at me play. And then all of a sudden I start hearing this music! And Richard is playing the fiddle along with my song! Richard asked me after the song, "Did you write that?" And I said, "Yes." And then he said, "Have you written anything else?" And I said, "Oh, shit. I have a lot of songs, if you want to hear another one." We did another one.

That was how I started performing. When Richard played along, that helped me because this subculture of Lubbock all know and love Richard Bowden. By Richard saying to everyone with his playing, "I accept what this guy is doing," that was my way of getting into the scene.

CHRIS: You had written these songs before, but it had not really occurred to you to perform before that night at the Burks'?

CARY: No. I pretty much was just playing around the house when I met Paul. Then I met Richard, and I was also encouraged by Jack and Mike Burk. If you're not careful with Jack Burk, he does not cut you any slack. He is not going to bullshit you and tell you that you are good if you aren't. As a matter of fact, he will give you a rash of shit about it.

Jack Burk is just a cotton farm boy originally from Grassland, Texas. But to me, in some odd way, Jack Burk is a step ahead of the game. Jack has the ability to see, and taught me to see, a different side of things. I was more conservative before I met Jack Burk. Jack opened my eyes to some things. Jack made me aware of how phony the newscasters all are. He made me aware for the first time that what you see on television is mostly just horseshit. Whatever the TV newscaster has to say is just being fed to him by whoever owns the station, Republican or a Democrat or whatever. I had never really thought about that. I guess I was such a young man that I just accepted TV news as being the gospel truth. I never questioned what was going on. Well, I can't really say that; I have questioned authority since I was a little bitty kid.

CHRIS: Tell me about growing up Cary Swinney.

CARY: I was born in Lubbock but I grew up in O'Donnell, home of Dan Blocker, who was Hoss Cartwright on the TV Western *Bonanza*. My parents are real nice, opened-minded people. We did go to the Church of Christ every Sunday just like everybody else, because that was where my mom and dad's parents went. You are raised with whatever you have. You really did not have a lot of choice in the matter of the church you went to when you live in a little town.

O'Donnell was really cool, because we lived right on the southern edge of town, so we had snakes and frogs and horny toads and rabbits. I had a Shetland pony named Prince, and my brother had a horse named Trixie. O'Donnell was a good twenty years behind the rest of the country, in some odd way like a Norman Rockwell painting. The town square was still alive and well at that time. It is all dead now. If you go back now, it makes you sad to even have to look at it. But at one time, there was a thriving little town there, for what it was. We had two or three grocers, dry cleaners. You believed in Santa Claus because they told you that he was real. God would send you to hell but Santa Claus would bring you gifts. I always wondered why didn't God take over for Santa Claus? God messed up right off the bat, if you ask me.

CHRIS: You mentioned earlier that you felt like you were much more conservative when you were younger, and that you were kind of a big, mean guy in high school.

CARY: I wasn't mean to other people. I just was trained to be aggressive. I was on the football team, and I played middle linebacker. We were trained to be mean. I am not saying that I was mean to people. I never picked on anyone in my life. But when you were a kid in a small town in West Texas, you were trained to be aggressive. And I thought this was all cool at the time, for some reason. It wasn't just me; it was the whole class. Every boy in school was on the football team. But mostly we were drinking a lot of booze on the weekends and doing everything we could to get some pussy. That was the name of the game, and it was very stupid. But we were kids in a small town. That's what you do.

I was probably considered kind of an oddball in my class, because I liked to play the guitar and write songs. I wasn't just a middle linebacker and the aggressiveness that goes with it. But that was a part of who I was.

It did not take but my freshman year at college to realize that I had been duped, and I had been duped in a big way. I thought, "I cannot believe that I have been indoctrinated into that shit! I've been fooled." And I fought it ever since. I was a fool in a lot of ways. At the same time, though, that conservative approach you and I got as a child probably did make you have manners and respect for other people. If I came out of it with anything, I did come out of it with that. But politically speaking, I have changed. I changed a lot, and I continue to change.

CHRIS: Much of your music seems to be inspired by your life in Lubbock. Talk about how you go about writing your songs.

CARY: It is just journalism, playing the role of the reporter, looking at what you see, and trying to figure out some way to put meter and rhyme to it. This happens to me when I do my songs in Lubbock; somebody will say, "At first you pissed me off because of something you said about" the president or Jesus or whatever, "because I didn't get the sarcasm"; and then they say, "I am sorry. I was wrong about what you're doing here."

But you have to watch that. I sometimes feel foolish because I say the things that I say. The foolishness is the part where they take you off to jail. But then you would be a damn fool not to say something. Do you just walk around with a hook in your nose, and let our newscasters decide what we believe? They are all a bunch of phony sonofabitches anyway. I have to say something. That's where a lot of my songs come from.

CHRIS: Talking about getting hauled off to jail, do you want to take this opportunity to clear up the legend of the cops cutting your show short at the Buddy Holly Festival?

CARY: I was singing onstage with Robin Griffin. There was a cop sitting in the shade, and he was not even paying attention to me at first. But then he started paying attention. I did my song "Jesus Silverstein," which is kind of throwing a dart at Jesus a little bit but it is just sarcasm. It did not go over well with the cop at all apparently. The next thing I know, another cop walks up, and another, and another, and another cop shows up. I guess they all got on the radio with each other, "We got some jackass over here that is out of control." They all lined up in front of the stage with their sunglasses, staring me down.

Back to "Why do I write songs?" When you are in an environment of these narrow-minded thinkers, you begin to feel like you are in a throwback. These Lubbock cops all have real short hair and they all wear the same kind of sunglasses that wrap around. I thought, "Wait a minute! These guys could be the bad guys!" And they're probably not, most of them. But it looked that way at my end!

The next thing I know, Don Caldwell, who was in charge of the festival that year, all of a sudden he was on a golf cart. People laugh about it now; they said he came around in the golf cart on two wheels he was driving so fast. Don comes around the corner and he literally puts on the skids. The cops were sitting around waiting for him to do something about me. "What are we gonna do about this smart-ass?" Caldwell comes straight up to the stage. He was all excited and his eyes are real wide open. "What the hell is going on over here!"

I said, "What do you mean 'What's going on?' I'm doing my act. You're the one who hired me to play." Don said to me, "Tone it down! I don't know what the hell you are doing over here but you have gotten everybody upset in this entire area!"

I thought, Goddamn! If I had been doing the same thing in Austin nothing would have happened! Nothing! Everybody would have gone about their business! Cannot do that kind of shit in places like Midland or Lubbock. It was blown out of proportion to a large degree. I don't think Don gave a shit one way or the other. Somebody had to be called who was in a position of authority, and he was the one running the show.

Jack Burk said, "The best thing that could have happened to you is if they cuffed you and hauled you off to jail." Because it would have brought to the forefront the fact that this was all silly. In other words, if the cops would have gotten their way it would have been like, "What did you throw me in jail for? For singing the words Jesus Silverstein? What did I do wrong exactly?" Of course, it didn't happen so it is all just speculation.

CHRIS: We just had to get that cleared up. You actually have sold more albums outside of the United States than you have at home. Why do you think that people overseas are more interested in your music than your own neighbors are?

CARY: I have sold more than I ever dreamed over in Europe. I think it's because Europeans have a tendency to write about diverse music. They will review my CDs, and they have a tendency to give me airplay that most American stations do not. There are stations in central Texas that do support the type of thing I do; KUT in Austin, KSYM out of San Antonio, KFAN. But how many hundreds of stations are in this state, and you have three I can think of which are playing my kind of music. And that is it! Those that do are all independent or public stations. The rest of the radio stations are all owned by the same one or two people. Corporate America controls most radio broadcasts, and my songs do not go over too well with corporate America. That's okay; they are not intended for that market.

CHRIS: Tell me about your day job.

CARY: My day gig is to do a commercial map of the City of Ruidoso, New Mexico. I am real lucky because I get to do it on my own terms. I don't have to be somewhere at a specific time. I spend a lot of time up there in the mountains around Ruidoso. I started hiking the area aggressively, every trail I could find. I haven't learned all of the trees and plants yet, but I have learned nearly all the birds that are up there. I do not take my guitar to Ruidoso, or anything that reminds me of the music.

CHRIS: Are you simply using your music to supplement your love of the outdoors? You have told me that Richard Bowden gets mad at you because you do not pursue music full-time. Why don't you?

CARY: If you do something all the time, it's a job. I don't want music to become a job. I have the luxury of being able to do the hikes and make money in that part of the world, and make money playing music, too. It is a balancing act that I do. Some guys really and truly want the fame. I do not think they give a shit about the money. I want to have fun. If I can make some money doing it, I take that too. I do not want to play three hundred gigs a year. I mean, that's a job! I don't want a job. I want to have fun when I go play.

Wally Moyers, the pedal-steel guitar player, made a comment to me. "Cary, every time I play with you, it's different." Good! The last thing I want to do is play the same old thing. And Richard does not want to play the same grind, the same lick constantly. That's no fun. I never know what the hell Richard Bowden is gonna play when we're together. That's what I like about it.

CHRIS: You and I once were talking about the tightness of Austin or L.A. audiences versus the looseness of a Lubbock audience. In Lubbock, it seems like the audience is participating more. They are much more likely to yell a big "Yeehah!" I have much more fun being in an audience in Lubbock than I ever do in Austin or in California.

CARY: Do you know that I hear that all the time? I swear to God, people from Austin and San Antonio will come to a show in Lubbock, and they always leave saying, "This was different! Why is it so different?" They get to Lubbock and there's not a helluva lot there. But then, "What happened? Why was that so much fun?"

I cannot explain that. I truly do not know why that is. It doesn't make any sense to me either. But I think the difference is because Austin is just saturated with professional musicians. I think that they might take it a little more seriously. Whereas in Lubbock, it is all about having fun and cutting loose.

Jesus Silverstein

from the album Human Masquerade

Jesus—
was a Jewish boy
who looked just like
but was so unlike
All the other boys

Born one night in Bethlehem
soon became the Holy Land
Jesus—
was a Jewish boy

Jesus—
is the son of God
he's a middle linebacker
a real nut cracker
on the Deity Squad

He can take ya' to the temple
of eternal man
and forgive ya' for your blunders
and stroke ya' like a lamb

Some said Jesus was a pretty good guy—
I never did meet him—I hope they
    wouldn't lie
would they?

Say . . . what if ol' Jesus' last name
would have been Silverstein?
ol' Jesus Silverstein . . .
It sure would have changed some
    things . . .
you know like when you're in your
    backyard . . .
and you're nailin' up a board . . .
and ya' hit your thumb with a ham-
    mer . . .
and ya' scream to the Lord,
"Jesus! Silverstein!"

Jesus—
he's a friend of mine
I break the bread
and bow my head
and drink the wine

I dig it on down and sing at High Mass
and if you don't like it—you can kiss
    my ass

Jesus—
he's a friend of mine

Desperate Searcher

from the album Human Masquerade

They tell me He created Adam and He
    created Eve
they tell me He created everything we
    see—
Oh, He, the great creator who fills the
    void within
He created us a Savior but who created
    Him?

Well, I don't know where I'm going and
    I don't know who I am
I don't know where we are—just where
    we've been
Sometimes I feel wonderful and some-
    times I feel bad
and sometimes I feel grateful for the
    good friends that I have

Chorus:
Oh, I am not alone
I can see it in the eyes of us children
    who have grown up
out there searchin'—for the answers—
    wherever they may be
Are you a desperate searcher who is
    searchin' just like me?

Envision all the questions with parents'
    answers that were lies?
Envision life with heaven as our prize
If the world is just some station
Mister, fill me to the brim
'cause I don't know where I'm going
and I don't know where I have been

Well, I went to church last Sunday, a
    lapse of self-esteem
I hoped to find what many say they see—
As I looked into their souls
I found that they were just like me
They are searching for the answers
wherever they may be

Chorus repeats

Hey, are you a desperate drunkard who's
    been drinkin' just like me?

Good Ol' Sunday Mornin'
from the album Martha

Good ol' Sunday mornin'
we hopped inside a Ford
Off to our father's father's church
to get ourselves some more
I guess it's bound to happen
ducks all in a row
Oh they dunk ya' down, 'til ya' think
    you've drowned
then they tell ya' all ya' need to know

Chorus:
Good ol' Sunday mornin'
Greasy bacon, eggs are fried
Put the pot roast in the oven
Slick your hair down
Go eat some humble pie

A puzzled child is staring
from a red crushed velvet pew
Out the window of the Sweet Street
    Church of Christ
was such a lovely view
I guess it's me who's crazy
for I never understood
How hellfire and damnation could be so
    doggone good

Chorus repeats

Does your clergy have an ego?
Are there things he's tried to hide?
You know he likes when people listen
oh he's never told a lie
Though the answers he's been given
are like an educated guess
They'll get you next to nothing when
    faith's put to the test

Chorus repeats

. . . Oh—Good ol' Sunday mornin'
Bees are buzzin', and so am I
Put the bird food in the feeder
Honey, let your hair down
Let's fly
Let's fly

Livin' in My Head

from the album Big Shots

If time were an old man
And I were young
I'd have my chaps on
My cap guns drawn

And love would be Mary
My 5-year-old Mary
And RC Cola
Would turn me on

Cowboys and injuns
And make-believe fun
I wish the days of my childhood
Had just now begun

And Roy and Gabby
Were ridin' the range
In a '52 Chevy
Drawin' quick . . . and takin' aim

Well I know it sounds crazy
To live in my head
But I'd rather be crazy
Than to be misled

By modern-day TV
And all that's been said
By anchormen
Jesus, let Elvis stay dead

Well there are days that I'm happy
And some days I'm sad
Most days I feel a little guilty
'Bout this good life I've had

You see, cowboys and injuns
Are a thing of the past
And make-believe westerns
Were never meant to last

So you live in your head
And I'll live in mine
You can have Nashville's newest
I'll take Patsy Cline

And then wrap me in a blanket
With an old black 'n' white TV
And turn on Gene Autry
And let me be

A Hero on the Square

from the album Big Shots

Well 1965 was sure a doosey
it's the year that ol' Dan Blocker came
    back home
he tipped his hat in the parade from a
    pony
all the old folks said it seemed he'd
    never gone

And later on that evening
he rode in the bed of an El Camino
borrowed from Ellis Chevrolet
in the grand ol' entry of the rodeo
while the "Stars and Stripes Forever"
    cleared the way

Everytime I hear the "Stars and Stripes
    Forever"
it takes me to a place I like to go
it's a world of Little League and cotton
    gins and Mexicans
and big yellow road-graders on dirt
    roads

So if you're ever on the highway towards
    Tahoka
and you find yourself with a little time
    to spare
make it a point to make a stop in ol'
    O'Donnell
to find a statue of Dan Blocker on the
    square

Sometimes I feel like a boy in a Rock-
    well painting
saddled up, with no place else to go
and since there ain't gonna be no ponies
    up in heaven
you can leave me stranded in an earth-
    bound rodeo

No, they ain't choppin' cotton like they
    used to
and ol' Dan Blocker's long since dead
but you can still find Hoss Cartwright
    on cable
and you can still find me livin' in my
    head

Yeah, if you're ever on the highway
    towards Tahoka
and you find yourself with a little time
    to spare
make it a point to make a stop in ol'
    O'Donnell
to find a statue, of a hero, on a square

DOUG SMITH is West Texas's premiere composer and pianist, although Doug says, "I prefer to call myself a piano player. Out here in West Texas, if an old boy says he's a pianist, folks tend to look at him awful funny." Smith's stunning compositional ability and powerful piano skills are the subject of the 2003 PBS special *There It Is*. He has recorded over a dozen albums of his piano compositions and has performed at New York's Carnegie Hall.

Doug Smith

DOUG: I started playing piano when I was two years old. It was on a little Wurlitzer organ about a couple feet long. I still have it in my studio at home. It belonged to my aunt. It was around Christmas time. As a toddler, they obviously didn't want me messing around with the instruments. It's beautiful to hear my grandmother tell the story. She says they were all in the kitchen cooking, and they heard this music coming from down the hall. Everybody had dumbfounded looks on their faces. They all went into the bedroom, and there I was playing music.

To my knowledge, I have always played music. I don't remember ever not playing, as long as I have lived. They say that I was playing two-note chords with my left hand and melodies with my right when I was two years old. There was no sitting down and experimenting, trying to get the sound. They were things that I had heard like Christmas songs, melodies, nursery rhyme songs; songs I had heard as a baby. "Twinkle,

Twinkle, Little Star" was the first song I ever played very recognizably, putting the melodies and the chords together with the left hand.

So when that happened, my aunt obviously gave me the organ. I took it home, and I was just infatuated with the thing.

I gave my first concert on that organ in the first grade. I was six years old. I could remember it like it was yesterday. It was at Purple Sage Elementary School in Kermit, where I grew up. My teacher had come over to the house, her and my mom were friends, and she heard me playing. She asked me if I would be willing to play for the class. I said, "Sure! Absolutely."

On Monday, I took my organ up there. And I was scared to death because she told the class that I was going to play music. I got my rig set up and began to play. To make a long story short: By the end of the day, every elementary school teacher in Purple Sage had brought their class in for me to play for twenty or thirty minutes. By the end of the day, I had played the whole day. The neatest thing I remember is, at the end of that day when I was walking out to my mom's car, fourth and fifth graders were coming up to me and saying, "Hey, Smith! That was really cool."

Right then, I realized that music connects me with people in a way that there is no other medium to make that connection with. To this day, everybody I am connected with is because of music. I have met the greatest people in my life as a result of people that love music.

I hear the music. Right now, I hear the music. I have this tune going through my head that I've been working on. It's in the forefront of my mind right now, right here in the middle of my forehead. I figure that the same way Michael Jordan was anointed to play basketball, I was anointed for piano and this music that I compose. Because I have never had a piano lesson in my life, if I think, "who to give the credit to?" I cannot point to a piano teacher, an instructor at the college with a doctorate degree in music, or any person. This music comes from the Divine. It is divine intervention. That has been my assumption my whole life; it had to come from God. Just like Mozart, Beethoven, Bach, all the masters did not really take the credit. God anointed these men to share the music with the world. Some people will say, "Ah, that's a bunch of crap!" But I think God works through people. God anoints certain people for certain things. And it is not just music; it is as wide as the universe.

I knew exactly what I wanted to do with my life. But my parents really wanted me to get in there and get the sheepskin, and they put a lot of pressure on me to do that. I was majoring in telecommunications at Texas Tech, and I was just comatose. Finally, after three and half years, I went to my folks and said, "This is over. Music is where I'm going, lock, stock, and barrel, feast or famine. I understand the circumstances I'm looking at, but this is the way it is with me." I took a couple of technical music courses in piano when I was at Tech, and flunked them both. It was very in-depth, as far as being able to interpret the masters, and obviously you had to read music.

But I still had all these creative ideas. I knew even though I could not read music or interpret Mozart that there was a place for me in this industry. I still believe that. Think of how many thousands of people will graduate this semester with music degrees that can interpret Mozart. Well, I don't give a damn to interpret Mozart. That is history to me. I am trying to forge a new sound and invent new music, a new approach to the piano.

I am able to make a living off of piano performances, although sometimes it is very meek. I do about three or four big performances a year, in concert halls or churches. But making music is exclusively all that I do. I mostly earn my livelihood through recording and selling my records. I cannot read or write music, so it is crucial that I get my copyrights. Everything that comes through my mind, I sit down and get it in structured form, copyright it, and publish it all myself.

My music is like my life's diary, a diary of my life through music. All of my music is related to life, things that have happened to me, relationships I have suffered through, friends who I have lost, things that have made my spirit move. That is what I write about.

West Texas is a perfect place for me. Because of its rustic beauty and space, I am almost forced to create. Out on my farm, when that sun comes up, I am parallel to it. When it goes down, I am parallel to it. It's almost like you are in the center of the universe!

People out here do not give a damn if I play a piano or not. They do not care if I have written five thousand songs. What a beautiful and humbling thing, for people to put you so far upon your ass that you are so humble you have to write. That's my case. I have been here all of my life. It's my home. But it is the ultimate challenge to survive as a piano player in West Texas. Growing up, do you know how much hell I caught playing the piano? Guys making fun of me?

COTTON FIELD AND POWER LINES.

I think that I have better insight now. I live outside Petersburg, Texas, now, northeast of Lubbock. When I got married and we were expecting our son, it dawned on me that I just did not want to be in the city. I wanted to be able to chase dogs, climb trees, throw clods, walk down a dirt road. So I moved out to Petersburg. My daddy was born and raised out there. My granddad farmed land out there. I have had family in Petersburg for a hundred years. And I thank God for it because I like living in the country. I am much more inspired. My writing has certainly taken on new depths since I have been out there.

West Texas is so barren and wide open and agricultural related, for people who are interested in music, all they have to do is hone in on an instrument and to begin to develop a sound. Time is to the musician what space is to the painter. The painter begins with a canvas. The musician begins with time and thought. You do have plenty of time out here in West Texas. I think that is a big part of the magic. Plenty of time to concentrate on creating the music you hear in your head.

Downé

DOWNÉ BURNS is an acclaimed painter who grew up in Lubbock. After studying art history and business at Texas Tech University for a brief time, he and his family moved to Santa Fe, where Downé began painting. After years of success in the cosmopolitan art world of Santa Fe, Downé and his wife returned to Lubbock, seeking "to get back to the basics of love."

Burns

DOWNÉ: My dad is a self-taught artist named Doreman Burns. When I was a kid, he always painted, but he just did it for his own enjoyment. So I was around painting, but I did not do much art when I was a kid. Dad had a little room in our house converted into his studio, and I drew a little bit when he would be back there.

We owned and ran B&B Music, a record store on University Avenue over by the Texas Tech campus. The record store was there from 1968 to '82, back in that era of Fat Dawg's and Main Street Saloon, all those great little music venues near campus. I was naturally exposed to all the locals trying to get on their feet at that time like Joe Ely and Jay Boy Adams. At that time B&B Music was really the top record store in town, so when all the bands like Pat Benatar, Foghat, or Cheap Trick would come to town to play the Lubbock Coliseum, we sold the tickets. At that time it was still common to get in-store record signings, so I always got to meet whatever big act was in town.

Being in that record store all the time, music was my biggest influence, everything from jazz, to rock 'n' roll, to country. Music created a real creative environment that I grew up in. Growing up like I did, I saw both sides of the music business: the creative side and the marketing side.

When I was a kid I thought I would go into music. But to make a long story short, once I graduated high school I realized I could not sing and I could not play an instrument. But my dad had always painted, and since I had determined that I was going to do something creative, I thought, "Bingo! I'll paint!" I can draw a little bit. It was as simple as that. I just thought, "I am going to be an artist." I asked Mom and Dad if I could convert one side of their garage into my studio. Of course, Mom thought I had lost my mind, but Dad said, "Go for it! You can do it."

Everybody here in Lubbock goes over to Santa Fe for vacations. Santa Fe is not a far-off place to us. Because we would go skiing there, I had been to Santa Fe many times and seen the galleries. So it's not like somebody from Lubbock saying, "I want to be an actor," and needing to go to Hollywood. If you are from Lubbock you may be thinking Hollywood is a long ways from home. Whereas, if you are going to be in the art world, the three art capitals are Santa Fe, New York, and Paris. And Santa Fe was close, right in the backyard, not too far from home. It was an easy transition. My wife Melissa and I took off to Santa Fe, and within a year we had so much success at it.

Dad was sick of the retail business. He had gotten out of the record business and owned a college gift store at that time and was getting tired of the whole rat race. I told him then, "Dad, I can make a living at this, and you're the real artist in the family. You're the one that has always pursued and practiced art. If I can do it, y'all need to just pack up and come over here." Next thing you know, they did. My folks just sold everything they had here in Lubbock, took off and moved into the hill country around Santa Fe, and hermitized for a few years. They both started painting. They still live outside of Albuquerque now. He paints full-time, and my mom paints full-time.

In the art world, people strictly know the art by the picture. I thought, "Let's take another approach. Let's develop a high-profile image that is identifiable as me, the artist." We did some off-the-wall advertising with me actually in the advertisement, not just the painting, which hadn't been done. We came up with the photographic image of me all in black, wearing a black cowboy hat. We shot a lot of black-and-whites of me in my cowboy getup, shades and a hat on, and a bunch of paintbrushes in my hand. We hand-colored the tips of the paintbrushes. That sort of stuff just hadn't been done. If not anything else, I knew it would get people's attention, and it did. It got a lot of attention. It definitely worked.

We started running ads in the Southwest art magazines. The minute all those galleries got hold of me and the bucks started rolling in, I put every bit of cash back into it. I signed a contract with *Southwest Art,* and we did a complete double-page ad in *Southwest Art* magazine every month for thirty-six months straight.

But I caught flak big-time. It definitely rubbed everybody within the Santa Fe art community raw. They didn't like that. My attitude was "Y'all can starve to death and play the starving artist role all you want." To me, I want to make a living at art. I want to enjoy this, and I also want to make some money at it. I have no interest in being an impoverished artist. I do not want to live that way, and that is what so many artists do. They want to play the whole part of the anguished, reclusive artist who does not want anything to do with big business, the commercial side, when deep down, that is exactly what they all want. They are miserable because they can't make a living at art. I never had that starving artist approach.

Immediately after I started advertising, I came up with a catchphrase: "An Important American Painter." It stuck, right off the bat. I was from nowhere but my ads always said, "Downé Burns: An Important American Painter."

I even had big local publications in the Santa Fe area that would not advertise me unless I dropped that byline. It was just too egotistical, they thought. So we didn't advertise with them. Anybody that knows me knew this wasn't an ego trip. I was trying to bring a whole new marketing idea. "Why are we all starving to death at this?"

With my dad running the retail record store, I grew up around regular dinnertime conversations like "How can we get more people in the store? How should we display the product?" Dad and I talked about it before moving over to Santa Fe. Like McDonald's comes up with an edible, pretty good hamburger, and then it's marketing from then on. How do we get this to the masses? That was my approach: If I can just come up with some good art that is marketable, and it doesn't have to be great art, then I'll just put it on the boilerplate, like a hamburger. If you're gonna make a living at it, then you gotta get it out there. We live in a day and age where everybody has discretionary income. The college kids that are living off pizza, everybody has got money to blow.

But eventually, it got to where people would realize that there wasn't a barrier at my studio in Santa Fe. I was willing to help anybody. I learned that from my dad. I have never been afraid of competition. When my dad had the record store, every other college guy wanted to open up a record store. Dad was always willing to tell them what they needed to do, and it would drive my mom crazy. "You're giving all the trade secrets away!" Dad would say, "No, you can help other people out and still survive."

I finally did build a pretty good reputation on one side of Santa Fe with some of the artists, some who were trying to get going. They were more than welcome to come to my studio, and I'd tell them everything that I did marketing-wise. My attitude was: "The more the merrier! It's America and there is room for all of us." I did have a big studio in a strip center there in Santa Fe for a while. We had converted part of it into a little makeshift gallery, and we did a bunch of shows for a while with unknown artists. I would do the whole production, print up the invitations and everything.

I will tell you a true blessing about being from Lubbock. I have learned that you just don't get that friendliness and helpfulness as much in other parts of the world. Melissa and I would have so many conversations while we were living over there in Santa Fe about "Where is that sense of community?" We missed that so much. I mean, we had so-called friends and all that, but when it got right down to the nitty-gritty, there was no one to be found. That was a big thing. That is why we came home to Lubbock finally.

Now this is worth everything to us. I want my kids to grow up in this environment, here in Lubbock. That security promotes part of the magic that is in the West Texas air. People are not as transient here; they are connected to this place and are going to stay here. Whereas when we lived in Albuquerque, I got so sick of the turnover; every time my son made a new friend on the block six months later they had moved to Illinois or who knows where.

Part of the typical downside of success, in a high-profile field like art, you do get caught up in the trappings. Like Waylon Jennings said: "Can't we get back to the basics of love?" Next thing you know, it's "a four-car garage and we're still building on." You cannot help it. You get in that circle. Everybody buying your artwork is wealthy, nine times out of ten. They are flying you around to all these galleries. You are being treated like a superstar. And being from Lubbock, much more of a simple background, all of the pomp and ceremony was very impressive; you couldn't help but start getting caught up in it all. Next thing you know, you have to play the part, you really do have to pretend. People think you are a millionaire. You are in all the magazines. It's all part of the fanfare. Now I can look back at it and see through different eyes because I know more now what's really going on. But they'd pick us up in limousines at the airport, there'd be somebody with my name on the sign. In the back of my mind, I am thinking, "Geez! I can't believe they are doing this! I am really not that big a deal."

But it is part of the image thing. And part of it, I had to stop and appreciate, because I had started doing it in my advertising. I understood that it's part of the Tinseltown idea. You can build stuff up in this country. If you get on a roll, you can really pump it up. You have to act like a rock star. You have to play the part.

After a while, that began to eat at Melissa and me, and it became a strain on our marriage. We finally had the nice cars and a pretty good-sized house. Then the next thing you know, you want to be on the board of this or that in your community; or your wife does. Especially, it starts there because now she's "somebody" because she is with me. Now she is sucked into the whole social thing.

It finally got to where, after several years, I remember thinking, "This is great and all, but how did I get here? This is not what I wanted. I am really not this person."

And I could not blame anybody else because I was doing it. I was participating and playing the part. I had created it. But you literally get to the point to where it's like, and this sounds stupid but this is how it gets, if we hadn't been out to at least three really expensive, high-profile, fancy restaurants in a week, then there was something wrong. You get to thinking in the back of your mind, "We have to be seen." You don't talk this out loud, but it does get that shallow, because of the social circle you finally get sucked into through your success, being a part of the country club. Success has a whole other side you get caught up in.

There came a point around 1993 or so that I started getting sick of painting. It is a cliché, but it starts feeling as if you have created a monster. Unfortunately, a lot of us that are successful in this day and age, and I am not saying "us" as me; just people in general, we get so many trappings around us. You just can't help it. I guess what I'm getting at is: it is all relative; people whose lifestyle is so "big-bucks," they are sweating the house payments just as much as anybody.

Finally, Melissa and I decided, "Let's go home, start over, revamp, get back to the basics and enjoy." We finally put an end to the business, shut everything down. I wasn't painting anything anymore over there in Santa Fe. I was really just selling posters. That was real lucrative. When you are hot and you are selling that paper, that's good bucks. You don't have to paint; you are just reproducing. You can get one image that is a hot seller and sell thousands a month on just that one image. That is just like printing money. That cut us loose from having to deal with all the galleries. I do not do any shows anymore. I got sick of that. I got tired of playing that part. We came home to Lubbock, and I really did not paint that much for the first year. I just kind of piddled around.

The house we had in Albuquerque was not a mansion by any means. But everything is inflated over there compared to Lubbock, so we were able to sell the house in Albuquerque with the same square footage for twice what our house in Lubbock costs. We got rid of the fancy cars and the whole bit. I bought me a truck. It was silly stuff, but I wanted to do this right. I grew up driving a pickup truck, and there I was driving a Mercedes for years, just playing that part. After a while it got to where I knew, "This is not me."

Now I am real fortunate. I look back and I realize I am so glad I went through all of it because now I have a real appreciation of, and this also sounds cliché, the little things. The big house, I have done that, and I have had the nice cars. Now I can stand back and go, "Okay, I have tasted of all of it. Now, this is what is really important to me."

This is how I want to do my art. I don't want a big studio. When we first moved back, I painted in the garage. I don't care if I have something to impress everybody with when they come into town to see my studio.

The studio in my home now is a cool setup. I finally came up with something new to paint. I got out of being burned out on painting. After being here in Lubbock, I started painting again.

But the other thing I did when we first got back, is I started this lawn service. We were still selling posters, but the distribution process was not as big, so we were not really in a financial bind. So just for something to do to keep busy, I started up a lawn service. I had mown lawns when I was younger, like everybody in Lubbock has done some lawn business. The lawn business is a big deal in this crazy town.

The lawn business was a therapy for me, and I've kept it going. It has been a great release because I love working in the yard. I paint three days a week and I run the lawn mowing service the other three workdays. I got a crew of three guys. I go out Mondays, Wednesdays, and Thursdays, every week, in my overalls, my cigar and cap. Everybody in the neighborhood knows me as the lawn guy. They would probably keel over if they ever saw me in that whole other world of art. Nobody in the neighborhood has any idea of what I did and who I am in the art community, and to me that is great. I like being another little pink house on the block. I am just another good ol' boy here.

Now, the art is way off. I ship all my paintings off to New York every Friday, and my distributor distributes it. I do not even answer my art-business phone. Melissa gets that one. If I do even answer that line, I use another name. I normally won't even pick it up. I do not want anything to do with the business side of it anymore.

BOB LIVINGSTON was instrumental in the creation of Austin's Cosmic Cowboy movement, as the bass player for Michael Martin Murphey, Jerry Jeff Walker, and Ray Wylie Hubbard, and as a founding member of the legendary Lost Gonzo Band. Bob is president of Texas Music International, a music education program that operates in Texas and abroad. He is also on the board of directors of the Texas Music Museum.

Livingston

BOB: I graduated from Lubbock High School in 1967, the Summer of Love. Lubbock was dry; there was no way to even get a beer. And I didn't even think of getting a beer back then, by God. I was a goodie-good kid. My parents both worked for the First Methodist Church in Lubbock. My father was the activities director and my mother was the general secretary of the church. I grew up in this church environment, but at the same time I had thoughts of rebellion, like preacher's kids do.

I was a football player, and Freddie Akers, who ended up coaching at the University of Texas, was my football coach at Lubbock High. An interesting fellow at Lubbock High was Rob Layne. He was the son of the famous Detroit Lions quarterback Bobby Layne, who lived there in Lubbock after he retired. Robby was the quarterback at Lubbock High, so Rob and I played football together. Robby was a complete over-the-top craze-o, one of these "go to Vegas every weekend to see Elvis" kind of guys. His dad was famous for that, too. Robby was a giant fan of and goods friends with Joe Ely, so I met Ely through Rob Layne. Although we were jocks, music was always a big part of our scene.

Joe Ely was definitely what would be considered a Lubbock hippie. He was getting in trouble a lot; Ely was almost like a hoodlum. But then he grew his hair down to his knees and would walk around town with one leg painted red and one leg painted white, stuff like that, just asking for it! Then he got in a rock band.

I got into music about that same time. My first band was called the New Grutchley Go-Fastees. It was me and Robbie Gamble and Johnny Tull, who is now a big-time lawyer in Dallas. Rob Gamble was better known as Papa Jelly Belly or just P. J. Belly. He later had a great blues club in Lubbock. Then he moved to Las Vegas and died of a heart attack. But we were kids in junior high school when we played together. It was like a jug band, basically. We played church functions. Church was big for me. I was this good guy that played football, but I played guitar in assemblies whenever I could. There really is nothing else to do in Lubbock!

My girlfriend was Penny Pearson, who is Tony Pearson's sister. Tony played in the Flatlanders. Her dad was Bobby Layne's best friend. We would play at private parties and Bobby Layne would tip me twenty bucks to play "Your Cheatin' Heart." So I was getting into playing and even writing some songs.

I graduated, and I went to Texas Tech and joined a fraternity just to have something to do, because my girlfriend had dumped me bigger'n Dallas when she got to college. I joined a fraternity because it gave you a place to party and drink beer. I never drank beer in high school, but by the time I got to Tech I was the champion beer drinker. We were having parties out in the cotton fields and getting so drunk. Suddenly I was pouring it down my throat.

Remember Ron's Ice Cream on College Avenue? Down the alley there was a folk club called Alice's Restaurant. But Ron's had a basement that was not in use at the time. When I was a sophomore at Tech, about 1968, I went and talked to Ron and said, "Let's open up a folk club down there." He says, "Okay. You can do it here for free. I'll split the door with you." We called it the Attic. I would play there for the frat guys, who would come down every Friday and Saturday and drink beer until they went crazy. I would play mostly covers of popular songs like "Proud Mary."

Then I went to see Ely perform, who was a folky at this time. He was playing solo, like Lubbock's version of Dylan. When he got away from his original rock band, Ely got into folk and country. There was Ely with his long hair, playing that old Gibson guitar of his with seashells glued all over it, and he played a high hat. He would play "I Got the Blues for My Baby by the San Francisco Bay" and "Candyman," all that old jug band stuff, cool, bluesy folk songs. I thought, "Yeah! That is so cool!"

I became more and more friendly with Ely, so I started booking him every Sunday night at my club. The frat guys would come down there to listen and say, "What is this shit? Come on! Play 'Proud Mary'!" I would stand up and threaten their lives if they didn't shut up. I was a big guy at that time; I had just finished playing football and I weighed close to 240 pounds. But I *loved* music, and here was Ely, who, to me, was God.

My brother was in a band. His name is Don Livingston and he played in a band called the Raiders with Charlie Hatchett, who was one of the first lead guitar player guys in Lubbock, and Gary Blakley and Stan Smith, who went on to be in the Sparkles. The Sparkles were the greatest rock 'n' roll band of all times! Better than the Beatles! It's unfortunate that they broke up. The Sparkles were a four-piece band; they played the Music Box and the Swinger, those clubs out on 19th Street, where it hits the Brownfield Highway. Lucky Floyd was the drummer and one of the greatest singers.

All the Sparkles did was play music. That was amazing to be able to only play music for a living, and not have another job. At that time in Lubbock, music was supported by the fraternities. They were the only people that would pay any sort of money. There were not that many clubs. If you could get a good frat-band you made money. The Sparkles would come down to Austin, and were the top party band at the University of Texas. It was cover stuff, but also one of their big hits was called "Do the Hip"; it was a dance. Those records are worth tons of money today, if you can find them. Usually you find them in Germany. People know more about Lubbock music in Germany than we know about it.

So there were these bands in Lubbock that were so good they blew your mind! Music started sinking in for me.

I think one reason why people came to music was because Lubbock was dry, as in no alcohol. You could not have any fun. You could not have long hair or you would get killed.

Another reason is that everything was so flat and hard-angled. Music seemed to round the flat edges off in Lubbock. You could soften things with your music. With music, you could come into your own little world and make it anything you want. We did not know about the rest of the world, we were so isolated. We just knew the pictures we saw on TV, and it was so different than our world that we tried to imitate what we saw.

Music was big in the circles that I ran in, and those people certainly were not leftists or alienated. All the high school kids went to the Music Box and the Swinger every weekend, and they danced their asses off. Even the rednecks like Robby Layne,

Tonky Murphey, Beau Boren, Grist Sands, Busty Underwood . . . these names! Where do you hear names like this? These guys were all rednecks but just loved music. We were starving for things to do.

I drew number 309 for the draft, a great number, and immediately left for Colorado. I quit school. I wanted to make records, to be a full-time musician. I did not know where I was gonna go, but I headed out.

My brother Don was Jesse Taylor's first guitar teacher. Don had been in a rock 'n' roll band but then became a folk singer in lounges. My brother was one of the first guys that made tons of money playing in Colorado after-ski joints. He said, "Come up and we can do a duo together." He was being paid a couple of hundred a night, plus he was making hundred-dollar tips. Back then, that was large money! So I got in on that. It was there that I was discovered by a guy named Randy Fred, who was an agent in L.A.

Randy said, "I can get you a record deal, boy," so I went out to California. I got a record deal with Capitol Records in 1969. Shortly after I got to California, I was driving down the L.A. freeway and I see a hitchhiker. He was from Germany. I said I'm from Texas. And he said, "Oh, really? I know only one other person from Texas and his name is Mike Murphey. He's a singer, too." See, before I had made it to California, I would go up to Red River, New Mexico, and play for drinks and tips in the bars there. All these great folkies played there in Red River, like Mike Murphey, Steve Fromholz, Ray Wylie Hubbard, B. W. Stephenson. I had never met Murphey but knew his songs from Red River, and I thought they were just the greatest songs I ever heard. I say to this hitchhiker, "If you ever see Mike Murphey again, give him my card." I never expected to hear from him again. That very night, I get a call from Mike Murphey! He says, "I'm living in this place called Wrightwood. Come up, I would love to meet you and talk."

I had a record deal. Murphey was playing in a band called Tex with Herb Steiner, the steel guitar player. Some people had recorded his songs, like the Monkees and Patti Page, and he was a writer for Screen Gems, but he had no record deal.

I moved up to Wrightwood, California, and started writing songs with Murphey. He and I formed a publishing company called the Mountain Music Farm, with Roger Miller and Guy Clark. We started writing songs and got paid a little bit, but not much ever happened with the company.

Murphey and I went on the road, and he asked me to play bass. The reason this is important is, up to this point, I was a folk singer and I was writing my own songs; I got a record deal on my own. Murphey says, "I got a tour back in Texas; come play bass with me." I said, "I don't know how to play bass." He said, "You'll learn. It's easy," and hands me the bass. From that point on, I stepped back from being out front to playing bass.

We went to Dallas and this fellow named Marty Caldwell that we knew says, "I know Bob Johnston, the guy that produced Bob Dylan, Simon and Garfunkel, Johnny Cash, Flatt and Scruggs, I mean you name it." So I said, "If you know him, have him come see us!" and by God he did! One Saturday afternoon, we were in the Rubyat in Dallas and played for Bob Johnston. We went to Nashville the next week and cut *Geronimo's Cadillac,* Murphey's first record.

Meanwhile, Gary Nunn had joined the Sparkles. Gary P. Nunn is from Brownfield, just outside of Lubbock. He ended up coming to Austin with the Sparkles, but they were playing all cover material. Murphey and I hit Austin and people started coming to see us at the Saxon Pub, when it was located over on I-35. That was *the* place in Austin at that point. Even before we made the *Cosmic Cowboy* record, Gary Nunn and Leonard Arnold and people in these rock bands started coming to see me and Murphey.

Here you have some Lubbock guys who are making part of this scene. The effect on Austin is that you have all these great musicians playing cover songs for fraternities at this point. Gary Nunn is just busting at the seams wanting to write his own songs. Nunn comes to see Michael Murphey playing his own songs, and Nunn is floored! He says, "I want to write and play my own songs."

Along about that time, I had been offered another job with Ray Wylie Hubbard's band Three Faces West for just tons of money, and Murphey was just crazy enough that I couldn't stand living with Murphey anymore. Gary Nunn was sitting there like this vulture, waiting for my job. He had heard Murphey needed a new bass player. I was so nervous, because I had seen Gary Nunn play with the Sparkles, and I thought he was the greatest. He was the bass player at that point, but he also sang and he played organ. Gary Nunn is a utility guy. So Gary got my job when I left Murphey.

Meanwhile, Bob Johnston says, "We gotta get Livingston back in the band." Murphey calls me and says, "I want you back in the band." So now Gary and I are in the same band playing with Michael Murphey. We started switching out instruments: I would play bass on one song, we would switch on the next song; I would play piano, he'd play organ; we both played mandolin. It was called the Interchangeable Band. Roland Swenson, the director of South by Southwest Music Festival, once sent me an e-mail saying, "I used to see you and Gary Nunn in the Interchangeable Band and that is why I'm doing South by Southwest to this day!" All these rock 'n' rollers started playing with these folkies, and that is where Cosmic Country came from.

Jerry Jeff Walker shows up in Austin. I had met him also at Red River, had hung out with him and Hubbard, so I called him up. I said, "Come and hang out. We're playing with Mike Murphey and have a little rehearsal studio." I remember the day Jerry Jeff comes and sticks his head in the door and you could see the light bulbs popping in his head. It was like "Instant band!" He had been in Red River writing all this good stuff, and had gotten a record deal with MCA and wanted to make it in Austin. Here we are, playing with Murphey, and Jerry Jeff's got an instant band. We went down to the first recording studio in Austin. All that they had was a sixteen-track tape recorder and burlap all over the walls; no soundboard. Couldn't even listen to playbacks. We cut the first Jerry Jeff record with "L.A. Freeway," "Charlie Dunn."

So Nunn and I are Murphey's touring band, but we made the record with Jerry Jeff. Jerry Jeff and Murphey played some of the same shows, so Nunn and I would play with both of them. We were onstage all day, and it was so much fun! We were twenty-something years old and thinking, "Are we actually making a record?" Nobody in Austin had a major record deal except Murphey and Jerry Jeff.

Then Willie Nelson hits town and comes to see us at a double concert at Mother Earth. I remember Eddie Wilson brought him, and Willie hears all the music, and sees half the people got long hair and beards and the other half are rednecks. They take him over to the Armadillo and it's the same way, and Willie said, "I'm moving here!"

The energy was just amazing. I wish I wasn't so stoned back then and would

BOB LIVINGSTON AND BAND.

have been able to take more advantage of the situation, because anything could have happened!

One little historic note: While I'm playing with Ray Wylie Hubbard and Three Faces West, Hubbard writes "Redneck Mother," but he was afraid to play it, afraid he was going to get beat up. We had barely long hair then but those were the days when some redneck might take exception. That was why he wrote "Redneck Mother" in the first place. I learn the song when I played with Hubbard. Then I go off and I play with Jerry Jeff, touring all over Kingdom Come. One night in Seattle, Jerry Jeff breaks a string and says, "Bob, play a song while I change this string." I thought, "Hmmm, I'll do 'Redneck Mother.'" People started pouring beer on their head, and they were all singing along by the second verse. They loved it! Jerry Jeff had me sing it again the next night. This is Jerry Jeff's plan to see how other people dig songs that he hadn't written. The third night he says, "Let's do that song 'Redneck Mother,' but this time, I'm going to sing it." So it became his song. We had already cut one record and it was just going through the roof. People love it. We were getting ready to do the second record, which ends up being ¡Viva Terlingua!

Gary Nunn had been to England with Murphey and he was hanging around not knowing what he was going to do. I said, "Gary, you have to come out here to Luckenbach and cut this record with us, for your own good." Nunn comes out and we cut the record and he says, "Here's a song I wrote when I was over in England. It's called the 'London Homesick Blues.'" So now we have "Redneck Mother" and "London Homesick Blues" on that record. Of course, "London Homesick Blues" became famous as the theme for Austin City Limits: "I wanta go home with the Armadillo . . ."

My big claims to fame are, at the end of "Redneck Mother" on ¡Viva Terlingua! I say, "That was a song by Ray Wylie Hubbard." And Gary Nunn sings "London Homesick Blues" on that album thanks to me. The recording in Luckenbach was the first time we had ever played that song; it was all live. It was so intense! People were hanging out of the rafters at the dance hall. Everybody from Austin had come over because we were cutting a live record. That had not been done before in this area of the world. They came all the way from New York City, this state-of-the-art, top-of-the-line mobile truck. What we were doing was funkier than hell, but they came. I mean, we were spaced out and Jerry Jeff was smashed, and he was writing songs on the spot.

CHRIS: The record sounds like that, which is one of the appealing things about it. It sounds like you are just sitting outside on the porch making stuff up.

BOB: *Absolutely!* I never understand it, when I listen to it lately, I think, "We were playing everything so slow and it's so weird and untogether." But people tell me, "That is what I love about it! I could do that!" And that record went gold, big-time. It is still a big-selling album.

Then we started the Lost Gonzo Band. Gary and I were the main singers and songwriters, along with John Inman. We left Jerry Jeff and started touring on our own. Then I got back with him, and Gary did his own thing. I had a family and I was able to make a living with Jerry Jeff; I mean, he was worldwide, so I just kept playing with him.

CHRIS: That brings us back here to Austin. What are you doing now?

BOB: My family is really interesting, strange, and cosmic. I got two boys who are real characters. My wife found a philosophical, cosmic place in India and took them over there to raise them in 1972. I would go over to India for six months, and then come back to the States and play. But I was starving to death half the time, paying for all that and just hanging out there, not working. I met a Fulbright Scholar named Frank Block over there in India. He told me about a program that the State Department has where they put you on the road if you are an expert in something. They have lawyers, musicians, artists, photographers, all kinds of people give programs for the State Department, disseminating information about American culture to win the hearts and minds of those folks. All over the world this program exists.

I'm trying to figure out how I can get gigs in India, because an American could not get a job there. India is such a closed society that anything you got, TVs, cars, whatever, is made there. They do not import anything, duty is so high. So a musician from the States cannot get a job as a touring band. But you can do it for the United States State Department.

I did a "History of American Folk and Country Music." I played some of my songs and did a lot of old cowboy stuff. That was in 1987, and I have done tours like that ever since.

As I did these tours, I would play with Indian players, the tabla and sitar, and they said at first [in an Indian-English accent], "You know, there is no way that the East and West can meet. No way, because we have different time signatures and all these different things. I don't think this will work. We will just play and then you play after." [Bob breaks out his guitar and begins strumming.] And I said, "I'm telling you it can meet!" They go, "I've heard it before and I don't know anything about this beat. It would not be good." And I go, "Look, just see if you can . . ." [Bob begins playing on his guitar the Bo Diddley beat chords that lead into Buddy Holly's classic "Not Fade Away."] [In the Indian accent:] "Oh you mean that beat! I know that beat! Oh, yes!"

I did this Buddy Holly, "I'm gonna tell you how it's gonna be . . ." accompanied by the sitar and tabla, and the people *love* it! I remember playing one time to an auditorium full of Indians, none of whom knew much of anything about America, many of the women with black scarves across their faces, all chanting with joy, "Love's for real! Not fade away!" They all understand that. They all understand "Love's for real, not fade away."

I put my cowboy stuff on and do this stuff all over India. I also went to Pakistan, Sri Lanka, Bangladesh, Nepal, Burma. My son Tucker and I went to Yemen, Syria, Kuwait, Jordan, Oman, all in the name of goodwill for America. We went to refugee camps in Pakistan. We went to Peshawar in the northwest frontier in the Hindu Kush, just east of the Khyber Pass. Here's a story for ya: The Russians are still in Afghanistan. I go into Peshawar to play, and the streets are filled with army trucks and rickshaws and bicycles and dead cats and camels and dirt; there is a gunsmith on every corner. People walking around with AK-47s. And refugee camps! Hundreds of thousands of Afghans are stowing away there. We were there to play at the university. I come in there and they say, "Bob, we got good news and bad news. The bad news is: There was a riot at the university and there is no gig there. But we are going to do it on the steps of the consulate."

We would play at the ambassador's house for an invited group of dignitaries from the government that might have gone to school in America, or at the U.S. consulate that invites certain people they are trying to target. They would introduce me, "Mr. Bob is here to play country music and to learn the country music of India." I did it as an educational program. I have had a thousand people come up to me and say, "I never knew what country music was until this very day."

Education has been big for me. When I came back here I got grants from the Texas Commission for the Arts, the Austin Arts Commission to do a similar program here in Texas. The money is used to pay the musicians so we can go out and perform at schools and do workshops. Through the grants, I have the money to pay my musicians to go into the schools during the day.

The program is called "Cowboys and Indians," and it is a meeting of East and West. It engenders a feeling of breaking down cultural barriers. It's Mahatma Gandhi and Sitting Bull meet Buddy Holly and Ravi Shankar. I have a tabla player, a sitar player, every once in a while my son Tucker plays with me, John Inman, Paul Pearcy on percussion. It's this cosmic thing, man.

Many musicians such as Meatloaf, Lee Ann Womack, Pat Green, and Cory Morrow were not originally from Lubbock but developed their love for music while attending Texas Tech University, Lubbock Christian College, or South Plains College. Some go on to make it big, like John Denver. Some simply fall in love with the local music scene and continue to live in relative anonymity. Like his better-known contemporaries Pat Green and Cory Morrow, WADE PARKS began playing music in restaurants and bars while attending Texas Tech University. Wade continues to perform acoustic music in Lubbock on weekends and seems content to do so.

Wade Parks

WADE: I grew up in Houston. My mom and dad are from Floydada, an hour northeast of Lubbock. Dad went to Texas Tech, and they lived in Lubbock for a while. I still have two aunts and uncles that live up here, so I have lots of cousins and family here.

My older sister came out here to go to Tech and she told me, "Wade, when you are ready to go to college, you need to check out Lubbock because it's fun." She knew Lubbock was a neat place. I came out here to go to college at Texas Tech. It took me the eight-year program to get out of college. I had been managing the Copper Caboose on 4th Street, which was a pool hall, game room, restaurant, and saloon over by the stadium. I used to book the Tejano bands there.

My brother Russell had turned me on to Jerry Jeff Walker and Robert Earl Keen in the late '80s. Russell came out here to go to graduate school at Tech. He was working at the rec center in the outdoor program there, and my brother told me, "You gotta meet this guy I work with. He's a bad-ass guitar player, and he sings some cool songs." This wound up being my friend Boone Law. His dad is a judge, Judge Law. Boone started writing songs and getting into that folk singer/songwriter scene by going to the Kerrville Folk Festival.

We got to hanging around with Boone and drank a lot of beer. The more we hung out with him, Boone would say, "Russell, we need to get him a guitar." I said, "What if I can't even play?" But all we were doing was banging on our guitars together. Boone got me to where I at least could strum a song. We started having big nights where everybody would come by and there would be eight or nine guitars, just for kicks, hanging out with buddies to play music. That's what's most fun, banging around, passing the time. It is cheap entertainment, an "experience," I guess you would say.

That same group that was picking guitars around the house started going out to see Cary Swinney at Great Scott's Barbecue, and that was where I met a lot of the local music folks. This little Mexican food place called Juan in a Million was the first place I saw Robin Griffin. At that time Robin was playing with Tony Adams and Braxton Howle, so it was the three of them and I was the only one there in the restaurant. It was just me and the bartender. Tony really didn't want to play to just one guy in the

SCENIC BUDDY HOLLY PARK.

audience, and Robin was saying, "This is our gig. We're playing!" I was just sitting there drinking my beer, waiting to see what was gonna happen. Robin talked them into playing, and I thought, "Man! That is *good* music!"

My buddies and I did not even know that element existed in Lubbock. We had heard so much about everything going on in Austin and how hot all the bands are down there. We kept thinking, "We should go to Austin. Imagine the bands!" Now I know better.

By this time, I was doing some gigs with a guy named Ryan Corpening. He is a killer guitar player. He lives in Amarillo now, playing up there. It was us two doing acoustic guitar songs. That was about the time when Robin Griffin left town. He had a different band at that time; that was Jay Hataway, Shawn Bailey, and Matthew McLarty. These guys are all awesome musicians. Ingrid Kaiter, who is Buddy Holly's niece, started singing with them, so that band stayed together. Ingrid then left the band to start a coffee shop in Levelland, so they were looking for a new singer.

This is what happened: Have you been over there to the Chicken Ranch? It's where Jay Hataway lives, and Mark Philbrick lives on the corner next door; in the adjoining backyard is an old chicken coop. They've got the structure of the coop still up, just the framework of the old chicken pen, but they've pioneered the shit out of it! They've got some old games that you can play, and areas that have couches. They have a room that's called the Gallery, where they've got some art up on the walls. It's just a makeshift structure but it's cool. Anyway, they have huge parties over there, and there's always someone sitting around playing, guys that Philbrick knows who you never see playing out on a stage anywhere but are just amazing pickers.

I had been hanging out some over at the Chicken Ranch and playing with those guys. One day, Jay Hataway called me and said, "We were wondering if you wanted to get together and play some music with us." And I said, "Cool! We usually pick on Thursdays and Fridays and sometimes on Tuesdays. Or are y'all gonna be getting together at the Chicken Ranch?" I thought he meant, "When do you want to hang out and play?"

Jay was like, "Uh, no, man. We want to put a combo together, and we want you for the front man." And I said, "Really?" So that was funny, how I even got into playing in a band. I thought he meant, "We're getting together tomorrow night, so bring some beer."

That's what they always say; the adage here in Lubbock is: "We play music because

there is nothing else to do." It's true. It's too windy to play ball. Music is a great way to get together. Another aspect of being out here is that if you don't interact with other people you can really go crazy from the loneliness. It's easy to become isolated in an environment like this. Maybe that has something to do with how social the music is. Somebody will throw a good party, and there'll be music there.

There is like a million bands here, it seems. They say there are more musicians per capita in Lubbock than anywhere else. I don't know. That may be just if you go to the music stores and ask. But there are more people advertising for bands, ads like "looking for a bass player" or "looking for a guitar player." You would think you were in Houston or some place bigger. And this is for a lot of different kinds of music.

I am much more comfortable here in Lubbock than in Houston. It took me awhile to feel that way. Once I realized that I could grow up enough to get a college degree, and then to find something like tuning your guitar, plugging in, playing on stage, and then the guy says, "Thanks for coming," and pays you, you think, "Wow. That was fun! That sounds like a pretty good idea!" But I'm more comfortable here in Lubbock. A lot of that might have to do with the music.

I have had a good time leaving town, like going up to Amarillo to watch Susan Gibson and the Groobees. To me, that's fun: To leave town and go see friends play, people that you know. It's fun to get out of Lubbock. I think everybody who lives out here in Lubbock ought to leave at least once a month. But I love it here.

I like living here. Strangely, my parents have said, "Are you sure you want to end up living in a place like this?" My mother actually called this place "godforsaken" not too long ago, and she's from here.

If I were living in Houston would I be pursuing music? I doubt it. I don't see the support for it. The people that are interested in music here in Lubbock are extremely interested in music. That's for sure. Whatever draws them to it, around here, they're serious about their music. But if you're asking about the music fans, that's me. I want to go see what else is going on.

I may not be in it forever, but I like this music biz here in Lubbock. I don't think sackers in a grocery store have this much fun.

COLIN GILMORE is a prominent Austin music performer and recording artist. Colin is Jimmie Dale Gilmore's son and grew up in Lubbock around such icons as the Hancock family, Jesse Taylor, Joe Ely, and Richard Bowden.

Gilmore

COLIN: I was in the Lubbock airport when I saw a poster on the wall about Lubbock's history, saying that Lubbock has a legacy of being very socially conservative and traditional but progressive in technology. Take Buddy Holly, there is a parallel there. In some ways Buddy was traditional. He sang nothing but love songs, and the music, while cutting-edge for the time, was based on real roots stuff. But at the time it was very radical, basing his music on the black culture, the blues, and on white country music, and also Mexican influences. Buddy Holly's music was roots, but to combine all those things at his time was very radical. And regarding technology, Buddy was really doing a lot of experimenting with the recording side of it, the engineering and mixing. That was one of his major influences on popular music.

Lubbock being technologically progressive and socially conservative might have given rise to all the artistic talent coming out of there. At the same time, it might have been what drove everybody away. All I can say is for myself, but I was always really turned off by Lubbock. I lived in Lubbock from the time I was four years old to when I was fourteen. By the time I got to be twelve or thirteen, I started listening to punk rock and heavy metal, and I started looking around Lubbock and thinking, "This place sucks! I don't want to live here. I don't like the people here." I was a bit disgusted at how my neighbors seemed to be in the twenty-first century materially, but the mentality had not changed a bit since way back when.

Now that I can look back at it and don't have to be there, Lubbock does seem kind of mysterious. Like watching a horror movie, you get this feeling of *"Wow!"* but are really glad you are not stuck in the middle of it.

CHRIS: You have a unique situation where both sides of your family have been in Lubbock for generations. Can you tell me a little bit about your grandfather?

COLIN: His name was William Brian Gilmore. I got my middle name Brian from him. He was a really great man. He grew up in Electra, Texas. He got his degree in Dairy and taught classes at Tech. He owned a dairy for a long time.

He was very active in getting Alcoholics Anonymous established in Lubbock. He was not an outspoken man, very humble, but a lot of people claim that he helped them achieve sobriety. He was an alcoholic himself, but when he died, he had over thirty-five years sober.

CHRIS: Common among many Lubbock artists is certainly a deep sense of spirituality. Of course, that spirituality is the backbone for someone in AA. I think people who listen to your father's music definitely hear spirituality there, the same with Joe, and Butch, and Terry Allen, and the Hancock family. It is all coming from a different direction but that spirituality is the backbone of a lot of it.

COLIN: Very much. I agree. My spiritual upbringing was very unorthodox. My first memories are of hanging out with the Hancock family and the Supernatural Family Band in Colorado, when our families were with Guru Maharaj Ji, a man from India who came over in the '70s as a teenager and had a huge following.

When I was growing up, I lived with my mom in Lubbock. We went to Agapé Methodist Church. That is my roots in Lubbock. My mother was always Christian, and now she goes to church pretty regularly, even though she was into Maharaj Ji for a time. She has never been a closed-minded type. My father never was much of a Christian. He has always been into Eastern philosophy, and now he is a Buddhist. There is a weird dichotomy going on.

My grandfather on my dad's side has always been very spiritual but I wouldn't say he was religious. He and my grandmother never really went to church much. But he was very active in AA and believed very strongly in God. He believed that each person's connection to God, whatever your religion might be, should be the most important thing in your life, even before family.

My grandparents on my mother's side have always been more traditional, orthodox, and very religious. My grandmother has always been very much a hard-core Christian. She has always gone to church regularly but she does not preach to other people. She advocates what she believes but she is a very strong believer in just being good to other people.

Most people from Lubbock have some kind of a Christian upbringing, Church of Christ, Methodist, or Baptist. But most of the people we know from Lubbock have had some connection to either Maharaj Ji or a religion other than Christianity.

CHRIS: You moved to Austin when you were fourteen to live with your dad. What are you doing these days?

COLIN: In high school, I was in a rockabilly band called Matt the Cat and the Gutter Rats with Marcia Ball's stepson and Alvin Crow's son. I was in a punk rock band called Sweat Lodge. Now I'm writing music and playing around Austin. People say they hear influences of everything from the Cars to the Clash to Dwight Yoakam. Country and punk rock are my main roots. I have gone on tour with my dad a couple of times. Each show I would get up and sing two songs. Other than that, I was a roadie and a driver.

I have my own band together now. I have recorded a couple of CDs which get some play around Austin. I definitely want a career in music. The reason that it has taken me so long is that I am a perfectionist. I tend to feel like it has to be exactly right or nothing at all. I am trying to overcome that so I can go forward and get stuff done.

CHRIS: Tell me some more about growing up among this community of Lubbock musicians.

COLIN: Richard Bowden and my mother got together when I was probably about two, and stayed together several years. They split up when I was five. Richard and I got to be really close. I traveled with him a bunch. All the traveling I did when I was young, I attribute to Richard. He took me to North Carolina, and New Mexico, and he took me to Mexico a couple of times. Now I have a love of traveling, and I think Richard brought that on. Richard is the kind of guy who, compared to a lot of adults I saw when I was young, tended to keep on living his own way. He lived out in the country and had a horse. A lot of people idealize that kind of lifestyle, but Richard stuck to it, whereas others just got regular jobs.

I am accidentally related to a lot of Lubbock musicians. I have always loved Jo Carol Pierce; she was married to my dad before my mom was. When I was young, I loved hanging around with Jo Carol. She lived in Austin, and I would come stay with her and my sister Elyse. Jo Carol is kind of the same way as Richard; she is not your average American at all.

My parents never married uninteresting people. My mother's third husband Danny Neal is not a musician, but he probably knows more Lubbock musicians than any of us put together. He owns a hair salon called the Bijou in an old theater in downtown Lubbock. He's an all-around great guy. Danny's played a huge part in the music scene, on the side, by introducing so many people. Danny is the type of guy who walks into a place and is friends with all the bikers and cowboys there, all the gays, all the musicians. He has introduced so many people to each other.

If you are one of those people born in Lubbock who is very unorthodox by nature or whose upbringing does not fit into that typical conservative way of looking at things, then you will desperately seek out like-minded companions to support you. If you don't have friends, you have nothing going for you in Lubbock.

This goes back to Lubbock being a spiritual place. Lubbock seems to me to be very simple. There is not much going on there. The land is nothing to look at. The streets are very predictable. They are all ordered "A-B-C" or "1-2-3." You never have any excuse to get lost in Lubbock. It seems like it is the same way with the mentality there. There is not much element of dissent there. When you are in the face of all that, in some ways it is hell. But also it can bring you back to yourself, because it is pure simplicity. If you want to have a quiet day and reflect on things, Lubbock is the place to do it. You can go out into an open cotton field and have all the peace and quiet you can stand.

CHRIS: A friend of mine once told me that they thought Lubbock is the perfect zendo.

COLIN: That is very possibly true. I remember when I was young, the moments of glory that I saw in Lubbock were on back porches. My parents would have parties centered around the back porch because that's where the bands would play.

Martha Fain is another person that I credit with partially raising me. She was Jesse Taylor's mother, and she was my babysitter. There was a period of time where I was staying at her house every day and every night, me and my younger sister Amanda.

That was the time when my parents were "unfit to raise anyone." Luckily they had Martha. We would sit around all day and watch soap operas and cartoons, and Kool-Aid and macaroni and cheese is all I ever remember eating at her house. She raised us on it.

She was real old, but she was one of the greatest people in the world. Dad told me that when he and Jesse were younger, they would bring all their hoodlum friends over, bikers, hippies. They were always in trouble with the law, and they sought refuge at Martha's house because she did not care what they were like. She would always take them in and stick up for them, no matter what. Talk about being wild and unorthodox, Jesse Taylor is really the one. He's the one that would hop on a train and never come back. Jesse lived life on the rough side. I guess having a son like Jesse, Martha would have to be open-minded to keep from going insane.

But I remember being at Martha's and feeling so complacent sitting on her back porch. It was a typical Lubbock backyard, just flat dirt. Her yard was kind of trashy, not much grass, an old beat-up swing set. But something about it was just absolutely beautiful, something about the lifestyle she lived. This neighborhood was fairly poor. She was very brave and strong just to be able to live by herself. My parents and all their friends, Jesse, Richard, Joe Ely, would all come over and drink a bunch of beer outside. They would set up a full electric band on the porch, and she was all for it.

My mom was a singer, too. She sang at Jug Little's Barbecue and at Stubb's. For a time she went by the name Loretta and the Leisure Brothers. She was also in the Ginger Blues Band. One time, she had been singing at Jug Little's for over three hours and Jug kept giving her more hundred-dollar bills, saying, "Please keep going! We have to keep the crowd happy." Finally she said, "No more, I'm tired!" The bouncer ended up chasing her around the place with a gun. Jug Little apologized about it later, but Mom said, "That's okay, I'm never going in there again."

CHRIS: What were your feelings when you left Lubbock to move to Austin?

COLIN: When I left Lubbock I was miserably depressed. I had just gotten out of eighth grade. I was sad to leave a few of my friends but most of the people I was very happy to leave. We were real troublemakers in Lubbock when we were teenagers because we realized that was all there was for us to do. People were doing drugs at thirteen, having sex at thirteen. I found Lubbock to be boring and very negative. I remember listening to Metallica all the time. Heavy metal is big in Lubbock, and it will probably never go out of fashion there.

CHRIS: How do you feel going back now?

COLIN: Generally I feel good. Recently, it has been a little depressing because of my granddad dying. That has taken a heavy toll and set me back to when I was just moving away from there: feeling trapped, nowhere to go, "Oh God! Get me out of here!" But at the same time, now that I can leave whenever I want and realize that the world is a much bigger place than Lubbock, it has a really special place in my heart. I still go there as often as I can. My family is still there.

CHRIS: Did you learn anything from living in Lubbock? What parts of your life did you get from Lubbock? Either positive things, or things you took as negative at the time but that you made something positive out of later?

COLIN: We talked about the dichotomy of people from Lubbock; the love-hate relationship with it. It's the same way I am with myself. Part of me wants to live the rock 'n' roll lifestyle and to have every day be up-and-going, interesting and different, meeting new people all the time. And part of me is just a small-town guy. I tend to spend most of my time out in the country with my parents. I can probably attribute some of that to my life in Lubbock. It is a dichotomy that oftentimes makes me in conflict with myself, but one that I have not shaken. Also, my rebellious side I attribute to Lubbock, and all the people I hung out with there who were desperately searching for something else.

Lubbock has produced a lot of country musicians, sure, but not what you would call traditional country. Joe Ely and my dad and Butch Hancock are not traditional country at all. And the biggest thing to come out of Lubbock since Buddy Holly has been Natalie Maines of the Dixie Chicks. Since Natalie joined the Chicks, they are mainstream, but they are shaking up the world of country music. To me, that is proof that the legacy goes on. Once something untraditional makes it out of there, like Waylon Jennings or Buddy Holly, the mainstream might pick up on it and make something huge out of it.

You are not going to turn Lubbock into a traditional place, even if 90 percent of the city is trying to make it that way. My brother-in-law Dan Yates once said that Lubbock is trying desperately to be like Dallas, but it never will be. Lubbock is always going to be a wild West Texas town and there is nothing they can do about it, try as hard as they will.

Winds of Heaven

from the EP 4 of No Kind

Well, the wind is yelling at windmills all
    around,
Spreading song like fire all over the
    sleepy town.
Western angel, take me in, never let me
    go again.
This is heaven now like heaven never
    knew herself before,
This is paradise on rolling plains,
Like heaven's kitchen floor,
And if you look outside the back screen
    door, and listen close and hard,
You'll see nothin' but the winds of
    heaven blowing,
Through heaven's backyard.

There's a girl on the corner of a street in
    my neighborhood,
With two eyes cryin' for as many as
    Jesus would,
For every wing broken, for every cloud
    out of reach,
For every word spoken, and nothin' left
    to teach.

Western angel, walk the line, turn her
    water into wine.
This is heaven now like heaven never
    knew herself before,
This is paradise on rolling plains like
    heaven's kitchen floor
And if you walk on out the back screen
    door, and hit the dusty town,
You'll see nothin' but the winds of
    heaven blowin' your heart around.

Renegades cast from heaven above,
    catch the world fire with your fool-
    hearted love
Cause I landed and I'm stranded in the
    hills of eternity,
Where I can't hear the wind and the
    wind can't hear me
Western angel if you take me home,
    never from you shall I roam.

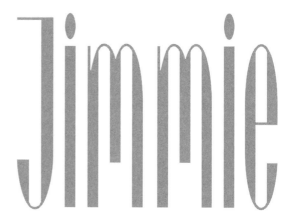

JIMMIE DALE GILMORE has been a central figure in the Lubbock and Austin music scenes for much of the last thirty years. Despite rarely being played on traditional country radio, Gilmore was named Country Music Performer of the Year by *Rolling Stone* magazine three times in the 1990s. Reunited in the twenty-first century with his friends Joe Ely and Butch Hancock as the Flatlanders, Gilmore is still touching souls with his mystical West Texas voice.

Dale Gilmore

JIMMIE: There is a paradox in my mind about Lubbock because in certain respects I don't think Lubbock is particularly unique. Because of my view of the interdependency of everything, I think it is always misleading and unreal to say that there was something special about *this* place in *this* time that produced this certain magic. I just don't think that it works like that.

I do believe that it seems like a disproportionate number of really creative people have come from Lubbock. Rather I should say, a large number of people have become known who came from that area. I don't think any place creates any more creative people than any other place.

I got to know Elvis' manager Colonel Tom Parker at the last of his life. He told me that to be a success and retain success in the music business, you have to have three things: talent, hard work, and luck. If any one of those things is missing, you can be a flash-in-the-pan, but for any real ongoing success, all three must happen. I think there is a large measure of this Lubbock phenomenon that is just luck, and that is the part that you cannot explain. There are talented people and people who work hard all over the place. I know lots that nobody ever heard of. I do not think you can pick out a single factor and say, "This is the explanation." I think it is more like, "So-and-so knew so-and-so, who knew so-and-so . . ." It is a cascade. Talking about why Lubbock is more magic or special than any other place is an artificial exercise, I think.

CHRIS: When you see groups of talented people like the Beats around Allen Ginsberg and Jack Kerouac, or the Lost Generation of Hemingway, Fitzgerald, and Stein, do you think that was luck?

JIMMIE: I absolutely believe that. It could have happened with a different group, at the same time, with just tiny things going differently. That is not to belittle anything that has been accomplished by any of those people. It reflects a tendency on my part to think that just regular, everyday people that nobody ever heard of in general are every bit as interesting and as talented as people that get all this spotlight put on them.

CHRIS: What if I told you that there are many young creative people living in Lubbock today who feel that local magic? Maybe it is because they see a direction to go, because they *believe* that there is something to all this?

JIMMIE: If there is something to inspire any young creative person, that is wonderful. I guess what I am saying is that I would prefer to see a premium put on the simple love of the art, the music, rather than the fame that comes from it. There are people that become famous only because of a giant drive to become famous, and there are other people who become famous because they happen to be good at what they do and blundered into the right circumstances.

To say that you were lucky enough to get to be aware of some really talented people that were to a large degree unnoticed, that is a whole different angle than saying, "Why does this place produce such special people," a different thought process. Many people already have this fixed idea that there is a special magical fountain of talent and genius in Lubbock. Reporters ask us, "What is it about Lubbock? Is it in the water?" Sometimes we will answer, "It was the flying saucers, the Lubbock Lights" or "It was the DDT spray trucks we all ran behind as kids." Those are the clichés; they are based on an unconscious presumption that there was a special magic in Lubbock that I just do not subscribe to.

CHRIS: Are you saying this phenomenon is merely a product of the observers, not any objective factors?

JIMMIE: It is a combination, I think. Like I said, I am aware that there are a disproportionate number of songwriters from that relatively small area, people that don't even know each other, people from several generations. But also, they are all generally within the realm of music that I am connected with personally, so that is why I know about them. It is true that, for some reason, there is an appealing flavor in the stream of creativity from this relatively small geographical area. But it also may partly be because they somehow had the vehicle to do so. That same thing might could have happened from any place if somehow the doors were open. If everything were truly equal, if the radio really and truly played all the genuinely talented people instead of somebody who happened to be the brother-in-law of somebody that had a hit song last month . . . see, those are the flukes that cannot be pinpointed.

I think something did happen that a string of interesting, talented, creative people came from this unlikely place of Lubbock. I just do not believe in all the clichés. I am not saying it isn't true there are a bunch of talented people who came from Lubbock.

CHRIS: Let's talk about some of your talented friends from Lubbock.

JIMMIE: I'll go through a short history of the way the whole scene developed. I was playing folk music just solo around Lubbock. Joe Ely and I had become acquaintances. He was playing solo too, and we were mutual fans of each other. I had met Joe when I was in high school but I didn't really know him until I started going to hear him play.

I met Buddy Holly's father, and he paid for me to do some demo recordings. We met through an English journalist whose name I don't even remember. This is so long ago, 1964 I'm talking about. Mr. Holley invited me over to their house one night while this writer was there. He had come to town and was amazed by how little known Buddy Holly was in Lubbock, because Buddy was an icon in England. This was about the same time the Beatles showed up in America.

It was this English journalist who introduced me to the Holley family. I did not know Buddy. I was a bit too young and had barely missed out on that section of the Lubbock development. But of course I was a fan. I had come from a country and western background, and Buddy's music probably appealed more to me as being rockabilly. My dad played guitar, and was a lover of honky-tonk music. Before we moved to Lubbock, when I was just a little bitty kid up in Tulia, he played in little local bands. He would play for money sometimes but not as his exclusive living.

When I met Mr. Holley, he liked my music and we became friends. At a certain point he said, "I don't really have a lot of money and I don't know much about the music business, but I think if you got some recordings together that maybe we could get some publishing going." He put out three or four hundred dollars. I had never seen that much money. I put a band together to do these recordings. I got the only musicians that I was aware of that were good. The band consisted of Joe Ely on bass, T. J. McFarland played drums, John Reed and Jesse Taylor on guitar, and Al Strehli on piano. But Al didn't really play in the band much. We did a lot of songs that Al had written, and part of the recordings we did with Al singing. I don't even know if those tapes still exist anymore. That was in the late '6os. The point is, that recording is what got us together. There was just something about that recording session. We all became such good friends. We already were friends, but we became a tight, close bunch of friends from that, and remain friends still. We had a friend named Tommy Nickel, or "T. Nickel." Our band was called the T. Nickel House Band because we practiced at Tommy Nickel's place, which was a big scene. We were like a combination of prehippie beatniks but with a Texan flavor.

Al Strehli was a huge inspiration to me because already back then, in his early twenties, he was writing music that to me stands with Bob Dylan and the Beatles to this day. Al is a poet more than just a songwriter. Al Strehli was a huge influence on me and all our circle of friends because his songs were so interesting and different.

Beginning with the T. Nickel House Band, Joe Ely and I have been partners in one way or another. We traveled together, hitchhiked and played as a duet all over the place. Both of us have spent a lot of time in Austin, together and separately.

The Hub City Movers was an extension of the T. Nickel House Band into Austin, a trio of me, John Reed, and T. J. McFarland. We had a following in Austin because we had a lot of friends. Our audience most of the times were just our friends, the people who we were living with. A lot of Lubbock friends were not musicians. In our circle, the music was always important but we never were exclusively a musicians' gang. These were creative people who were interested in everything. The music did bring a larger circle of friends together as something we held in common. But it was not the cause of our group forming.

The Hub City Movers was insane psychedelic country folk-rock. We were sloppy, never rehearsed, which was partly my fault. The Hub City Movers were the last house band at the Vulcan Gas Company; we played every Wednesday night. The history of Austin music intertwines with the Lubbock musicians. Folk and hard-core country mixing with the blues and rock 'n' roll, that was what the Austin music scene was about.

In the meantime, we had become friends with Jim Franklin the artist and Eddie Wilson, who founded the Armadillo World Headquarters. Franklin was with Eddie at a Hub City Movers gig at a place called the Cactus, which burned down later on. I believe the Cactus was right on the current spot of Threadgill's. During the break we all went out back in the alley, and Eddie saw that old armory across the way. He got the idea to go check on it, and it became the Armadillo World Headquarters. In the evolution from the Vulcan Gas Company to the Armadillo World Headquarters, we were part of that little circle of friends. The Hub City Movers played the grand opening of the Armadillo.

CHRIS: How did you end up back in Lubbock to put together the Flatlanders?

JIMMIE: Things started changing for me, personally, my whole perspective. What I was reading and becoming interested in was all shifting around. I went back to Lubbock.

Butch Hancock and I had been friends since we were twelve years old at Atkins Junior High School and all the way through school. At this time, Butch had been living in San Francisco, working for an architect as a photographer. I had been in Austin, for the preceding year or so, doing the Hub City Movers thing. And Joe had been touring Europe with a show called *Stomp,* a musical theater revue.

It so happened that we all came back to Lubbock within a few days of each other. I was hanging out with both of them, but separately. Butch and Joe did not know each other then, but I kept telling Joe, "You have to meet this old friend of mine that has been writing some really good songs." One night I took him over to Butch's house and from that night on the sparks that flew have affected my life and all of our lives ever since. It was a group of friends that later became called the Flatlanders. And that group of friends are still intertwined with each other.

During most of the period when the Flatlanders were living together in Lubbock, we did not have lots of actual gigs. Joe and I played more gigs as a duet than the band ever played together. We all lived in a house on 14th Street together and played primarily for fun. Sitting around the living room having fun was what the Flatlanders was all about. There are probably thirty people that could legitimately claim to be members of the Flatlanders, but they just were not there when we did the recording. That group on the original record became stamped as who the Flatlanders were, and most people don't even know about Tony Pearson and Steve Wesson. Butch, Joe, and I are a lot of the times the only ones that are thought of as the Flatlanders, and that is a misperception of the historical facts.

Some short time after Butch and Joe and I started hanging out together, Tony Pearson, who is one of my best friends from high school, was playing mandolin and Tony introduced me to Tommy Hancock. Tony took us over to his house, and in that period we started hanging out with the Hancock clan. That marked another platform, another stepping-off place.

We originally called ourselves the Supernatural Playboys. Tony Pearson had started a health food store called the Supernatural Food Company, and we hung around there playing music. When we went to Nashville later on to record the album, the Nashville people did not want to use that name Supernatural Playboys. So, stupidly I think, we decided to agree with them.

CHRIS: Where did the name Flatlanders came from?

JIMMIE: We changed it while we were in Nashville making the record. Somebody said in conversation, "It is so weird that it took a bunch of flatlanders to come to Nashville and show them how to play hillbilly music." And Steve Wesson said, "That's it! Flatlanders!" When Steve said that, all the rest of us liked it.

The original record was *Jimmie Dale and the Flatlanders* because I was actually the only one that signed the contract with them, which was dumb on my part. I really can't say that I was stupid; that was just what went on at the time. But we ended up completely cheated by that whole deal. On the other hand, we came out of the deal with a record. We did make a record in a Nashville studio, which was a good thing.

But those guys in Nashville did not have the slightest inkling that they could have made a huge splash with us, because at that time music like the Byrds, the Nitty Gritty Dirt Band, Poco, and the Flying Burrito Brothers, that amalgam of country

FLATLANDERS' HOMECOMING, SEPTEMBER 2001.

with the folk-rock hippie world, was getting big. We were the real thing, but they did not know what was going on at all. All they knew was that they liked this music but could not figure out any possible way of marketing it. They were dumb.

CHRIS: How did they discover your music in the first place?

JIMMIE: We had met Sylvester Rice, who was friends with all the KLLL deejays and was tied in with the radio world of Lubbock. Syl introduced us to Country Lou Dee, Lou Driver, who was on KDAV in Lubbock. It was Lou and Syl who organized us into making the demo tapes. We recorded them in Odessa.

We knew nothing about the music business. Joe was the one that knew the most about it, but he had no connection really with the country music world. Joe had been more involved with the rock world. On the other hand, we were not really particularly ambitious to begin with. We were not trying to do anything big. We did it just for fun. After we recorded the Flatlanders record, there was a period when we thought, "Oh, boy! We'll sell millions!" But that never had been the drive to begin with; it was not why the band was put together. It was a fluke that this even happened. It was a joke! You can tell from the name of the band. It was just for fun. It was just silly.

CHRIS: It is startling music. People listen to the Flatlanders and it is not what they expect to hear. People don't know exactly how to categorize it. After all these years, the Flatlanders have put out two more albums of new music, which have received quite a bit of acclaim.

JIMMIE: The real point now is that Joe and Butch and I like working together, and we want to do something that we enjoy doing. Now we all have more free time to spend together, and a little more understanding, both of the business and ourselves. We work together better than we did when we were younger.

We never were really serious about writing together until this later phase. Use to be, when we would get together we would end up being silly and writing a bunch of goofy songs. We all have improved musically, and in every other way. Plus the fact that all three of us were able to become successful independent of each other, Joe more so than us, but Butch and I both have done our own thing to the point that we have established ourselves as independent entities.

We enjoy working together, and there is a magic to the Flatlanders that even now is greater than the individual pieces. I feel like we are extremely blessed and lucky to have that. A lot of people our age are burned out and don't really have any avenue to do anything different. But with us, we are still the Flatlanders. We still can do that any time we want to and it is always fun.

Braver Newer World

from the album Braver New World

Tell me now that you know how
To greet the dawn each day.
Fearless and unfettered, stand
Before the sun and pray.
There's no controversy
Let silence judge your plea
For justice or for mercy.
They both will set you free.

Chorus:
It's a braver, newer world you've found,
Rolling 'round and 'round and 'round
    and 'round
It's a braver, newer world you've found.

Show me now that you know how
To play the winning game.
Laughing 'til the sky stands still
With neither praise nor blame.
There's still time for heaven,
Though we're already there.
The daily bread will leaven
All hope, all pain, all care.

Chorus repeats

Teach me now that you know how
To learn the learner's art.
Open with the master's myth
And play with all your heart.
Listen to your singing,
Love will be your voice.
The gift that you are bringing
Is all for all, your choice.

Chorus repeats

Midnight Train

from the album After Awhile *(also appears on the Flatlanders'* Wheels of Fortune*)*

That midnight train
Is a long and a slow one
Your seat is reserved
The brakeman is tired
Timetable set with exceptions for no one
No luggage allowed
No ticket required

It will be there
Right on time at the station
Even if midnight
must come at high noon
You will not know
That train's destination
And you'll not leave late
Nor one minute too soon

You may sit beside Fear
And go worse than lonely
Or travel with Trust
With Love and Faith restored
These choices you have
And these choices only
When that train rolls in
And you step aboard

Now, that whistle blows
It's already whinin'
If you listen close
You can hear it soft and clear
And that headlight burns
Yes, it's already shinin'
And you might as well choose
Right now
It's Love or Fear

MAC DAVIS established himself as a successful songwriter in 1969 and 1970 when Elvis Presley scored Top Ten hits with three of Mac's songs: "In the Ghetto," "Memories," and "Don't Cry Daddy." Throughout the 1970s, Davis recorded several hit songs of his own, including "I Believe in Music," "Baby Don't Get Hooked on Me," and "It's Hard to Be Humble," and he made Lubbock famous with his song "Texas in My Rearview Mirror." From 1974 to 1976, he starred in his own NBC variety show, *The Mac Davis Show*. He was awarded Favorite Male Performer at the first People's Choice Awards in 1973. The Academy of Country Music named him Entertainer of the Year in 1975. Davis also has starred in movies such as *North Dallas Forty* and *The Sting II*, and played the title role in the original Broadway production of *The Will Rogers Follies*. On July 31, 2004, Lubbock honored Mac Davis by renaming downtown 6th Street "Mac Davis Lane."

Mac Davis

MAC: When I was a little boy, I was starting to learn to read on my own so my parents put me in Mrs. Jacksman's private school at five years old because I was too young to go to public school. When I was old enough to go to public school, they put me in the third grade, because I already knew how to read and write. I graduated early from Lubbock High School at age sixteen because I had skipped two grades.

I went to college in Atlanta at Emory University but did not last very long in college. I moved to Los Angeles in 1966. I have lived in L.A. ever since.

CHRIS: At what point did you decide to be a musician and performer?

MAC: When I was a kid in Lubbock, I saw Buddy Holly driving down the street with a bunch of girls in his convertible. That was the exact moment I decided I wanted to be a singer. It says it right there in the song: "If Buddy Holly could make it that far, I figured I could too." That had a lot to do with it; that and ol' Elvis.

CHRIS: Did you see music as your ticket out of Lubbock?

MAC: No, I never saw it that way. Music is just what I love. I loved music and thought, "This is something that I can do." Music was something I was born with. Any natural musical ability and talent with words that I have and was able to develop was a gift from God.

CHRIS: Do you think Buddy Holly is the impetus for all the talent that has arisen in Lubbock over the years?

MAC: No, I think there is talent in every little town and city in the world. It either pops up or it doesn't. I am not taking credit away from Buddy Holly. I just think it was there all the time. I think there are a lot of people probably sitting there right now in Lubbock just waiting to be discovered.

CHRIS: What was Buddy's influence on you?

MAC: He was a little older than me. I used to go to Lawton's Roller Rink down on College Avenue and watch him play. I roller-skated, but also I would take the skates off and hang around for the fight later when Buddy would play. I got a big kick out of that movie on Buddy's life, when they showed the teenyboppers standing around in their poodle skirts and roller skates on. In all honesty, most everybody took off their skates real quick when the music started, for a couple of reasons, to dance and in case a fight started you did not want to be on roller skates.

I have nothing but good memories about Lubbock when I was a kid. I don't do too many interviews anymore, but I always had a stock answer when people would ask what Lubbock was like. I would always say that if I was going to have a flat tire without a spare, Lubbock is where I would like to be.

CHRIS: I have heard you felt like some people in Lubbock misinterpreted "Happiness Is Lubbock, Texas, in My Rearview Mirror," that some people thought you were putting down your hometown. Obviously, the song is your reconciliation with Lubbock. Please comment on that song, in particular.

MAC: I got a little grief. I remember coming into Lubbock, the last time I played a big date there, and seeing a sign coming into town that said, "You're right, Mac Davis. Happiness is Lubbock, Texas. Period." I thought, "Wait a minute; didn't they hear the end of the song?"

Basically, that song is explaining what every teenage kid goes through in life. If you lived in Dallas, then it is "Happiness is Dallas in my rearview mirror." Every kid is going through that rebellion in their teens and they want to get away from home and start their own life. Then all of a sudden, it's like that old saying: "When I was fifteen, my daddy was the dumbest guy I had ever met in my life. It's amazing how much that ol' guy has learned in the last twenty years." We all have a turning point in our lives where you look back and your roots are very important to you.

Everything started happening for me in Los Angeles. L.A. was where I met Elvis and where I got my television show. But now I live a pretty quiet life. I do come back to Lubbock every once in a while. In fact, it's kind of fun because frankly nobody knows who I am anymore when I come to Lubbock, because I am pretty much retired. Other than doing *The Will Rogers Follies,* I have been retired for over fifteen years. So when I come to Lubbock, almost nobody knows me. You go through the other side of fame for twenty years, and it is nice to be anonymous once in a while, to sit back and observe and not have to be on your toes all the time.

CHRIS: You have been fortunate to do just about everything, TV, Broadway, tours, songwriting, movies. What do you enjoy the most?

MAC: I am a songwriter. I love the process of sitting down and writing a song, coming up with a melody and different words. I tell everybody that my tombstone will say: "Mac Davis, De-Composing."

I consider myself a songwriter at heart. Everything else has been gravy.

In all honesty, my favorite song I have ever written is "Texas in My Rearview Mirror." It's what I am and who I am, and besides it has a good rhyme scheme and melody. I cannot tell you how many other songwriters come up to me and say they love that song. I'll give you an example: Clint Black is a friend of mine. One time we were talking about the line where I said, "If Buddy Holly could make it that far, I figured I could too." Clint said to me, when he was seventeen and he was playing at some bar in Houston, lying about his age, and wondering if he was ever going to make it and whether it was all worth it, Clint said that every time that he would hear that song played he would think, "If Mac Davis can make it that far I figure I can too." So it inspired a lot of people that were just like I was when I was a kid. Like I said, I think every kid feels that way whether they live in Dallas or New York or wherever; they can't wait to get away from home. All of a sudden they grow up and think, "I didn't have it so bad."

CHRIS: You mentioned your relationship with Elvis earlier; Elvis had several hit songs which you wrote. How did that come about?

MAC: Actually, I had another big hit with Elvis a long time after he died. The remix of "A Little Less Conversation" was a big hit in 2002. I wrote that specifically with

Aretha Franklin in mind, but that was my first record I had with Elvis. It just happened to fit into this movie that Elvis was doing at the time. That is how the songwriting business works. Some people write specifically for an artist, and some like me just write the song and if I get lucky, somebody cuts it. But I don't pursue that. That is the part of the music business that I hate. The one part of being a songwriter that I do not like is the part of trying to get a song recorded, being a salesman. I am not much of a salesman. I write them and half the time just sit around and play them for my friends. Once in a while, somebody like Elvis cuts one.

But I am retired now. I was recently inducted into the Songwriter Hall of Fame, but that doesn't mean anything to my teenage kids. These things are very nice, but the one honor that is going to be the most important to me is my little Mac Davis Day in Lubbock. "Lubbock in My Rear View Mirror" pretty much said it; I'll be coming back to Lubbock, but at least I'll be coming back alive.

My favorite thing about Lubbock is that if you get lost, you can stand up on your bumper and look around and you will see where it is you are trying to get to. It's a beautiful place. You get outside Lubbock and drive around and you can find beauty out there. But what is great about Lubbock is the people; they are the salt of the earth. I wrote the song "It's Hard to Be Humble," but it's not really. I'm very grateful that Lubbock has acknowledged my contributions. I have also written a sequel to that song: "It's Hell to Get Old."

CHRIS: Do you have any advice for Lubbock artists who may be thinking, "If Mac Davis could do it, I figure I can too"? What would that advice be?

MAC: I would tell them to get themselves a day job that they really are good at. I am serious, I tell that to all songwriters and singers. There is about one in a million of us, whether we are good or not, that really get lucky and are in the right place at the right time. I bet there are a hundred songwriters in Lubbock right now that are really good. But to be at the right place at the right time, that is the hard part. Therefore, you need to find your second most favorite thing in the world and pursue it and be good at it, so you always have that to fall back on. You still have your guitar and you can entertain your family and friends and have a great time, play local gigs, do whatever you want. But you still have that good job to fall back on. Because there is nothing worse than a bitter starving artist walking around saying, "Won't nobody give me a chance, and I'm starving for my art." Sorry, you need to find something else you do just as well. But do continue to pursue the music and to pursue it with great vigor, because then you will get pleasure out of it whether you make it or not.

Texas in My Rear View Mirror

from the album Texas in My Rear View Mirror

I was just fifteen and out of control
Lost to James Dean and Rock-n-Roll
I knew down deep in my country soul that
    I had to get away
And Hollywood was a lady in red
Who danced in my dreams as I tossed in
    bed
I knew I'd wind up in jail or dead
If I had to stay

I thought happiness was Lubbock, Texas, in
    my rear view mirror
My mama kept calling me home but I just
    did not want to hear her
And the vision was gettin' clearer in my
    dreams

So I lit out one night in June
Stoned on the glow of the Texas moon
Hummin' an old Buddy Holly tune called
    Peggy Sue (Pretty, pretty Peggy Sue)
With my favorite jeans and a cheap guitar
I ran off chasin' a distant star
If Buddy Holly could make it that far
I figured I could too

And I thought happiness was Lubbock,
    Texas, in my rear view mirror
My mama kept calling me home but I just
    did not want to hear her
And the vision was gettin' clearer in my
    dreams

But the Hollywood moon didn't smile the
    same old smile that I'd grown up with
The lady in red just wanted my last dime
And I cried myself to sleep at night
Too dumb to run, too scared to fight
And too proud to admit it at the time

So I got me some gigs on Saturday nights
Not much more than orchestrated fights
I'd come home drunk and I'd tried to write
But the words came out wrong
Hell bent and bound for a wasted youth
Too much gin and not enough vermouth
And no one to teach me how to seek the
    truth before I put it in a song

And I still thought happiness was Lubbock,
  Texas, in my rear view mirror
My mama kept calling me home but I just
  could not, would not hear her
And the vision was gettin' clearer in my
  dreams

Well I thank God each and every day
For giving me the music and the words to
  say
I'd have never made it any other way. He
  was my only friend
And now I sleep a little better at night
and when I look in the mirror in the
  mornin' light
The man I see was both wrong and right
And he's going home again.

I guess happiness was Lubbock, Texas, in
  my rear view mirror
But now happiness is Lubbock, Texas,
  growing nearer and dearer
and the vision is gettin' clearer in my
  dreams
And I think I finally know what it means
And when I die you can bury me in
  Lubbock, Texas, in my jeans

Selected Discographies

All songs written by Terry Allen

1975 *Juarez*, 1980, LP album, Fate Records; 1992, CD and audiocassette reissue, Fate Records; 2004, CD reissue (liner notes by Dave Alvin), Sugar Hill Records #1077.

1. Juarez Device (aka "Texican Badman")
2. Characters/A Simple Story
3. Cortez Sail
4. Border Palace
5. Dogwood
6. Writing on Rocks across the USA
7. Radio . . . and Real Life
8. There Oughta Be a Law against Sunny Southern California
9. What of Alicia
10. Honeymoon in Cortez
11. Four Corners
12. Run South
13. Jabo/Street Walkin' Woman
14. Cantina Carlotta
15. Despedida (The Parting)
16. Camino

1978 *Lubbock: on everything*, LP double-record album, Fate Records; 1992, CD reissue, Special Delivery/Topic Records, London; 1995, CD reissue, Sugar Hill Records #1047.

1. Amarillo Highway
2. High Plains Jamboree
3. The Great Joe Bob (A Regional Tragedy)
4. The Wolfman of Del Rio
5. Lubbock Woman
6. The Girl Who Danced Oklahoma
7. Truckload of Art
8. The Collector (and the Art Mob)
9. Oui (A French Song)
10. Rendezvous USA
11. Cocktails for Three
12. The Beautiful Waitress
13. Blue Asian Reds (For Roadrunner)
14. New Delhi Freight Train
15. FFA
16. Flatland Farmer
17. My Amigo
18. The Pink and Black Song
19. The Thirty Years Waltz (For Jo Harvey)
20. I Just Left Myself

1980 *Smokin' the Dummy*, LP album, Fate Records; 1995, CD reissue, Sugar Hill Records #1057 (with *Bloodlines*).

1. The Heart of California
2. Whatever Happened to Jesus (and Maybelline)?
3. Helena Montana
4. Texas Tears
5. Feeling Easy
6. The Night Cafe
7. Roll Truck Roll
8. Red Bird
9. The Lubbock Tornado

1984 *Bloodlines*, LP album, Fate Records; 1995, CD reissue, Sugar Hill Records #1057 (with *Smokin' the Dummy*).

1. Bloodlines (I)
2. Gimme a Ride to Heaven Boy
3. Cantina Carlotta
4. Ourland
5. Oh Hally Lou
6. Oh What a Dangerous Life
7. Manhattan Bluebird
8. There Oughta Be a Law against Sunny Southern California
9. Bloodlines (II)

1987 *Amerasia*, LP album, sound track for film *Amerasia* by Wolf-Eckert Buhler, recorded with the Panhandle Mystery Band, Lubbock, Texas, and Surachal Jantimorn and Caravan, Bangkok, Thailand, Fate Records; 2003, CD reissue of sound track by T. Allen (liner notes by David Byrne), Sugar Hill Records #1076.

1. Amerasia
2. My Country 'Tis of Thee
3. The Burden
4. Back Out of the World
5. Swanlake
6. Display Woman/Displaced Man
7. Lucy's Tiger Den
8. Chop Sticks/Thai Sticks
9. Nobody's Goin' Home (Friendship Highway)
10. Metrapab
11. Church Walking
12. Food Stall
13. Canal
14. Sawahdi (Christmas Song)
15. Orphans
16. Pataya
17. Let Freedom Ring

1992 *The Silent Majority (Terry Allen's Greatest Missed Hits)*, CD, Sugar Hill Records #1079.

1. Advice to Children
2. Yo Ho Ho
3. Home on the Range
4. I Love Germany
5. The Burden
6. Big Ol' White Boys
7. Arizona Spiritual
8. Oh Tired Feet
9. Rollback
10. Cocktail Desperado
11. 3 Finger Blues
12. Oh Mom
13. High Horse Momma
14. New Delhi Freight Train
15. Loneliness (Rockin' by Momma Lonesome Rose Lonely Road)
16. Heart's Road

1993 *Pedal Steal/Rollback*, CD, two sound tracks by T. Allen, Fate Records #7655260.

1. Fenceline
2. Rodar Parar Atras
3. Rollback
4. Figure Ate
5. Home on the Range
6. Further Away
7. French Home
8. Pedal Steal—In Memory of Wayne Gailey

1996 *Human Remains*, CD and audiocassette, Sugar Hill Records #1050.

1. Gone to Texas
2. Room to Room
3. Back to Black
4. Wilderness of This World
5. Little Sandy
6. Buck Naked
7. What of Alicia
8. That Kind of Girl
9. Galleria Dele Armi
10. Crisis Site 13
11. Peggy Legg
12. After the Fall
13. Flatland Boogie

1999 *Salivation*, CD, Sugar Hill Records #1061.

1. Salivation
2. The Doll
3. Billy the Boy
4. Southern Comfort
5. Rio Ticino
6. Red Leg Boy
7. Cortez Sail
8. Xmas on the Isthmus
9. Ain't No Top 40 Song
10. The Show
11. Give Me the Flowers

Selected Compilations Featuring Songs by Terry Allen

1994 *Songs from Chippy,* produced by Joe Ely and Terry Allen; written and performed by Joe Ely, Terry Allen, Butch Hancock, Robert Earl Keen, Wayne Hancock, Jo Harvey Allen, and Jo Carol Pierce; Hollywood Records HR-61609-2.
Songs by Terry Allen:
  6. Gonna California
  8. Fate with a Capital F
 16. Boomtown Boogie

1986 *The Sounds from True Stories* (movie soundtrack CD), Sire Records #255151.
Song by Terry Allen:
Cocktail Desperado (cowritten with David Byrne)

All compositions by Mac Davis

1971   *I Believe in Music*, Columbia C-30926.

1. I Believe in Music
2. Hollywood Humpty Dumpty
3. Little Less Conversation
4. In the Eyes of My People
5. Watching Scotty Grow
6. Yesterday and You
7. Christmas Carol
8. Sarah between the Lines
9. Something's Burning
10. Poem for My Little Lady

1972   *Baby Don't Get Hooked on Me*, Columbia KC-31770.

1. Dream Me Home
2. Lonesomest Lonesome
3. Everybody Loves a Love Song
4. Naughty Girl
5. Friend Lover Woman Wife
6. Half and Half (Song for Sarah)
7. Spread Your Love on Me
8. Whoever Finds This I Love You
9. Poor Boy Boogie
10. Baby Don't Get Hooked on Me
11. Words Don't Come Easy

1973   *Mac Davis*, Columbia KC-32206.

1. Way You Look Today
2. Everything a Man Could Ever Need
3. Sunshine
4. I'll Paint You a Song
5. Woman Crying
6. Feel Like Crying
7. I Hope You Didn't Chop No Wood
8. Lovin' You Lovin' Me
9. Beginning to Feel the Pain
10. Your Side of the Bed

1973   *Stop and Smell the Roses*, Columbia KC-32582.

1. Stop and Smell the Roses
2. Soft Sweet Fire
3. Sweetest Song
4. Two Plus Two
5. Birthday Song
6. One Hell of a Woman
7. Poor Man's Gold
8. Rufus Was a Redneck
9. Kiss It and Make It Better
10. Good Friends and Fireplaces

1974 *All the Love in the World*, Columbia KC-32927.
1. Rock-n-Roll (I Gave You the Best Years of My Life)
2. I Still Love You (You Still Love Me)
3. Boogie Woogie Mama
4. Magic Mystery
5. Every Woman
6. If You Add All the Love in the World
7. Freedom Trail
8. Smiley
9. Fall in Love with Your Wife
10. Emily Suzanne
11. Biff the Friendly Purple Bear

1975 *Burning Thing*, Columbia KC-33551.
1. Burning Thing
2. I Feel the Country Callin' Me
3. Put Another Notch in Your Belt
4. Special Place in Heaven
5. Honeysuckle Magic
6. You're Gonna Love Yourself
7. I Still Love You
8. Hits Just Keep On Coming
9. Sweet Dreams and Sarah
10. Rufus Was a Redneck
11. Jimmy Brown Song

1976 *Forever Lovers*, Columbia PC-34105.
1. Good Times We Had
2. I'm Just in Love
3. Forever Lovers
4. Tears in My Baby's Eyes
5. I'm a Survivor
6. Baby I Just Ain't the Man for You
7. Please Tell Her That I Said Hello
8. I Won't Want to Own You
9. Love Lamp
10. Every Now and Then

1976 *Thunder in the Afternoon*, Columbia PC-34313.
1. Thunder in the Afternoon
2. Picking Up the Pieces of My Life
3. Morning Side
4. Plastic Saddle
5. Do It
6. Please Be Gentle
7. Jennifer Johnson
8. Where Did the Good Times Go
9. Play Me a Little Traveling Music
10. When I Dream

1978 *Fantasy*, Columbia KC-35284.

1. Music in My Life
2. You Are
3. I Don't Want to Get Over You
4. Dreams That Last Forever
5. Shee Moe Foe
6. Fantasy
7. For No Reason at All
8. Sad Girl
9. Melting in the Moonlight
10. If There Were Only Time for Love

1979 *It's Hard to Be Humble*, Casablanca NB-7207.

1. It's Hard to Be Humble
2. Greatest Gift of All
3. Let's Keep It That Way
4. It Was Time
5. Gravel on the Ground
6. Tequila Sheila
7. I Will Always Love You
8. Why Don't We Sleep on It
9. I Wanta Wake Up with You
10. I Know You're Out There Somewhere

1980 *Texas in My Rear View Mirror*, Casablanca NB-7239.

1. Texas in My Rear View Mirror
2. Hooked on Music
3. Remember When
4. Me'n Fat Boy
5. Hot Texas Night
6. Sad Songs
7. Hello Hollywood
8. Rodeo Clown
9. Secrets
10. In the Eyes of My People

1981 *Midnight Crazy*, Casablanca NB-7257.

1. Midnight Crazy
2. Dammit Girl
3. I Got the Hots for You
4. You're My Bestest Friend
5. Comfortable
6. Fantasies
7. You Are So Lovely
8. Kiss and Make It Better
9. Something's Burning
10. Float Away

1982 *Forty 82*, Casablanca NB-7274.

1. Lying Here Lying
2. It's Written All over Your Face
3. Late at Night
4. Love You Ain't Seen the Last of Me
5. Beer Drinkin' Song
6. She's Steppin' Out
7. Good Old Boys
8. Shame on the Moon
9. Spending Time Making Love and Going Crazy
10. Quiet Times

1982 *Beginning*, Plantation PLP-49.

1. Honey Love
2. With a Little Touch of Love
3. I Wish I'd Said That
4. You're Ridin' for a Fall
5. Standing in the Need of Love
6. Be a Good Little Girl When I'm Gone
7. Pick Hit of the Week
8. Don't Say No

1983 *Who's Lovin' You*, Columbia FC-38950.

1. Silence on the Line
2. It Was Always You
3. Crazy Again
4. Closest Thing to Love
5. Hey Girl
6. I Wanna Make It with You Tonight
7. Country Love
8. Who's Lovin' You
9. Two of a Kind
10. When It's Just You and Me

1984 *Volume XC*, Allegiance AV-5019.

1. Sweet Was Our Love
2. Boys Ain't Supposed to Cry
3. Little Dutch Town
4. Be a Good Little Girl While I'm Gone
5. Let 'Em Try
6. Pick Hit of the Week
7. Weep Little Girl Weep
8. Don't Say No
9. I Wish I'd Said That
10. Work

1984 *Losers*, Allegiance AV-5031.

1. Losers
2. Man Don't Cry
3. Once Was the Time of Man
4. Standing in the Need of Love
5. Hey Monkey
6. Honey Love
7. Lookin' at Linda
8. You're Ridin' for a Fall
9. Poor Loser
10. With a Little Touch of Love

1984 *Soft Talk*, Mercury #818131.

1. Caroline's Still in Georgia
2. Good News Bad
3. Patch of Blue
4. Most of All
5. Soft Talk
6. Springtime Down in Dixie
7. Nickel Dreams
8. Put a Bar in My Car
9. Deep Down
10. I've Got a Dream

1985 *Till I Made It with You*, MCA #5590.

1. Never Made Love (Till I Made It with You)
2. Too Big for Words
3. Shake Ruby Shake
4. Rainy Day Lovin'
5. Regrets
6. Special Place in Heaven
7. Save That Dress
8. I Think I'm Gonna Rain
9. I Feel That Country Callin' Me
10. Sexy Young Girl

1986 *Somewhere in America*, MCA #5718.

1. Somewhere in America
2. It Ain't Cool to Be Crazy about You
3. Bottom Line Blue
4. Ode to a City Girl
5. After the Lights Go Down Low
6. Looking at You
7. I Need a Hug
8. Naughty Girl
9. Last Dance at the Old Texas Moon
10. You Make the Living Worthwhile

1994 *Will Write Songs for Food*, Columbia CK-64444.

1. Southern Cookin'
2. In the Ghetto
3. Full Moon
4. Everyone but Me and You
5. Same Old Song and Dance
6. Texas in My Rear View Mirror
7. Back from the Dead
8. Plain Old Love
9. Watchin' Scotty Grow
10. It Only Hurts When I'm Awake
11. If She Hadn't Broken My Heart
12. Life Is Hard
13. Brand New Lease on Life

1977 *Joe Ely*, MCA Records MCA-2242; 2000, CD rerelease, MCA Records MCAD-10219.

1. I Had My Hopes Up High (Joe Ely)
2. Mardi Gras Waltz (Joe Ely)
3. She Never Spoke Spanish to Me (Butch Hancock)
4. Gambler's Bride (Joe Ely)
5. Suckin' a Big Bottle of Gin (Butch Hancock)
6. Tennessee Is Not the State I'm In (Butch Hancock)
7. If You Were a Bluebird (Butch Hancock)
8. Treat Me Like a Saturday Night (Jimmie Gilmore)
9. All My Love (Joe Ely)
10. Johnny's Blues (Joe Ely)

1978 *Honky Tonk Masquerade*, MCA records MCA-2333; 2000, CD rerelease, MCA Records MCAD-10220.

1. Cornbread Moon (Joe Ely)
2. Because of the Wind (Joe Ely)
3. Boxcars (Butch Hancock)
4. Jericho (Butch Hancock)
5. Tonight I Think I'm Gonna Go Downtown (Jimmie Dale Gilmore, John Reed)
6. Honky Tonk Masquerade (Joe Ely)
7. I'll Be Your Fool (Joe Ely)
8. Fingernails (Joe Ely)
9. West Texas Waltz (Butch Hancock)
10. Honky Tonkin' (Hank Williams)

1979 *Down on the Drag*, MCA Records MCA-698; 1991, CD rerelease, MCA Records MCAD-10221.

1. Fools Fall in Love (Butch Hancock)
2. BBQ and Foam (Ed Vizard)
3. Standin' at the Big Hotel (Butch Hancock)
4. Crazy Lemon (Joe Ely)
5. Crawdad Train (Joe Ely)
6. In Another World (Butch Hancock)
7. She Leaves You Where You Are (Joe Ely)
8. Down on the Drag (Butch Hancock)
9. Time for Travelin' (Joe Ely)
10. Maria (Joe Ely)

1980 *Live Shots*, MCA Records MCA-5262; 1993, CD rerelease, MCA Records MCAD-10816.

1. Fingernails (Joe Ely)
2. Midnight Shift (Jimmie Ainsworth, Earl Lee)
3. Honky Tonk Masquerade (Joe Ely)
4. Honky Tonkin' (Hank Williams)
5. Long Snake Moan (traditional, arranged and adapted by Joe Ely)
6. I Had My Hopes Up High (Joe Ely)
7. She Never Spoke Spanish to Me (Butch Hancock)
8. Johnny's Blues (Joe Ely)
9. Fool's Fall in Love (Butch Hancock)
10. Boxcars (Butch Hancock)

1981 *Texas Special*, SouthCoast Records EP EPS-1736; included as extra tracks on the 1993 *Live Shots* MCA CD rerelease.

1. Crazy Lemon (Joe Ely)
2. Not Fade Away (Norman Petty, Charles Hardin)
3. Treat Me Like a Saturday Night (Jimmie Gilmore)
4. Wishin' for You (Butch Hancock)

1981 *Musta Notta Gotta Lotta*, MCA Records MCA-5183; 1991, CD rerelease, MCA Records MCAD-815.

1. Musta Notta Gotta Lotta (Joe Ely)
2. Dallas (Jimmie Gilmore)
3. Wishin' for You (Butch Hancock)
4. Hold On (Joe Ely)
5. Rock Me Baby (Shorty Long, Susan Heather)
6. I Keep Gettin' Paid the Same (Joe Ely)
7. Good Rockin' Tonight (Roy Brown)
8. Hard Livin' (David Halley)
9. Road Hawg (Butch Hancock)
10. Dam of My Heart (Joe Ely)
11. Bet Me (Joe Ely)

1984 *Hi-Res*, MCA Records MCA-5480; not available on CD.

1. What's Shakin' Tonight (Eddie Beethoven, Joe Ely)
2. Cool Rockin' Loretta (Eddie Beethoven, Joe Ely)
3. Madame Wo (Joe Ely)
4. Dream Camera (Joe Ely)
5. Letter to Laredo (Joe Ely)
6. She Gotta Get the Gettin' (Joe Ely)
7. Lipstick in the Night (Joe Ely)
8. Imagine Houston (Joe Ely)
9. Dame Tu Mano (Joe Ely)
10. Locked in a Boxcar with the Queen of Spain (Joe Ely)

1987   *Lord of the Highway,* Hightone Records HT-8008; 1990, CD rerelease, Hightone Records HCD-8008.

1. Lord of the Highway (Butch Hancock)
2. Don't Put a Lock on My Heart (Eddie Beethoven)
3. Me and Billy the Kid (Joe Ely)
4. Letter to LA (Joe Ely)
5. No Rope Daisy-O (Joe Ely)
6. My Baby Thinks She's French (Joe Ely)
7. Everybody Got Hammered (Joe Ely)
8. Are You Listenin' Lucky? (Joe Ely)
9. Row of Dominoes (Butch Hancock)
10. Silver City (Joe Ely)
11. Screaming Blue Jillions (CD only) (Joe Ely)

1988   *Dig All Night,* Hightone Records HT-8015; 1990, CD rerelease, Hightone Records HCD-8015.

1. Settle for Love (Joe Ely)
2. For Your Love (Joe Ely)
3. My Eyes Got Lucky (Joe Ely)
4. Maybe She'll Find Me (Joe Ely)
5. Drivin' Man (Joe Ely)
6. Dig All Night (Joe Ely and Mitch Watkins)
7. Grandfather Blues (Joe Ely)
8. Jazz Street (Joe Ely)
9. Rich Man, Poor Boy (Joe Ely)
10. Behind the Bamboo Shade (Joe Ely)
11. I Didn't Even Do It (CD only) (Joe Ely)

1990   *Live at Liberty Lunch,* MCA Records MCAD-10095.

1. Me and Billy the Kid (Joe Ely)
2. Are You Listenin' Lucky? (Joe Ely)
3. Grandfather Blues (Joe Ely)
4. Barbecue and Foam (Ed Vizard)
5. Row of Dominoes (Butch Hancock)
6. Dallas (Jimmie Dale Gilmore)
7. Where Is My Love? (Randy Banks)
8. She Gotta Get the Gettin' (Joe Ely)
9. Drivin' to the Poorhouse in a Limousine (Joe Ely)
10. Cool Rockin' Loretta (Eddie Beethoven and Joe Ely)
11. Musta Notta Gotta Lotta (Joe Ely)
12. Letter to L.A. (Joe Ely)
13. If You Were a Bluebird (Butch Hancock)

1993 *Love and Danger*, MCA Records MCAD-10584.

1. Sleepless in Love (Joe Ely)
2. Pins and Needles (Joe Ely)
3. Love Is the Beating of Hearts (Joe Ely)
4. Slow You Down (Joe Ely)
5. Highways and Heartaches (Joe Ely and David Grissom)
6. The Road Goes On Forever (Robert Earl Keen)
7. Settle for Love (Joe Ely)
8. Whenever Kindness Fails (Robert Earl Keen)
9. She Collected (Joe Ely)
10. Every Night about This Time (Dave Alvin)

1995 *Letter to Laredo*, MCA Records MCAD-11222.

1. All Just to Get to You (Joe Ely and Will Sexton)
2. Gallo Del Cielo (Tom Russell)
3. Run Preciosa (Joe Ely)
4. Saint Valentine (Joe Ely)
5. Ranches and Rivers (Joe Ely)
6. Letter to Laredo (Joe Ely)
7. I Saw It in You (Joe Ely)
8. She Finally Spoke Spanish to Me (Butch Hancock)
9. I Ain't Been Here Long (Bruce Gambill)
10. That Ain't Enough (Joe Ely)
11. I'm a Thousand Miles from Home (Joe Ely)

1998 *Twistin' in the Wind*, MCA Records MCAD-70031.

1. Up on the Ridge (Joe Ely)
2. Roll Again (Joe Ely)
3. It's a Little Like Love (Joe Ely)
4. Twistin' in the Wind (Joe Ely)
5. Queen of Heaven (Joe Ely, Jo Carol Pierce, T. J. Nabors)
6. Sister Soak the Beans (Joe Ely)
7. I Will Lose My Life (Joe Ely)
8. You're Workin' for the Man (Joe Ely)
9. Nacho Mama (Joe Ely)
10. Behind the Bamboo Shade (Joe Ely)
11. Gulf Coast Blues (Joe Ely)
12. If I Could Teach My Chihuahua to Sing (Joe Ely, Kimmie and Gabe Rhodes)

1999 *Live @ Antone's,* Rounder Records ROUN 3171.

1. The Road Goes On Forever (Robert Earl Keen)
2. All Just to Get to You (Joe Ely, Will Sexton)
3. Gallo del Cielo (Tom Russell)
4. Ranches and Rivers (Joe Ely)
5. Workin' for the Man (Joe Ely)
6. Me and Billy the Kid (Joe Ely)
7. Up on the Ridge (Joe Ely)
8. Rock Salt and Nails (Utah Phillips)
9. Nacho Mama (Joe Ely)
10. Dallas (Jimmie Dale Gilmore)
11. Thousand Miles from Home (Joe Ely)
12. Road Hawg (Butch Hancock)
13. Everybody Got Hammered (Joe Ely)
14. My Eyes Got Lucky (Joe Ely)
15. Oh Boy! (Petty, Tilghman, West)

2003 *Streets of Sin,* Rounder Records ROUN 3181.

1. Fightin' for My Life (Butch Hancock)
2. I'm on the Run Again (Joe Ely)
3. A Flood on Our Hands (Joe Ely)
4. All That You Need (Joe Ely)
5. Run Little Pony (Joe Ely)
6. Streets of Sin (Joe Ely)
7. 95 South (Joe Ely)
8. Carnival Bum (Joe Ely)
9. Twisty River Bridge (Joe Ely)
10. That's Why I Love You Like I Do (Joe Ely)
11. Wind's Gonna Blow You Away (Butch Hancock)
12. I Gotta Find Ol' Joe (Joe Ely)

Selected Compilations Featuring Songs by Joe Ely

1972 *Jimmie Dale and the Flatlanders, Featuring Joe Ely and Butch Hancock,* 8 track tape, Plantation PLP-20; 1990, CD rerelease on Rounder Records (ROUN 5534) as *The Flatlanders: More a Legend Than a Band.*

1. Dallas (Jimmie Dale Gilmore)
2. Waiting for a Train (Jimmie Rodgers)
3. You've Never Seen Me Cry (Butch Hancock)
4. She Had Everything (Butch Hancock)
5. Rose from the Mountain (Louis Driver)
6. Tonight I Think I'm Gonna Go Downtown (Jimmie Dale Gilmore, John Reed)
7. Jolé Blon (Clark Bentley)
8. One Day at a Time (Willie Nelson)
9. Bhagavan Decreed (Ed Vizard)
10. The Heart You Left Behind (Angela Strehli)
11. Keeper of the Mountain (Al Strehli)
12. Hello Stranger (A. P. Carter)

1995 *Songs from Chippy*, produced by Joe Ely and Terry Allen; written and performed by Joe Ely, Terry Allen, Butch Hancock, Robert Earl Keen, Wayne Hancock, Jo Harvey Allen, and Jo Carol Pierce; Hollywood Records HR-61609-2.
Selections by Joe Ely:

1. Good Night Dear Diary
4. Buildin' More Fires Than She's Been Puttin' Out
8. Fate with a Capital "F" (Joe Ely and Terry Allen)
10. Cup of Tea (Joe Ely and Jo Harvey Allen)
14. Oil Wells (narration by Jo Harvey Allen and Joe Ely)

15. Cold Black Hammer
16. Boomtown Boogie (Joe Ely, Terry Allen, Jo Carol Pierce, Butch Hancock)
19. Whiskey and Women and Money to Burn
23. Goodnight

1998 *Los Super Seven* (artists include Freddy Fender, Flaco Jimenez, Cesar Rosas and David Hidalgo of Los Lobos, Rick Trevino, and Ruben Ramos), RCA records #67689.
Featuring Joe Ely:

7. Plane Wreck at Los Gatos (Deportee) (Woody Guthrie)

2002 The Flatlanders, *Now Again*, New West Records NW6040, produced by Joe Ely; unless otherwise noted, all songs by Butch Hancock, Joe Ely, and Jimmie Dale Gilmore.

1. Goin' Away (Utah Phillips)
2. Julia (Butch Hancock)
3. Wavin' My Heart Goodbye
4. Down in the Light of the Melon Moon
5. Right Where I Belong
6. My Wildest Dreams (Hancock, Ely, Gilmore, and Dan Yates)

7. I Thought the Wreck Was Over
8. Yesterday Was Judgment Day
9. Now It's Now Again
10. All You Are Love
11. You Make It Look Easy
12. Pay the Alligator
13. Filbert's Rise
14. South Wind of Summer

2004 The Flatlanders, *Wheels of Fortune,* New West Records NW6049, produced by Joe Ely.

1. Baby Do You Love Me Still? (Butch Hancock)
2. Wheels of Fortune (Butch Hancock)
3. Midnight Train (Jimmie Dale Gilmore)
4. Wishin' for You (Butch Hancock)
5. Eggs of Your Chickens (Butch Hancock)
6. I'm Gonna Strangle You Shorty (Joe Ely)
7. Back to My Old Molehill (Joe Ely)
8. Deep Eddy Blues (Jimmie Dale Gilmore)
9. Neon of Nashville (Joe Ely)
10. Once Followed by the Wind (Butch Hancock)
11. Go to Sleep Alone (Jimmie Dale Gilmore)
12. Indian Cowboy (Joe Ely)
13. Whistle Blues (Al Strehli)
14. See the Way (Jimmie Dale Gilmore, Butch Hancock)

2005 Los Super Seven, *Heard It on the X* (artists include Rodney Crowell, Freddy Fender, John Hiatt, Lyle Lovett, Raul Malo, Delbert McClinton, Rick Trevino, and Joe Ely), Telarc Records TELARC 83623.
Song by Joe Ely:

6. Let Her Dance (Joe Ely)

1988 *Fair and Square,* Hightone Records HCD-8011.

1. White Freightliner Blues (Townes Van Zandt)
2. Honky Tonk Masquerade (Joe Ely)
3. Fair and Square (David Halley)
4. Don't Look for a Heartache (J. D. Gilmore)
5. Trying to Get to You (Singleton and McCoy)
6. Singing the Blues (M. Endsley)
7. Just a Wave, Not the Water (Butch Hancock)
8. All Grown Up (J. D. Gilmore)
9. 99 Holes (Butch Hancock)
10. Rain Just Falls (David Halley)

1989 *Jimmie Dale Gilmore,* Hightone Records HCD-8018.

1. Honky Tonk Song (Mel Tillis)
2. The Doors Are Open Wide (J. D. Gilmore)
3. See the Way (J. D. Gilmore and Butch Hancock)
4. Beautiful Rose (J. D. Gilmore)
5. Dallas (J. D. Gilmore)
6. Up to You (J. D. Gilmore)
7. Red Chevrolet (Butch Hancock)
8. Deep Eddy Blues (J. D. Gilmore)
9. That Hardwood Floor (J. D. Gilmore and Butch Hancock)
10. When the Nights Are Cold (Butch Hancock)

1990 *Two Roads: Butch Hancock & Jimmie Dale Gilmore, Live in Australia,* Virgin VOZCD-2036.

1. Hello Stranger (A. P. Carter)
2. Ramblin' Man (Butch Hancock)
3. Her Lover of the Hour (Butch Hancock)
4. Tonight I Think I'm Gonna Go Downtown (J. D. Gilmore and John Reed)
5. Two Roads (Butch Hancock)
6. Wheels of Fortune (Butch Hancock)
7. One Road More (Butch Hancock)
8. Blue Yodel Number 9 (Jimmie Rodgers)
9. Down by the Banks of the Guadalupe (J. D. Gilmore)
10. Dallas (J. D. Gilmore)
11. Already Gone (Butch Hancock)

12. Special Treatment (Paul Kelly)
13. Howlin' at Midnight (Lucinda Williams)
14. Firewater Seeks Its Own Level (Butch Hancock)
15. West Texas Waltz (Butch Hancock)

1991 *After Awhile,* Elektra/Nonesuch #61148.
1. Tonight I Think I'm Gonna Go Downtown (J. D. Gilmore and John Reed)
2. My Mind's Got a Mind of Its Own (Butch Hancock)
3. Treat Me Like a Saturday Night (J. D. Gilmore)
4. Chase the Wind (J. D. Gilmore)
5. Go to Sleep Alone (J. D. Gilmore)
6. After Awhile (J. D. Gilmore)
7. Number 16 (J. D. Gilmore)
8. Don't Be a Stranger to Your Heart (J. D. Gilmore, Rich Smith, David Hammond)
9. Blue Moon Waltz (J. D. Gilmore)
10. These Blues (J. D. Gilmore)
11. Midnight Train (J. D. Gilmore)
12. Story of You (J. D. Gilmore)

1993 *Spinning around the Sun,* Elektra #61502-2.
1. Where You Going (J. D. Gilmore, David Hammond)
2. Santa Fe Thief (A. B. Strehli, Jr.)
3. I Was the One (C. Demetrius, B. Peppers, H. Blair, A. Schroeder)
4. So I'll Run (A. B. Strehli, Jr.)
5. I'm So Lonesome I Could Cry (Hank Williams)
6. Mobile Line/France Blues (traditional, arranged and adapted by J. D. Gilmore)
7. Nothing of the Kind (Butch Hancock)
8. Just a Wave (Butch Hancock)
9. Reunion/with Lucinda Williams (Jo Carol Pierce, Harry Porter)
10. I'm Gonna Love You (J. D. Gilmore)
11. Another Colorado (J. D. Gilmore)
12. Thinking about You (J. D. Gilmore)

1996 *Braver Newer World,* Elcktra #61836-2.
1. Braver Newer World (J. D. Gilmore)
2. Come Fly Away (A. B. Strehli, Jr.)
3. Borderland (J. D. Gilmore, David Hammond)
4. Headed for a Fall (J. D. Gilmore, David Hammond, Kevin Welch)
5. Long, Long Time (J. D. Gilmore, David Hammond)
6. Sally (A. B. Strehli, Jr.)
7. There She Goes (J. D. Gilmore)
8. Where Is Love Now (Sam Phillips)
9. Black Snake Moan (Blind Lemon Jefferson)

10. Because of the Wind (Joe Ely) 11. Outside the Lines (J. D. Gilmore)

2000 *One Endless Night,* Rounder Records/Windcharger #3173.
1. One Endless Night (J. D. Gilmore, David Hammond)
2. Down by the Banks of the Guadalupe (Butch Hancock)
3. No Lonesome Tune (Townes Van Zandt)
4. Goodbye Old Missoula (Willis Alan Ramsey)
5. Georgia Rose (Walter Hyatt)
6. Your Love Is My Rest (John Hiatt)
7. Blue Shadows (J. D. Gilmore, Hal Ketchum)
8. Defying Gravity (Jesse Winchester)
9. Ripple (Jerry Garcia, Robert Hunter)
10. Ramblin' Man (Butch Hancock)
11. Darcy Farrow (T. Campbell, S. Gillette)
12. Mack the Knife (Berthold Brecht, Kurt Weill, Marc Blitzstein)

2005 *Come On Back,* Rounder Records #3719.
1. Pick Me Up on Your Way Down (Harlan Howard)
2. Saginaw, Michigan (Lefty Frizzell)
3. Blue Yodel No. 9 (Jimmie Rodgers)
4. Don't Let the Stars Get in Your Eyes (Slim Willet, Cactus Pryor, Barbara Tramell)
5. Four Walls (George Campbell, Marvin Moore)
6. I'll Never Get Out of This World Alive (Hank Williams)
7. Walking the Floor over You (Ernest Tubb)
8. I'm Movin' On (Hank Snow)
9. Don't Worry 'bout Me (Marty Robbins)
10. Train of Love (J. R. Cash)
11. Jimmie Brown the Newsboy (A. P. Carter)
12. Gotta Travel On (Billy Grammer)
13. Peace in the Valley (Thomas A. Dorsey)

Selected Compilations Featuring Songs by Jimmie Gilmore

1972 *Jimmie Dale and the Flatlanders, Featuring Joe Ely and Butch Hancock,* Plantation PLP-20; 1990, rereleased on CD as *The Flatlanders: More a Legend Than a Band,* Rounder ROUN 5534 (for song list, see Joe Ely discography, this volume).

2002 The Flatlanders, *Now Again,* New West Records NW6040 (for song list, see Joe Ely discography, this volume).

2004 The Flatlanders, *Wheels of Fortune,* New West Records NW6049 (for song list, see Joe Ely discography, this volume).

All songs written by David Halley

1992 *Stray Dog Talk,* Dos Records #7007.

1. Tonight
2. Darlene
3. Live and Learn
4. If You Ever Need Me
5. Dreamlife
6. Hard Livin'
7. When It Comes to You
8. Walk the Line
9. Rain Just Falls
10. Opportunity Knocking
11. Further

1993 *Broken Spell,* Dos Records #7003.

1. Sky
2. Losing Your Grip
3. Hometown
4. It's Just as Well
5. Prayer
6. Close to Your Heart
7. Bill W.
8. Man of Steel
9. Girlfriend
10. King of Things
11. Slowing Down

All songs by Butch Hancock, unless otherwise noted; published by Rainlight Music, ASCAP, unless otherwise noted.

1978 *West Texas Waltzes & Dust-Blown Tractor Tunes,* Rainlight RLT 1114.

1. Dry Land Farm
2. Where the West Winds Have Blow'd
3. You've Never Seen Me Cry
4. I Wish I Was Only Workin'
5. Dirt Road Song
6. West Texas Waltz
7. They Say It's a Good Land
8. I Grew to Be a Stranger
9. Texas Air
10. Little Coyote Waltz
11. Just One Thunderstorm

1979 *The Wind's Dominion,* Rainlight RLT 1644.

1. Sea's Deadog Catch (by Milo Flagg)
2. Capture, Fracture, and the Rapture
3. Long Road to Asia Minor
4. Smokin' in the Rain
5. Fightin' for My Life
6. Personal Rendition of the Blues
7. Row of Dominoes
8. Once Followed by the Wind
9. Wild Horses Chase the Wind
10. Own and Own
11. Mario y Maria
12. Eternal Triangles
13. Only Born
14. Gift Horse of Mercy
15. Wind's Dominion

1980 *Diamond Hill,* Rainlight RLT 7777.

1. Golden-Hearted Ways
2. You Can Take Me for One
3. Neon Wind
4. Diamond Hill
5. Corona Del Mar
6. Ghost of Give and Take Avenue
7. Some Folks Call It Style
8. Her Lover of the Hour
9. Wheels of Fortune

1981 *Firewater Seeks Its Own Level*, Rainlight RLT 1001.

1. No Hiding Place
2. Like the Light at Dawn
3. Firewater
4. I Keep Wishing for You
5. If You Were a Bluebird
6. One More Road
7. Man on a Pilgrimage
8. The Wind's Dominion

1981 *1981: A Spare Odyssey*, Rainlight RLT 1981.

1. Horseflies
2. 1981: A Spare Odyssey
3. Dawgs of Transition
4. Two Roads
5. Angels on the Lam
6. 'Cause You Never Compromise
7. Sharp Cutting Wings (by Lucinda Williams)
8. I Wish You Were with Me Tonight
9. Voice in the Wilderness

1985 *Yella Rose*, with Marce Lacouture, Rainlight RLT 1137.

1. Perfection in the Mud
2. Yella Rose
3. Like a Kiss on the Mouth
4. Ain't No Mercy on the Hiway
5. So I'll Run
6. Two Roads
7. Sharp Cutting Wings
8. Tell Me What You Know

1986 *Cause of the Cactus*, with Marce Lacouture (self-released audiocassette only).

1. Leo 'n' Leona
2. Fools Fall in Love
3. Neon Wind
4. Because of the Wind (by Joe Ely)
5. Own 'n' Own
6. Dry Land Farm
7. Prisoner of the Moon
8. Banks of the Guadalupe (by J. D. Gilmore)
9. Moments of Their Day
10. Farmer (author unknown)
11. Already Gone

1987 *Split & Slide/Apocalypse Now, Pay Later* (self-released audiocassette only).

1. Fools Fall in Love
2. Split 'n' Slide I
3. Red Chevrolet
4. Pancho 'n' Lefty (by Townes van Zandt)
5. Own 'n' Own
6. Mr. Mudd 'n' Mr. Gold (by Townes van Zandt)
7. Mario y Maria
8. Leo y Leona
9. Split 'n' Slide II

1989 *Own & Own* (contains previously released material republished by Sugar Hill), Sugar Hill Records #1036.

1. Dry Land Farm
2. Wind's Dominion
3. Diamond Hill
4. 1981: A Spare Odyssey
5. Firewater Seeks Its Own Level
6. West Texas Waltz
7. Horseflies
8. If You Were a Bluebird
9. Own & Own
10. Fools Fall in Love
11. Yella Rose
12. Like a Kiss on the Mouth
13. Ghost of Give-and-Take Avenue
14. Tell Me What You Want to Know
15. Just a Storm
16. Just Tell Me That
17. When Will You Hold Me Again

1991 *No 2 Alike* (fourteen self-produced audiocassettes, tape of the month club).

1. Little Coyote
2. Unknown Love
3. Only Born
4. I Wish You Were with Me Tonight
5. Long Road to Asia Minor
6. Split and Slide (1)
7. Mountains of Resistance
8. Solstice
9. Her Personal Rendition of the Blues
10. I Wish I Was Only Workin'
11. Rawhide/Raw Nerves
12. I Played Along
13. Coolin' Down
14. Wheels of Fortune
15. Just a Wave
16. I Think Too Much of You
17. Nothin' of the Kind
18. 99 Holes in My Head
19. Stronger Bonds
20. Her Lover of the Hour
21. There Is a Place to Go
22. Golden Guitar Lounge
23. Standin' at a Big Hotel
24. Dry Land Farm
25. Tennessee Is Not the State I'm In
26. She Never Spoke Spanish to Me
27. Boxcars
28. Like a Row of Dominoes
29. Suckin' a Big Bottle of Gin
30. Wild Horses Chase the Wind
31. Roadhawg
32. She Finally Spoke Spanish to Me
33. Voice in the Wilderness
34. The Gift Horse of Mercy
35. Sweet Mother of Pearl
36. Golden-hearted Ways
37. Eternal Triangles
38. Angels on the Lam
39. Once Followed by the Wind
40. Dawg of Intermittent Love
41. Seven Cities of Gold
42. Fightin' for My Life

110. It's Just a Storm
111. Don't Let Go Till It Thunders
112. Welcome to the Real World Kid
113. 14th Street
114. One Road More
115. Honky-tonk Tavern
116. Down This Road and Back Again
117. The Stars in My Life
118. She Had Everything
119. You've Never Seen Me Cry
120. If You Were a Bluebird
121. The Shadow of the Moon
122. When the Nights Are Cold
123. West Texas Waltz
124. Wishing for You
125. All My Illusions
126. Love's Transfusion
127. Lord of the Highway
128. Outward Bound
129. I Grew to Be a Stranger
130. Red, White & Blue
131. Back on the Track
132. High Moon
133. Another Diamond Hill
134. Deep Blue Eddy
135. Down to Earth Again
136. Only Makes Me Love Ya' More
137. Don't Let the Mountains Down
138. Pal-o-mine
139. Last Long Silver Dollar
140. Roads Ends Are Found

1993 *Own the Way over Here* (published by Sugar Hill), Sugar Hill Records #1038.
1. Talkin' about That Panama Canal
2. Only Born
3. Smokin' in the Rain
4. Corona Del Mar
5. Like the Light at Dawn
6. Gift Horse of Mercy
7. Neon Wind
8. Perfection in the Mud
9. Only Makes Me Love You More
10. Already Gone
11. Away from the Fountain

1995 *Eats Away the Night* (published by Sugar Hill), Sugar Hill Records #1048.
1. To Each His Own
2. Moanin' of the Midnight Train
3. Eileen
4. One Kiss
5. Pumpkineater
6. If You Were a Bluebird
7. Junkyard in the Sun
8. Boxcars
9. Baby Be Mine
10. Welcome to the Real World, Kid
11. Eats Away the Night

2000 *You Coulda Walked around the World,* Rainlight RLT 37.

1. Chase	8. Low Lights of Town
2. Barefoot Prints	9. Red Blood
3. Roll Around	10. One Good Time
4. Long Sunsets	11. Circumstance
5. Black Irish Rose	12. Naked Light of Day
6. All Curled Up	13. You Coulda Walked around
7. Hidin' in the Hills	the World

Collections with One or More Songs by Butch Hancock

1972 *Jimmie Dale and the Flatlanders, Featuring Joe Ely and Butch Hancock,* Plantation PLP-20; 1990, rereleased on CD as *The Flatlanders: More a Legend Than a Band,* Rounder ROUN-5534 (for song list, see Joe Ely discography, this volume).

1990 *Two Roads: Butch Hancock & Jimmie Dale Gilmore, Live in Australia,* Virgin VOZCD-2036 (for song list, see Jimmie Dale Gilmore discography, this volume).

1995 *Songs from Chippy,* produced by Joe Ely and Terry Allen; written and performed by Joe Ely, Terry Allen, Butch Hancock, Robert Earl Keen, Wayne Hancock, Jo Harvey Allen, and Jo Carol Pierce; Hollywood Records HR-61609-2.
Songs by Butch Hancock:
  5. Wind's Gonna Blow You Away
 12. Low Lights of Town
 20. Morning Goodness (Butch Hancock and Robert Earl Keen)

2002 The Flatlanders, *Now Again,* New West Records NW6040 (for song list, see Joe Ely discography, this volume).

2004 The Flatlanders, *Wheels of Fortune,* New West Records NW6049 (for song list, see Joe Ely discography, this volume).

Bobby Keys plays saxophone on these albums by various artists:

1969

Delaney & Bonnie, *Accept No Substitute,* Elektra CCM-2832

Rolling Stones, *Let It Bleed,* Abkco #9004

1970

Delaney & Bonnie, *On Tour with Eric Clapton,* Atco #33326

George Harrison, *All Things Must Pass,* Capitol/EMI #30474

Joe Cocker, *Mad Dogs & Englishmen,* A&M #5531

1971

B. B. King, *In London,* MCA MSP-10843

Barbra Streisand, *Barbra Joan Streisand,* Sony #30792

Delaney & Bonnie, *Motel Shot,* Atco Records #33359

Dr. John, *The Sun, Moon & Herbs,* Wounded Bird Records WOU 362

Harry Nilsson, *Nilsson Schmilsson,* RCA SF-8371

Humble Pie, *Rock On,* MCA MSP-520240

Rolling Stones, *Sticky Fingers,* Atlantic/Virgin #39525

Rolling Stones, *Get Your Leeds Lungs Out!,* Mighty Diamonds MD2004

Yoko Ono, *Fly,* Apple SVBB-3380

1972

Delaney & Bonnie, *D & B Together,* Columbia/Legacy CK85743

Carly Simon, *No Secrets,* Elektra/Wea #75049

Harry Nilsson, *Son of Schmilsson,* RCA SF-8297

John Lennon, *Sometime in New York City/Live Jam,* Capitol #93850

Rolling Stones, *Exile on Main Street,* Atlantic/Virgin #39524

1973

Donovan, *Cosmic Wheels,* Epic EPC 65450

Marvin Gaye, *Let's Get It On,* Motown #4400640212

Ringo Starr, *Ringo*, Capitol #95637
Shawn Phillips, *Bright White*, Wounded Bird Records WOU 4402
Rolling Stones, *Goats Head Soup*, Atlantic/Virgin #39519

1974
Country Joe McDonald, *Paradise with an Ocean View*, Fantasy #9495
Carly Simon, *Hotcakes*, Elektra/Wea #1002
Etta James, *Come a Little Closer*, MCA MSP-9363
Harry Nilsson, *Pussy Cats*, RCA CLP-10570
Harry Nilsson, *Son of Dracula*, RCA ABL-10220-AS
John Lennon, *Walls and Bridges*, Capitol #46768
Lynyrd Skynyrd, *Second Helping*, MCA #11648
Ringo Starr, *Goodnight Vienna*, Capitol #80378
Martha Reeves, *Martha Reeves*, MCA #414
Rolling Stones, *Headin' for an Overload*, Totonka PI5053A/PI5054

1975
Harry Nilsson, *Duit on Mon Dei*, RCA APL-10817
Joe Cocker, *Jamaica Say You Will*, Castle Music UK CLACD-237
John Lennon, *Rock 'n' Roll*, Capitol #46707
Keith Moon, *Two Sides of the Moon*, MCA #2136

1976
Harry Nilsson, *That's the Way It Is*, RCA RS-1062
Joe Cocker, *Live in L.A.*, Castle Music UK CLACD-189
Leo Sayer, *Endless Flight*, RPM SB1004
Ron Wood and Ronnie Lane, *Mahoney's Last Stand*, Pilot #29
Van Dyke Parks, *Clang of the Yankee Reaper*, Warner Bros./ADA #26185
Warren Zevon, *Warren Zevon*, Elektra/Wea #1060

1978
Joe Cocker, *Luxury You Can Afford*, Wounded Bird Records WOU 4641

1979
Ron Wood, *Gimme Some Neck*, Columbia CD35702

Ian McLagan, *Troublemaker,* Mercury SRM 13786

1980
Billy Preston, *Late at Night,* Motown IM46019
Rolling Stones, *Emotional Rescue,* Atlantic/Virgin #39523

1981
Ron Wood, *1-2-3-4,* CBS #85227
Ian McLagan, *Bump in the Night,* Mercury SRM 14007

1987
Chuck Berry, *Hail! Hail! Rock 'n' Roll,* MCA #6217
Joe Ely, *Lord of the Highway,* Hightone HCD-8008

1988
Keith Richards, *Talk Is Cheap,* Virgin #86079

1991
Keith Richards, *Live at the Hollywood Palladium,* Virgin #86262
Rolling Stones, *Flashpoint,* Columbia/Virgin #45670

1993
The Crickets, *Double Exposure,* Rollercoaster RCCD 3006

1995
Jerry Lee Lewis, *Young Blood,* Elektra/Wea #61795
Rolling Stones, *Stripped,* Virgin #41040

1998
Sheryl Crow, *The Globe Sessions,* A&M #540959
Rolling Stones, *No Security,* Virgin #46740

2003
John Hiatt, *Beneath This Gruff Exterior,* New West NW60452

1996 *West Texas Heaven,* Justice Records #2201, all songs by Kimmie Rhodes, except "Home John" by Jimmy Day, BMI.

1. West Texas Heaven
2. Hard Promises to Keep
. Wild Roses
4. Just to Be Near You
5. Maybe We'll Just Disappear
6. Be Mine
7. Git You a Job
8. I Never Heard You Say
9. The Corner of the Bar
10. Home John
11. I'm Gonna Fly
12. Las Roses Sauvagas
13. I'm Not an Angel

1997 *Jackalopes, Moons & Angels,* Last Call Records #3024442, all songs by Kimmie Rhodes, unless noted.

1. Contrabandistas (Joe Gracey and Billie Earl Smith)
2. I'm His Little Chevrolet
3. Sweetheart You're a Lot Like Texas
4. Man in the Moon
5. 1,000 Magicians
6. Daddy's Song
7. It'll Do
8. Angels Get the Blues
9. Just One Love
10. I Just Drove By
11. Bad Times for Me
12. Trying for My Heart

2000 *Rich from the Journey,* Sunbird Records #1.

1. Rich from the Journey (Rhodes)
2. Thank You for Another Day (Rhodes, Kevin Savigar)
3. Shine All Your Light (Rhodes, Beth Nielsen Chapman)
4. Big Ol' Train (Rhodes, Bob Reagan)
5. Espiritu Santo Bay (Rhodes, Walt Wilkins)
6. I'm So Amazed (Rhodes, Gabe Rhodes)
7. There Is a Place (Rhodes, John Keller)
8. Yellow Sand (Rhodes, Kevin McCormick)
9. God's Acre (Rhodes)
10. The Wonderful Sound (Rhodes, Savigar)
11. This Is the Gift (Rhodes)
12. Bells of Joy (Rhodes)

2003   Kimmie Rhodes and Willie Nelson, *Picture in a Frame,* Sunbird Records #70007.

1. Picture in a Frame (T. Waits, K. Brennan)
2. Valentine (Willie Nelson)
3. Just One Love (K. Rhodes)
4. 'Til I Gain Control Again (R. Crowell)
5. Love Me Like a Song (K. Rhodes)
6. I Just Drove By (K. Rhodes)
7. Contrabandistas (J. Gracey, B. E. Smith)
8. It Always Will Be (Willie Nelson)
9. We've Done This Before (K. Rhodes, G. Nicholson)
10. Rhinestone Highway (K. Rhodes)

2004   *Lost & Found,* Sunbird Records #8.

1. Road to Jubilee (Rhodes, Keller)
2. Take Me Down (Rhodes)
3. Over the Edge (Rhodes)
4. Catfish Song (Townes Van Zandt)
5. Past Never Happened (Rhodes, Savigar)
6. Heart of a Believer (Rhodes)
7. Daddy's Heaven (Rhodes, Nicholson)
8. War Prayer (Rhodes, Nicholson)
9. I'm Not an Angel (Rhodes)
10. Keep Me in Your Grace (Rhodes, McBride, Randall)
11. Born in a Barn (Rhodes)
12. Lines (Rhodes, Waylon Jennings)
13. Somebody Cares for Me (Rhodes, Roboff)

2004   *Love Me Like a Song,* Sunbird Records #70003.

1. Darkness Lifting (Rhodes, Cates)
2. I Have Everything (Rhodes, Savigar)
3. Only Love Can Save Me Now (Rhodes)
4. Love Me Like a Song/with Willie Nelson (Rhodes, Nicholson)
5. Send Me the Sun/with Emmylou Harris, Beth Nielsen Chapman (Rhodes)
6. Midnight Song (Rhodes)
7. Play Me a Memory (Rhodes, Tench, Tillis, Nicholson)
8. Louis' World (Rhodes)
9. We've Done This Before/with Willie Nelson (Rhodes, Nicholson)
10. Witness to the Crime (Rhodes, Nicholson)
11. Love and Happiness for You/with Emmylou Harris (Rhodes, Harris)
12. November December (Rhodes)
13. The One to Walk You Home/with Benmont Tench (Rhodes, Tench, Nicholson)

2005   *Windblown,* Sunbird Records #70010, all songs by Kimmie Rhodes.

1. Windblown
2. Oh Padre
3. Lost in You Again
4. That's My Heart
5. Desert Train
6. Laredo Cantina
7. Little Angelina
8. Diablo Gallo
9. Angelino
10. Clear Blue Sky

All compositions by Doug Smith, unless otherwise noted; all recordings published by Doug Smith Music.

1989 *Doug Smith,* Doug Smith Music 001-RGP.

1. Passion
2. Linda
3. Gunslinger
4. Patent Pending
5. Capital
6. Look at the Moon
7. Air Waves
8. Zot
9. Knockout
10. No Jones'n Allowed

1996 *The Human Element,* Doug Smith Music DM-01.

1. The Human Element
2. Cotton Strippin'
3. I'll Go Away
4. Farewell to Petersburg
5. Smitty's Waltz
6. Moon over Quitaque
7. Ghost Windows
8. The Leavin' Song
9. One Perfect Circle
10. Just a Thought Rollin'
11. Iron Horses

1997 *Piano Player,* Doug Smith Music DSP-197.

1. Again and Again and Again
2. Dominoe
3. Time on 27th
4. Different Dimensions
5. Ivory and Steel
6. Late in the Evening
7. Park Tower
8. Tamara's Song
9. The Last Real Medley

1998 *Hope,* Doug Smith Music DRS-1998.

1. Song for Suns
2. The Hartz Horizon
3. See, Sea, Strut
4. Less Pomp, More Circumstance
5. Tumbleweed Rag
6. Stone Road
7. Miles to Go
8. Hope

9. Kinda Like Home

10. Rat House Blues

11. Dreams Come True

12. The Final Destination

13. West Texas

2000 *Live*, Doug Smith Music DRS-2000.

1. Song for Suns

2. Stone Road

3. Rat House Blues

4. Linda

5. The Hartz Horizon

6. West Texas

7. Tumbleweed Rag

8. Strings

9. The Final Destination

10. Dreams Come True

11. Faith

12. Less Pomp, More Circumstance

13. Passion

2001 *Confirmation*, Doug Smith Music DRS-2001.

1. Confirmation

2. Passion

3. Swinney Blues

4. Olayinka's Dream

5. Tamara's Song

6. Can You Hear What I Feel

7. My Heart Belongs to You

8. Angelic Ascension

9. Love Endures

10. Arrival

11. Strippin' Cotton

12. The Leavin' Song

2003 *There It Is* (CD & DVD), Doug Smith Publishing DRS-2003.

1. The Final Destination

2. Last Date (Floyd Cramer)

3. Confirmation

4. West Texas

5. Tumbleweed Rag

6. Linda

7. Faith

8. Swinney Blues

9. The Leavin' Song

10. Song for Suns

11. Waitin' for Tom

CD Bonus Tracks:

12. Moon over Quitaque

13. Passion

14. Amazing Grace (traditional)

1986 *Stranger Blues,* Antone's Records EP (included as extra tracks on CD rerelease of *Soul Shake*).

1. Voodoo (Arril and Coleman)
2. Stranger Blues (B. Robinson)
3. Wang Dang Doodle (W. Dixon)

1987 *Soul Shake,* Antone's Records #0006.

1. I Wouldn't Treat a Dog (Price/ Walsh/Barri/Omaritan)
2. Your Sweetness (Angela Strehli)
3. Be Bop Man (I. Ross)
4. It Hurts Me Too (Tampa Red)
5. Take It from Me (Angela Strehli)
6. Mean Mistreater (Bobby Robinson)
7. Soul Shake (Margaret Lewis, Myra Smith)
8. 20% Alcohol (J. B. Hutto)
9. Tough Times (John Brim)
10. Back in My Arms Again (Holland/ Dozier/Holland)
11. In Spite of What You Do (Angela Strehli)
12. Big Town Playboy (Eddie Taylor)

1993 *Blonde and Blue,* Rounder Records ROUN 3127.

1. Two Bit Texas Town (Angela Strehli)
2. Never Like This Before (Booker T. Jones, Isaac Hayes, David Porter)
3. Can't Stop These Teardrops (Angela Strehli)
4. You Don't Love Me (Walter Jacobs)
5. I'm Just Your Fool (Walter Jacobs)
6. Say It's Not So (Angela Strehli)
7. Um, Um, Um, Um, Um, Um/Duet with Don Covay (Curtis Mayfield)
8. Go On (Angela Strehli)
9. Gotta Find Me a Lover--24 Hours a Day (Eugene Record, Carl Davis)
10. Sun Is Shining (Elmore James)
11. Going to That City (Sister O. M. Terrell)

1997   Stevie Ray Vaughan and Double Trouble, *Live at Carnegie Hall*, Sony/Epic #68163, featured vocalist.

1998   *Deja Blue*, House of Blues #161399.
1. Cut You Loose (Mel London)
2. Stand by Your Woman Man (Angela Strehli)
3. Deja Blue (Angela Strehli, Mike Schermer, Joe Kubek)
4. Man I Can Love (Angela Strehli)
5. Boogie Like You Wanna (Charlie Bradix)
6. Give Me Love (Angela Strehli)
7. Still a Fool (Angela Strehli)
8. Close Together (Jimmy Reed)
9. Hey, Miss Tonya (Angela Strehli)
10. Too Late/with Doug Sahm (Tarheel Slim and Little Anne)
11. Where the Sun Never Goes Down (Willie Mae Williams)

All songs written by Cary Swinney, published by Cary Swinney/Johnson Grass Music Pub.

1997 *Human Masquerade*, Johnson Grass JGPC-75760-2.

1. Human Masquerade
2. Death Is Strange
3. Fools Like Me
4. Jesus Silverstein
5. Hair in the Windshield
6. Love Is Never Caged
7. When I Was a Kid
8. Country Music Music
9. Will They Bury You with Your Shoes On?
10. Desperate Searcher
11. What If God Is a Woman?
12. The Problem with Humans
13. Dream Song

2000 *Martha*, Johnson Grass JGPC-75734-2.

1. Good Ol' Sunday Mornin'
2. Seventh of September
3. Neanderthal Man
4. Letter to Alaska
5. Mr. Guilt
6. They Don't Serve Barbecue in Hell
7. Joey, Abdul and Me
8. Martha, Our Son's Insane
9. The Bike Ride
10. Johnson Grass Farm
11. Twelve Januarys

2005 *Big Shots*, Johnson Grass JGPC-75784-2.

1. Noah's Ark
2. Dawson County
3. A Hero on a Square
4. American History
5. Santa Fe Afternoon
6. Livin' in My Head
7. Parades Down Main Street
8. Fatherless Child
9. Bigshots
10. Almost Persuaded
11. Birdwatcher
12. Galileo, Charlie and Thom

Original Interviews

All interviews conducted exclusively by Christopher J. Oglesby. There were follow-up conversations for additional material and clarifications in many cases.

ADAMS, JAY BOY. February 8, 2002. Office of Roadhouse Coaches, Comfort, Texas.

ALLEN, JO HARVEY. June 17, 1998. Stubb's BBQ dining room, Eighth and Red River, Austin, Texas.

ALLEN, TERRY. March 26, 1998. Etta's Place Bed and Breakfast, Fort Worth, Texas.

BONE, PONTY. June 22, 2000. Ponty Bone's home, South Austin, Texas.

BOWDEN, RICHARD. March 5, 1998. Stubb's BBQ back porch, Eighth and Red River, Austin, Texas.

BURNS, DOWNÉ. September 15, 2000. Downé's Studio, Lubbock, Texas.

CALDWELL, DON. February 3, 1998. Don Caldwell's office, 19th Street, Lubbock, Texas.

DAVIS, MAC.* July 2, 2004. Via telephone, Davis at home in Los Angeles, California.

ELY, JOE. June 9, 1998. Joe Ely's vehicle, various locations in Austin, Texas.

ELY, SHARON. October 15, 2000. Central Market Café, south location, Austin, Texas.

GILMORE, COLIN. October 19, 2000. Author's home, South Austin, Texas.

GILMORE, JIMMIE DALE. December 1, 2000. Central Market Café, south location, Austin, Texas.

HALLEY, DAVID. June 15, 2003. David Halley's home, Austin, Texas.

HANCOCK, BUTCH. June 27, 2002. Jimmie Dale Gilmore's home, Spicewood, Texas.

HANCOCK, TOM X. June 5, 2000. Tom X Hancock's home, Austin, Texas.

JAGGERS, BRUCE. September 15, 2000. Moose Magoo's Restaurant and Bar, 82nd Street, Lubbock, Texas.

KEYS, BOBBY. April 12, 2005. South Austin Recording Studio, Austin, Texas.

LIVINGSTON, BOB. December 4, 2000. Texas Music International, The Artplex, Austin, Texas.

MAINES, LLOYD. November 21, 2000. Cedar Creek Studios, South Austin, Texas.

PARKS, WADE. November 20, 2000. Wade Parks's home, south of Lubbock, Texas.

PIERCE, JO CAROL, and GUY JUKE. August 31, 2000. Threadgill's restaurant, original location, North Lamar, Austin, Texas.

RHODES, KIMMIE. October 30, 2000. Central Market Café, south location, Austin, Texas.

SMITH, DOUG. May 15, 2000. Montelongo's Restaurant, Clovis Highway, Lubbock, Texas.

STREHLI, ANGELA. April 23, 2005. Via telephone, Strehli at home in Marin County, California.

SWINNEY, CARY. April 4, 2000. Author's home, South Austin, Texas.

TAYLOR, JESSE. February 12, 1998. Shaggy's Bar and Grill, South Congress Avenue, Austin, Texas.

* Author's Note: My interview with Mac Davis was adjunct to a prearranged press conference in preparation for "Mac Davis Day" in Lubbock. Thank you to Steve Long for facilitating my extra time with Mr. Davis prior to the press call and to Marcy Jarrett, executive director of the Lubbock Convention and Visitors Bureau, for allowing my questions to carry over into the scheduled conference call.